JOURNAL FOR THE STUDY OF THE NEW TESTAMENT SUPPLEMENT SERIES
100

Executive Editor
Stanley E. Porter

JSOT Press
Sheffield

To Tell the Mystery

Essays on New Testament Eschatology in Honor of Robert H. Gundry

edited by
Thomas E. Schmidt
and
Moisés Silva

Journal for the Study of the New Testament
Supplement Series 100

Copyright © 1994 Sheffield Academic Press

Published by JSOT Press
JSOT Press is an imprint of
Sheffield Academic Press Ltd
343 Fulwood Road
Sheffield S10 3BP
England

Typeset by Sheffield Academic Press
and
Printed on acid-free paper in Great Britain
by Bookcraft
Midsomer Norton, Somerset

British Library Cataloguing in Publication Data

A catalogue record for this book is available
from the British Library

ISBN 1-85075-486-1

CONTENTS

PREFACE

I first met Bob Gundry at the Santa Barbara Airport in June of 1972 on the occasion of my being interviewed for a position at Westmont College. As I got out of the plane and set foot on one of the driest regions on earth, I happened to be holding an umbrella firmly in hand—the result of my having been conditioned by two years of Manchester weather—and the incongruous sight drew an uncontrollable chuckle from Bob's wife, Lois (both of them, of course, had also lived in Manchester). My other vivid impression from that meeting, however, was shaking Bob's hand and feeling as though I had known him for a very long time. That immediate sense of camaraderie has never left me, not the least reason for which is that he took me under his wing and proved to be a totally faithful friend.

When I began teaching that fall, one of my assignments was an introductory New Testament course for which Bob had written his widely used text, *A Survey of the New Testament* (though I was given complete freedom in choosing a textbook, that volume seemed ideally suited for the course). Bob took the opportunity to ask me for possible changes that might be made in subsequent editions of the book. I do not recall having many suggestions, but one specific comment stands in my mind, namely, my recommendation that his treatment of redaction criticism might be expanded and the subject treated more positively. A few years earlier I had been deeply impressed by the work of Ned B. Stonehouse, particularly since it seemed to anticipate some of the concerns of redaction criticism. Upon reading Bob's book, it struck me that his handling of that discipline was much too brief.

Next thing I knew, he was publishing his controversial commentary on Matthew, which of course applied redaction-critical concerns well beyond what most people might have imagined. Unfortunately, I cannot take much credit for this turn of events. What really led him to treat Matthew as he did was close attention to the text. And some details about his method might be of interest to the readers of the present *Festschrift*.

Knowing that Bob had a contract to write a commentary on Matthew, I volunteered to go over the instalments of his first draft and offer suggestions. (My motives were not particularly altruistic—I figured the exercise would be important for my own education.) Bob informed me that, if he was to meet his deadline, he would need to write at the rate of one page of the Nestle–Aland Greek text per week. He proceeded, in typical fashion, to hand me every Friday a batch of material written in longhand. The amount and insightfulness of the comments astounded me, and I often wondered, as I sat in my library cubicle next to his, what forces—quiet, but perhaps supernatural—were at work on the other side of the partition.

Most people familiar with his work are probably unaware of the fact that Bob began his commentary on Matthew without any commitment to the Marcan Hypothesis. It was 'merely' a matter of sitting in front of a Greek synopsis of the Gospels, and trying to account in detail for the distinctiveness of the Matthean text, that led him to the firm conclusion that Mark had indeed served as a source for Matthew. As for his specific explanations of the Matthean distinctives, they were often compelling and sometimes puzzling, but the general validity of his approach, as well as its consistency, originality and value, seemed to me undeniable.

I mention these things because they illustrate, in a striking way, some of Bob's remarkable traits. One of them—particularly noticeable to those of us plagued by mental disorganization—is his constancy and discipline, the determination to set a clear goal and drive inexorably toward it. Another is his ability to assimilate vast amounts of information, a feature especially evident in his recent commentary on Mark.

Most important, however, is the independent thinking apparent in all his work—and that within the context of an unwavering commitment to the authority of Scripture. For me, as a young scholar in the early 1970s, nothing was so refreshing as to converse with someone who did not divorce the nuts-and-bolts work of New Testament criticism from the responsibility of broad theological reflection. Indeed, Bob Gundry's contribution has to be measured not only by the quantity and quality of his output but also—and perhaps primarily—by the example of Christian scholarship he has provided to our generation. It is therefore a distinct pleasure for me to have a part in the production of this volume.

Moisés Silva

My introduction to Bob Gundry came in 1978 when he visited his daughter Judy, who lived in a neighboring apartment and was one of my first friends at Fuller Seminary in Pasadena, California. Like Moisés, I was immediately impressed with Bob's warmth and his offer of hospitality should I ever journey north to Santa Barbara. A few subsequent meetings, including a visit to the Westmont College campus, convinced me that I could aspire no higher than to work alongside Bob some day.

It was during those early visits that I met the rest of Bob's wonderful family, which could incidentally produce a well-rounded *Festschrift* with little outside help. His wife, Lois, has mastered the rudiments of several languages, including Bob's handwriting, to render thousands of pages into publishable form over the years. Daughter Judy went on for a doctorate in New Testament at Tübingen and there married theologian Miroslav Volf. Daughter Connie earned a seminary degree in Old Testament and excavates in Israel with her husband, Harvard-educated archaeologist Ron Tappy. Son Mark is completing doctoral studies in theology at Boston College. Surely, then, no tribute would be complete without commendation of Bob for his *versatility* in the dissemination of theological knowledge. The family is a bit weak in church history—but the first grandchild has just appeared.

I left Pasadena in 1981 for doctoral work at Cambridge University and fell out of touch with Bob. Then one day in the Tyndale House lounge, one of Bob's former students—Kevin Vanhoozer—looked up from a letter and casually mentioned that there was a New Testament opening at Westmont if anyone was interested. Someone was indeed interested, and one of the high points in my life came two months later when I sat in Bob's living room and heard him offer me the job. So it has been from a close vantage point that I have had occasion to admire his character and his scholarship.

From the first success in the publication of his dissertation, written under the supervision of F.F. Bruce, Bob showed scholarly promise. A steady stream of journal articles and professional papers attest to his breadth of interests and his diligence despite a heavy undergraduate teaching load, draining committee assignments, and infrequent sabbaticals. In the past decade, his reputation has blossomed to international prominence, as scholars representing a variety of traditions have come to appreciate Bob's unusual combination of innovation and thoroughness. There has not been time to gauge fully the impact of his work on

Mark, the first major exegetical commentary on that Gospel by an American scholar. But early indications are that it is a landmark work, certain to influence our general view of Mark's purpose and our detailed understanding of the text.

My professional identity as The Other New Testament Professor at Westmont has innumerable advantages to console the fragile ego. No hotheaded young ox was ever yoked to a more steady and dependable partner. Bob is always a gentleman, never patronizing, ever solicitous and prayerful for the well-being of his colleagues. He is always ready to recommend bibliography, to serve as a sounding board for ideas, and to return a manuscript promptly with detailed comments and corrections. Indeed, I am not sure that I fully appreciated his role as private editor *par excellence* until we chose secrecy for this volume and I had to offer my contribution without first passing it beneath his careful eye.

In my ten years at Westmont, the department has hired six people, and those six represent hundreds of good scholars who have wanted very much to work here. Bob's presence is clearly a major factor. In interview after interview, it is evident that his work is known and admired by young scholars in various theological sub-disciplines. By their testimony, Bob demonstrates that evangelical biblical scholarship need not be a contradiction in terms, that good thinking is welcomed by other good thinkers, irrespective of ideology.

It is fitting, then, that a volume dedicated to Bob Gundry represent scholarship from several countries, from several traditions, and from several generations. Why eschatology? I remember that aforementioned day in Bob's living room when he told me that it did not matter all that much to him, but just for the record—in case the board of trustees wanted to know—*was I premillennial?* I replied that I was, but that I had never cared much for experts on things that have not happened yet and that eschatology for me was best expressed in the words of the old hymn, 'I want to be ready when He comes'. Bob seemed to like that answer, and I never heard from the trustees. But I have since observed that Bob treats 'things that have not happened yet' with the same seriousness and energy he applies to other theological concerns. From his early book *The Church and the Tribulation*, to his monograph *Sōma in Biblical Theology*, to his recent analysis of Mark's apocalypse, and in many other published works, Bob has demonstrated that the eschatology at the core of the New Testament is worthy of careful study.

It is, therefore, in gratitude for association with a fine scholar and a good man that I join Moisés Silva and all of the contributors to present this volume to Bob Gundry.

Thomas E. Schmidt

ABBREVIATIONS

AB	Anchor Bible
AnBib	Analecta biblica
AT	Arbeiten zur Theologie
ATAbh	Alttestamentliche Abhandlungen
ATR	*Anglican Theological Review*
BAGD	W. Bauer, W.F. Arndt, F.W. Gingrich and F.W. Danker, *Greek–English Lexicon of the New Testament*
BETL	Bibliotheca ephemeridum theologicarum lovaniensium
BEvT	Beiträge zur evangelischen Theologie
BGBE	Beiträge zur Geschichte der biblischen Exegese
Bib	*Biblica*
BNTC	Black's New Testament Commentaries
BSac	*Bibliotheca Sacra*
BZ	*Biblische Zeitschrift*
CBQ	*Catholic Biblical Quarterly*
CGTC	Cambridge Greek Testamony Commentary
CNT	Commentaire du Nouveau Testament
ConBNT	Coniectanea biblica, Old Testament
CRINT	Compendia rerum iudaicarum ad novum testamentum
CTJ	*Calvin Theological Journal*
EBib	Etudes bibliques
EGT	*Expositor's Greek Testament*
EKKNT	Evangelisch-Katholischer Kommentar zum Neuen Testament
EvQ	*Evangelical Quarterly*
FB	Forschung zur Bibel
FRLANT	Forschungen zur Religion und Literatur des Alten und Neuen Testaments
GNB	Good News Bible
HBT	*Horizons in Bible Theology*
HNT	Handbuch zum Neuen Testament
HNTC	Harper's NT Commentaries
HR	*History of Religions*
HTKNT	Herders theologischer Kommentar zum Neuen Testament
HTR	*Harvard Theological Review*
ICC	International Critical Commentary
Int	*Interpretation*
JAAR	*Journal of the American Academy of Religion*
JB	*Jerusalem Bible*
JBL	*Journal of Biblical Literature*

JJS	*Journal of Jewish Studies*
JSJ	*Journal for the Study of Judaism in the Persian, Hellenistic and Roman Period*
JSNT	*Journal for the Study of the New Testament*
JSNTSup	*Journal for the Study of the New Testament* Supplement Series
JSOTSup	*Journal for the Study of the Old Testament* Supplement Series
JTS	*Journal of Theological Studies*
MeyerK	H.A.W. Meyer, Kritisch-exegetischer Kommentar über das Neue Testament
MTZ	*Münchener theologische Zeitschrift*
NCB	New Century Bible
NClarB	New Clarendon Bible
NEB	*New English Bible*
NedTTs	*Nederlands theologisch tijdschrift*
NICNT	New International Commentary on the New Testament
NIDNTT	C. Brown (ed.), *The New International Dictionary of New Testament Theology*
NIGTC	The New International Greek Testament Commentary
NIV	*New International Version*
NJB	H. Wansbrough (ed.), *New Jerusalem Bible*
NovTSup	*Novum Testamentum* Supplements
NRSV	New Revised Standard Version
NTAbh	Neutestamentliche Abhandlungen
NTM	New Testament Message
NTS	*New Testament Studies*
RB	*Revue biblique*
REB	Revised English Bible
RHPR	*Revue d'historie et de philosophie religieuses*
RSV	*Revised Standard Version*
RTL	*Revue théologique de Louvain*
SANT	Studien zum Alten und Neuen Testament
SBLDS	SBL Dissertation Series
SBM	Stuttgarter biblische Monographien
SBS	Stuttgarter Bibelstudien
SJT	*Scottish Journal of Theology*
SNT	Studien zum Neuen Testament
SNTSMS	Society of New Testament Studies Monograph Series
ST	*Studia theologica*
TDNT	G. Kittel and G. Friedrich (eds.), *Theological Dictionary of the New Testament*
THKNT	Theologischer Handkommentar zum Neuen Testament
TNTC	Tyndale New Testament Commentaries
TynBul	*Tyndale Bulletin*
TU	Texte und Untersuchungen
WBC	Word Biblical Commentary
WF	Wege der Forschung
WS	Walberberger Studien (Theol. Reihe)
WTJ	*Westminster Theological Journal*

To Tell the Mystery

WUNT	Wissenschaftliche Untersuchungen zum Neuen Testament
ZAW	*Zeitschrift für die alttestamentliche Wissenschaft*
ZB	Zürcher Bibelkommentare
ZKT	*Zeitschrift für katholische Theologie*
ZNW	*Zeitschrift für die neutestamentliche Wissenschaft*

LIST OF CONTRIBUTERS

Michael Goulder
Professor of Biblical Studies, University of Birmingham, England

Birger Gerhardsson
Professor of Exegetical Theology Emeritus, Lund University, Sweden

Donald A. Hagner
George Eldon Ladd Professor of New Testament, Fuller Theological
Seminary, Pasadena, CA, USA

I. Howard Marshall
Professor of New Testament, University of Aberdeen, Scotland

Judith Gundry-Volf
Associate Professor of New Testament, Fuller Theological Seminary,
Pasadena, CA, USA

Jan Lambrecht, SJ
Professor Emeritus, Katholieke Universiteit, Leuven, Belgium

Moisés Silva
Professor of New Testament, Westminster Theological Seminary,
Philadelphia, PA, USA

Prof. James D.G. Dunn
Lightfoot Professor of Divinity, University of Durham, England

J. Ramsey Michaels
Professor of Religious Studies, Southwest Missouri State University,
Springfield, MD, USA

Gordon D. Fee
Professor of New Testament Studies, Regent College, Vancouver, BC,
Canada

D.A. Carson
Research Professor of New Testament, Trinity Evangelical Divinity
School, Deerfield, IL, USA

Thomas Schmidt
Associate Professor of New Testament, Westmont College, Santa
Barbara, CA, USA

BIBLIOGRAPHY OF ROBERT H. GUNDRY

Books

The Use of the Old Testament in St Matthew's Gospel with Special Reference to the Messianic Hope (NovTSup, 18; Leiden: Brill, 1967).

A Survey of the New Testament (Grand Rapids: Zondervan, 1970; rev. edns, 1981, 1994).

The Church and the Tribulation (Grand Rapids: Zondervan, 1973).

Sōma in Biblical Theology with Emphasis on Pauline Anthropology (SNTSMS, 29; Cambridge: Cambridge University Press, 1976) (repr. Academie Books; Grand Rapids: Zondervan, 1987).

Panorama do Novo Testamento (Sao Paulo: Sociedade Religiosa Edicões Vida Nova, 1978) (Portuguese translation of A Survey of the New Testament).

Pregled Novog Zavjeta (Zagreb: EBI, n.d.) (Serbo-Croatian translation of A Survey of the New Testament).

A Survey of the New Testament (Seoul: Emmaus, 1992) (Korean translation).

Mark: A Commentary on his Apology for the Cross (Grand Rapids: Eerdmans, 1993).

Matthew: A Commentary on his Literary and Theological Art (Grand Rapids: Eerdmans, 1982 [rev. edn: Matthew: A Commentary on his Handbook for a Mixed Church under Persecution (Grand Rapids: Eerdmans, 1994)]).

Articles

'למטלים': 1QIsaiah a 50,6 and Mark 14,65', RevQ 2 (1960), pp. 559-67.

'The Narrative Framework of Matthew XVI.17-19: A Critique of Professor Cullmann's Hypothesis', NovT 7 (1964), pp. 1-9.

'The Language Milieu of First-Century Palestine: Its Bearing on the Authenticity of the Gospel Tradition', JBL 83 (1964), pp. 404-408.

' "Ecstatic Utterance" (NEB)?', JTS NS 17 (1966), pp. 299-307.

' "Verba Christi" in I Peter: Their Implications concerning the Authorship of I Peter and the Authenticity of the Gospel Tradition', NTS 13 (1967), pp. 336-50.

' "In my Father's House are Many Monai" (John 14.2)', ZNW 58 (1967), pp. 68-72.

'The Form, Meaning and Background of the Hymn Quoted in I Timothy 3.16', in W.W. Gasque and R.P. Martin (eds.), Apostolic History and the Gospel: Biblical and Historical Essays Presented to F.F. Bruce (Exeter: Paternoster Press, 1970), pp. 203-22.

'Further Verba on Verba Christi in First Peter', Bib 55 (1974), pp. 211-32.

'Recent Investigations into the Literary Genre "Gospel" ', in R.N. Longenecker and M.C. Tenney (eds.), New Dimensions in New Testament Study (Grand Rapids: Eerdmans, 1974), pp. 97-114.

'Jesus is Coming Again: Posttribulationalism', *Christian Life* 36 (May, 1974), pp. 22,
    59-61 (reprinted in *When is Jesus Coming Again* [Carol Stream, IL: Creation
    House, 1975], pp. 53-63).
'Quotations in the NT', *The Zondervan Pictorial Encyclopedia of the Bible* (Grand
    Rapids: Zondervan, 1975), V, pp. 7-11.
'The Moral Frustration of Paul before his Conversion: Sexual Lust in Romans 7.7-25',
    in D.A. Hagner and M.J. Harris (eds.), *Pauline Studies: Essays Presented to
    F.F. Bruce* (Grand Rapids: Eerdmans, 1980), pp. 228-45.
'Trouble Ahead for the Church? An Interview with Robert Gundry', *The WatchMan*
    1/1 (August, 1980), pp. 8-9.
'A Response to "Matthew and Midrash"', *JETS* 26 (1983), pp. 41-56.
'A Surrejoinder to Douglas J. Moo', *JETS* 26 (1983), pp. 71-86.
'A Response to "Methodological Unorthodoxy"', *JETS* 26 (1983), pp. 95-100.
'A Surrejoinder to Norman L. Geisler', *JETS* 26 (1983), pp. 109-15.
'Grace, Works, and Staying Saved in Paul', *Bib* 66 (1985), pp. 1-38.
'On Interpreting Matthew's Editorial Comments', *WTJ* 47 (1985), pp. 319-28.
'Body', *Harper's Bible Dictionary* (San Francisco: Harper & Row, 1985), p. 138.
'The Hellenization of Dominical Tradition and Christianization of Jewish Tradition in
    the Eschatology of 1-2 Thessalonians', *NTS* 33 (1987), pp. 161-78.
'The New Jerusalem: People as Place, Not Place for People', *NovT* 29 (1987),
    pp. 254-64.
'A Responsive Evaluation of the Social History of the Matthean Community in Roman
    Syria', in D.L. Balch (ed), *The Social History of the Matthean Community in
    Roman Syria* (Minneapolis: Fortress Press, 1991), pp. 62-67.
'Matthean Foreign Bodies in Agreements of Luke with Matthew against Mark:
    Evidence that Luke Used Matthew', in F. van Segbroeck *et al.* (eds.), *The Four
    Gospels: Festschrift Frans Neirynck* (BETL, 100; Leuven: Leuven University
    Press/Peeters, 1992), pp. 1467-95.
'On True and False Disciples in Matthew 8.18-22', *NTS* (forthcoming).
'The Essential Physicality of Jesus' Resurrection according to the New Testament', in
    J. Green and M. Turner (eds.), *Jesus of Nazareth, Lord and Christ: Essays on the
    Historical Jesus and New Testament Christology* (FS I. Howard Marshall; Grand
    Rapids: Eerdmans, 1994).
'Style and Substance in Philippians 2.6-11', in *Crossing the Boundaries: Essays in
    Biblical Interpretation in Honour of Michael D. Goulder* (Leiden: Brill, 1994).

Book Reviews

The Reality of the Resurrection, by M.C. Tenney, *Christianity Today* 7 (1963), p. 1089.
*The Reality of Christianity: A Study of Adolf von Harnack as Historian and
    Theologian*, by G.W. Glick, *Christianity Today* 11 (1967), p. 1152.
The Theme of Jewish Persecution of Christians in the Gospel according to St Matthew,
    by D.R.A. Hare, *JBL* 87 (1968), pp. 346-47.
History and Theology in the Fourth Gospel, by J.L. Martyn, *Christianity Today* 12
    (1968), p. 1210.
The Eucharist, by L. Bouyer, *Christianity Today* 13 (1969), p. 875.
Neotestamentica et Semitica: Studies in Honor of Principal Matthew Black, ed.
    E.E. Ellis and M. Wilcox, *Christianity Today* 14 (1970), p. 350.

Matthew's Advice to a Divided Community: Mt. 17,22–18,35, by W.G. Thompson, *Int* 26 (1972), pp. 99-100.

The Anchor Bible: Matthew, by W.F. Albright and C.S. Mann, *Christianity Today* 16 (1972), pp. 880-81.

Theological Dictionary of the New Testament. VII. *Sigma*, ed. G. Friedrich, *Christian Scholar's Review* 2 (1973), pp. 388-89.

The Jewish Leaders in Matthew, by S. van Tilborg, *JBL* 92 (1973), pp. 138-40.

Wisdom, Christology, and Law in Matthew's Gospel, by M.J. Suggs, *Int* 27 (1973), p. 369.

Glory at the Right Hand: Psalm 110 in Early Christianity, by D.M. Hay, *JBL* 93 (1974), pp. 472-73.

Mark: Evangelist and Theologian, by R.P. Martin, *The Reformed Journal* 24 (1974), pp. 30-31.

New Testament Foundations: A Guide for Christian Students. I. *The Four Gospels*, by R.P. Martin, *The Reformed Journal* 26 (1976), pp. 28-29.

Matthew: A Scribe Trained for the Kingdom of Heaven, by O.L. Colpe, *JBL* 96 (1977), pp. 605-606.

The Formula Quotations in the Infancy Narrative of Matthew, by G.M. Soares Prabhu, *Bib* 58 (1977), pp. 591-94.

A History of the Exegesis of Matthew 16.17-19 from 1781 to 1965, by J.A. Burgess, *JBL* 97 (1978), pp. 142-43.

The Meaning of the Millennium: Four Views, ed. R.G. Clouse, *Themelios* 4 (1978), p. 39.

The Origin of Christology, by C.F.D. Moule, *JBL* 97 (1978), pp. 313-14.

The Gospel of Luke, by I.H. Marshall, *Theology Forum Brief* 6 (April 1981), pp. 3-4.

The Royal Son of God, by B.M. Nolan, *Bib* 61 (1980), pp. 585-88.

God's People in Christ: New Testament Perspectives on the Church and Judaism, by D.J. Harrington, *TSF Bulletin* 5 (1981), p. 24.

Matthew, by J.P. Meier, *JBL* 101 (1982), pp. 298-91.

The Gospel according to Matthew, by F.W. Beare, *TSF Bulletin* 6 (1982), pp. 19-20.

The Sermon on the Mount, by R.A. Guelich, *The Reformed Journal* 33 (1983), pp. 18-20.

Christ the Lord: Studies in Christology Presented to Donald Guthrie, ed. H.H. Rowden, *Christian Scholar's Review* 13 (1983), pp. 62-63.

A Genre for the Gospels: The Biographical Character of Matthew, by P.L. Shuler, *The Reformed Journal* 33 (June 1983), pp. 28, 30.

The Rapture, by H. Lindsey, *Books for Better Living* 1 (1983), pp. 10-11.

Typology in Scripture: A Study of Hermeneutical TYPOS Structures, by R.M. Davidson, *JBL* 103 (1984), pp. 109-10.

Colloquy on New Testament Studies: A Time for Reappraisal and Fresh Approaches, ed. B.C. Corley, *Christian Scholar's Review* 14 (1984), pp. 91-93.

Galatians: Dialogical Response to Opponents, by B.H. Brinsmead, *JAAR* 53 (1985), p. 139.

Jesus on the Mountain, by T.L. Donaldson, *Bib* 67 (1986), pp. 402-404.

Jesus and the Laws of Purity, by R.P. Booth, *JBL* 107 (1988), pp. 325-27.

'Spirit and Gospel' in Mark, by M.R. Mansfield, *JBL* 108 (1989), pp. 152-54.

Slow to Understand: The Disciples in Synoptic Perspective, by B.L. Melbourne, and *The Concept of Disciple in Matthew's Gospel*, by M.J. Wilkins, *JBL* 109 (1990), pp. 533-35.

Messianic Exegesis: Christological Interpretation of the Old Testament in Early Christianity, by D. Juel, *Christian Scholar's Review* 20 (1990), pp. 183-84.

The Structure of Matthew's Gospel: A Study in Literary Design, by D.R. Bauer, *Bib* 71 (1990), pp. 126-29.

Lohnmetaphorik und Arbeitswelt in Mt 20,1-16: Das Gleichnis von den Arbeitern im Weinberg im Rahmen rabbinischer Lohngleichnisse, by C. Hezser, *JBL* 111 (1992), pp. 340-41.

The Corinthian Women Prophets, by A.C. Wire, *JAAR* 61 (1993), pp. 392-94.

ALREADY?[1]

Michael Goulder

It is a theological commonplace that in New Testament times the kingdom of God had both come already, and also not yet.[2] This familiar paradox sits uncomfortably alongside Paul's aggressive sarcasm in 1 Cor. 4.8: 'Already you are sated! Already you have become rich! Apart from us you have begun to reign (ἐβασιλεύσατε)! And I wish you had begun to reign that we might begin reigning with you (συμβασιλεύσωμεν)'. It is evident that some of the Corinthians (not perhaps 'those of Paul') supposed the kingdom of God to have begun already (ἤδη),[3] and that this notion arouses the apostle's anger and contempt. He remarks at the end of the chapter, 'For the kingdom *of God* is not in talk (ἐν λόγῳ), but in power' (4.20),[4] and towards the end of the epistle he says, 'And this I say, brethren, that flesh and blood cannot inherit the kingdom of God' (15.50). So there does not seem to be much *Already* for St Paul.

Paul did not like talkers about the kingdom for a number of reasons. First, there is the contrast between their presumption and his hard life.

1. This paper is offered as a small tribute to Bob Gundry, whose bold and imaginative work in New Testament studies I have constantly admired, and whose kindly friendship I have much enjoyed. In many things we have been allies, too.

2. I have not traced this idea earlier than C.H. Dodd, *The Parables of the Kingdom* (London: Nisbet, 1935), pp. 35-36.

3. C.K. Barrett, *A Commentary on the First Epistle to the Corinthians* (London: A. & C. Black, 2nd edn, 1971), p. 109, 'for them there is no "not yet" to qualify the "already" of realised eschatology'; H. Conzelmann, *1 Corinthians* (ET Hermeneia; Philadelphia: Fortress Press, 1975 = MeyerK; Göttingen: Vandenhoeck & Ruprecht, 1969), pp. 87-88; G.D. Fee, *The First Epistle to the Corinthians* (NICNT; Grand Rapids: Eerdmans, 1987), p. 172, 'Paul's perspective...is one of "already but not yet" held in tension: theirs is one of "already" with little room for "not yet"'.

4. Barrett, *1 Corinthians*, p. 118, renders λόγῳ by *eloquence*; but cf. Fee, *1 Corinthians*, p. 191.

22   *To Tell the Mystery*

He went hungry and thirsty and unclad, toiling at work with his own hands (4.11), while they were 'sated' (κεκορεσμένοι) and 'rich' (ἐπλουτήσατε). The contrast recalls the tensions in Thessalonica, where the same phrase, ἐργαζόμενοι ταῖς ἰδίαις χερσίν, comes in 1 Thess. 4.11, cf. ἐργαζόμενοι, 2 Thess. 3.8; it looks as if money has been shared round, and there are free lunches for all.[5] No doubt the 'enrichment' was also on the spiritual level, and this meant long periods of the precious Saturday night church gathering being given over to 'tongues', tendentious expositions of Scripture ('words of wisdom'),[6] and so-called angelic revelations ('words of knowledge').[7] Claims of being 'strong' (ἰσχυροί) and 'glorified' (ἔνδοξοι) at 4.10 sound like the aspirations to σοφία and γνῶσις in chs. 12–13.[8] Besides these there is the arrogance and lawlessness that Paul deals with in chs. 5–6. The kingdom was a nightmare.

Who then were the kingdom enthusiasts? It is clearly not Paul's own idea, for he sends Timothy with the letter, 'who will remind you of my ways in Christ' (4.17). They are 'puffed up' (4.18-19), which sounds like those in 4.6 who are 'puffed up for the one [leader] against the other' (ὑπὲρ τοῦ ἑνὸς φυσιοῦσθε κατὰ τοῦ ἑτέρου).[9] This leads on to 4.7, 'For *who* makes you different?...why do you *boast* as if you did not receive?',[10] and so to the *Already* sequence in 4.8. The kingdom people

5.   Barrett (*1 Corinthians*, p. 109), Conzelmann (*1 Corinthians*, p. 87) and Fee (*1 Corinthians*, p. 172) all assume a metaphorical meaning, without argument. But κορέννυμι at least is naturally used of physical eating, and parallels from Philo prove little, since Philo is the great spiritualizer. The contrast with 4.11, and the verbally identical 1 Thess. 4.11, are strong indications of a series of good meals.
6.   דברי חכמה; cf. my 'Σοφία in 1 Corinthians', *NTS* 37 (1991), pp. 516-34.
7.   Cf. my forthcoming 'Vision and Knowledge': *knowledge* is bracketed with *mysteries* in 1 Cor. 13.2; *knowing* is paralleled with *seeing in a reflector dimly* in 13.12.
8.   In 1.17-31 Paul aligns the μωρία and ἀσθενές of his gospel against the σοφία of human beings, in comparison to which it is ἰσχυρότερον (1.25, 27); in 10.22, 'Are we ἰσχυρότεροι than God?' closes the discussion of claims to γνῶσις in 8–10. So Corinthian claims to be ἰσχυροί seem to be claims to have σοφία and γνῶσις. The δόξα with which they claim to be ἔνδοξοι is no doubt that of the realized kingdom with the same correlates.
9.   Fee (*1 Corinthians*, p. 170) correctly notes that the grammatical form excludes the general 'for one against another', and requires the specific '*the* one' *the* other'; though he mistakes the force of the passage and thinks Apollos is referred to.
10.   The 'difficulty' felt by Barrett and Fee over the point of 'who' arises from their missing the meaning of the passage (as is also done by Conzelmann). The 'For'

were the Cephas group of 1.12;[11] they boasted that their leader alone was a proper apostle, that having him made them different; they were puffed up for him against Paul (and his friend Apollos).[12] They 'examined' Paul (4.3-4) instead of treating him and Peter as equal stewards of the mysteries of God; in 9.3-4 Paul returns to 'those who examine' him, and explicitly asserts his parity with 'the other apostles and the brothers of the Lord and [in particular] Peter'. He writes a long excursus about his planting and Apollos's watering, and so on in ch. 3, and he then says, 'I have transposed (μετεσχημάτισα) this onto myself and Apollos for your sake, brethren, that in us you may learn the principle, Not beyond what is written' (4.6). The issue was really between his followers and those of Peter, but he transposed it and spoke as if it were between himself and Apollos, to be diplomatic (δι' ὑμᾶς); the Jerusalem party wanted the Gentile converts to keep the standard *halakha*, 'taught words of human wisdom' (2.13), but the principle established by Paul and Apollos was *the Bible and the Bible only*, 'not beyond what is written'.[13]

So Paulines did not like talk of the kingdom; it encouraged unreality and false spirituality. Paul himself does not mention it often, and when he does he is rather negative about it:

For the kingdom of God is not food and drink (Rom. 14.17).
For the kingdom of God does not consist in talk (1 Cor. 4.20).
The unrighteous will not inherit the kingdom of God (1 Cor. 6.9).
Neither the immoral...will inherit the kingdom of God (1 Cor. 6.10).
Flesh and blood cannot inherit the kingdom of God (1 Cor. 15.50).
Those who do such things shall not inherit the kingdom of God (Gal. 5.21).
No fornicator...has any inheritance in the kingdom of Christ and of God (Eph. 5.5).

shows the link to 4.6: some Corinthians were puffed up and boasted in having a special leader *who* made them different. This was not Paul; and Apollos was even less special than Paul. So who can it have been?

11. Barrett and Conzelmann (and many critics) identify the enthusiasts as 'Gnostics'. This is not a helpful description. The attempt is now widely made to use the word Gnosticism with a defined sense, including dualism in the godhead (cf. K. Rudolph, *Die Gnosis* [Leipzig: Koehler & Amelang, 1977; ET Edinburgh: T. & T. Clark, 1983], pp. 59-113); and there is no evidence in 1 Corinthians of such a belief. The text does refer to four groups at Corinth at 1.12, and it is likely that the enthusiasts of 4.8-21 are (at least) one of these.

12. For Apollos's position as a friend and ally of Paul, see my 'Σοφία', n. 6.

13. See my 'Σοφία', n. 6.

That is seven out of twelve references to the kingdom in the
Pauline Epistles,[14] all negative, and mostly excluding from *future*
inheritance. Four of them come out of the context of kingdom 'talk' in
1 Corinthians.

Not too much can be inferred from the Romans text, 'For the
kingdom of God is not eating and drinking, but righteousness and peace
and joy in the Holy Spirit'. Someone might say today in a charismatic
church, where there is no thought of the kingdom being already present,
'The kingdom of God is not dancing and hand-clapping but charity and
kindness'. Paul is concerned to break up the miserable pattern of the
Roman church's *agape*, with Gentiles despising the newly returned
Jewish Christians for their legalism over food-laws, while the latter have
a meatless meal and 'judge' the lawless Gentiles. The kingdom is not
squabbles about meat and wine, he says, but righteousness and peace
and joy in the Spirit. An exact parallel is to be found in 1 Cor. 4.20,
'*For the kingdom of God* is *not* in word *but* in power'. It is not here
already (4.8); all that is here is talk—it will be here in power when the
Lord comes. All that is going on at Rome is talk about the kingdom and
a reality of uncharity over the *agape*; when it comes it will be in the
fulness of righteousness, peace and joy, of which we now have a
foretaste in the Spirit.[15]

The other five Pauline references to the kingdom are:

> When [Christ] delivers the kingdom to God the Father (1 Cor. 15.24).
> He has transferred us to the kingdom of his beloved Son (Col. 1.13).
> Among my fellow-workers for the kingdom of God (Col. 4.11).

14. I have included Ephesians, Colossians and 2 Thessalonians with the Paulines,
believing Paul to have written them. My thesis that Paul opposed talk of the kingdom,
and placed it consistently in the future, would be even clearer without them, for late in
his life he tried a compromise, with 'the kingdom of Christ'.

15. J.D.G. Dunn (*Romans 9–16* [WBC, 38B; Dallas: Word Books, 1988],
pp. 822-23) defends a present force for the kingdom in this text and in 1 Cor. 4.20
alone in the Pauline corpus, apparently without noticing 1 Cor. 4.8, where the *already*
is denigrated. He correctly infers that the kingdom language lay to hand in the
common Christian tradition, and that it has been suppressed in favour of 'righteousness' and 'Spirit'; his suggestion is that Paul dropped it fearing charges of
sedition—but would these not apply for the evangelists too? Dunn makes the
kingdom an ideal entity, with God-given δικαιοσύνη and εἰρήνη, well removed from
the free meals, suspended work, visions and miracles implied in the Corinthian letters.
Paul prefers to speak of the Spirit because that indicates a spiritual phenomenon, and
one that is but an ἀρραβών or ἀπαρχή of what is to come.

God, who calls you into his own kingdom and glory (1 Thess. 2.12).
That you may be made worthy of the kingdom of God (2 Thess. 1.5).

Of these the last three are ambiguous, but if anything a future reference is easier.[16] In 1 Thessalonians it is natural to think that God calls those who walk worthily into his kingdom *and glory* hereafter. In 2 Thessalonians the persecutions are a proof of the righteous judgment of God, to make the Thessalonians worthy of the kingdom [hereafter, it seems], for which they are suffering now. In Colossians 4 Luke and the others are fellow-workers εἰς τὴν βασιλείαν τοῦ θεοῦ, which can be read as either present or future.

In 1 Corinthians 15 and Colossians 1 we have a complicating factor, the kingdom *of Christ*. In the former the distinction is clear. The kingdom of God is not in operation in the present age, nor can it be (15.50): it will begin with Christ's parousia (15.23-24).[17] In the meantime Christ has taken *his* kingdom in heaven, with his resurrection and exaltation, and is in process of subduing all his supernatural enemies (15.25). Paul gives no hint throughout 1 Corinthians of any interest in the kingdom of Christ as a force in the present world. In Colossians 1, however, we have already been rescued from the power of darkness and transferred to the kingdom *of the Son of his love*. This looks like a characteristic softening of the apostle's line to meet the opposition part way. He will not allow that the kingdom *of God* is here; but he can live with kingdom talk if it is just the kingdom *of Christ*, until he has a better grip on the church. We saw a parallel weakening in Eph. 5.5, where no gross sinner has any inheritance in the kingdom of *Christ and God.*

This apparent refusal to allow that the kingdom of God is in any sense present is confirmed if 2 Thessalonians is genuine.[18] Here Paul (if it is he, the Pauline tradition if it is not) describes as *deceit* (2.3, 10) the notion that 'the Day of the Lord has come' (2.2).[19] The Day of the Lord can

16. So Dunn, *Romans*, p. 822.

17. Taking εἶτα as *thereupon*; so Barrett, *1 Corinthians*, p. 357; Conzelmann, *1 Corinthians*, p. 271; Fee, *1 Corinthians*, p. 755.

18. I have argued its genuineness in 'Silas in Thessalonica', *JSNT* 48 (1992), pp. 87-106.

19. ἐνέστηκεν means *is present* in Rom. 8.38, 1 Cor. 3.22, Gal. 1.4., but *is imminent* in 1 Cor. 7.26. Paul thought the Day of the Lord to be imminent (coming like a thief in the night, 1 Thess. 5.1-2), so if 2 Thessalonians is Pauline the RSV translation *has come* will be correct (so E. Best, *A Commentary on the First and Second Epistles to the Thessalonians* [London: A. & C. Black, 1972], pp. 275-77); he will have objected to teaching that the kingdom is present.

only mark the initiation of the kingdom; the issue is between Paulines who say it is in the future and others who suppose it to have arrived. The controversy is strongly reminiscent of 1 Cor. 4.8-21; only this time Paul settles it by appeal to the series of programmed phases that he finds in the book of Daniel. First must come a period of *persecution* (Dan. 1–6) and *lawlessness* (Dan. 9), as God's plan is held up by *the delaying angel* (Dan. 10.21). Then we must endure *the man of sin who exalts himself against all divinity* (Dan. 11.36), and seats himself *in the Temple* (Dan. 11.31). It is not until afterwards that the Lord will kill the man of sin, and the resurrection will take place (Dan. 12.2). This phasing of the future was to be further developed by the Pauline movement, in Mark 13 par. and Revelation; it is an effective rebuff to any claim of a realized kingdom.[20]

So Paul speaks with a single voice throughout, and we can understand why: talk about the kingdom of God ended in unreality and unspirituality, sponging free meals, arrogant talk, boasting about Peter as the real apostle, interminable and dangerous hot air at church meetings, defiance of basic morality and much other wrong-headedness (about sex, idol-meat, women's ministry, the resurrection, etc.). He is quite clear about it. The kingdom of God cannot come in this age; it belongs entirely in the future. There is no *Already* about it at all.

John is even more negative. The kingdom does not occur at all in the Epistles, and it comes in only three verses in the whole Gospel:

> Unless one is born anew, he cannot see the kingdom of God (3.3).
> Unless one is born of water and the Spirit, he cannot enter the kingdom of God (3.5).
> My kingdom is not of this world; if my kingdom were of this world, then my servants would fight...but my kingdom is not from the world (18.36).

It is all negatives. The subject is only introduced in ch. 3 because the dialogue is with Nicodemus, a pattern Pharisaic Jewish-Christian, one of those always talking about the kingdom.[21] The trouble with Jerusalem Christians like him is that they have not even *begun* the spiritual life. Their crass questions, gross misunderstandings, greasy approaches in half-belief and general preference for the night over the light, all show that their talk of the kingdom is nothing but froth. They cannot see it, let

---

20. On this see my 'Silas in Thessalonica', with bibliography.
21. See my 'Nicodemus', *SJT* 44 (1991), pp. 153-68.

alone enter it, without a baptism that is a new beginning in faith. In 18.36 it is not the kingdom of *God* that is at issue, but the absurdity of seeing any threat from Jesus' spiritual kingship to the secular Empire. The whole idea has no place in John's theological agenda.

The contrast with the Synoptic Gospels is striking, since the Kingdom is there so central: no doubt Jesus proclaimed the kingdom of God. Since his closest followers ran the Jerusalem mission for the first decade of the Church's life, we may work with the hypothesis that, like them, Jesus himself thought that the kingdom *had come*. It is not easy to see how the Petrine mission could have made the realized kingdom so central a theme of its preaching and practice unless they believed Jesus had taught it, and the struggle between the two missions provides a key to resolve a longstanding scholarly tension.[22]

I have argued elsewhere that Mark is a reliable Pauline,[23] and if so he will have seen the Kingdom as a future entity in redactoral passages:

> The time is fulfilled and the kingdom of God is at hand (ἤγγικεν, 1.15).[24]
> ...before they see the kingdom of God has come with power (9.1).

---

22. The tension goes back a long way, to Albrecht Ritschl's Kingdom built by human obedience, which was challenged by Johannes Weiss's and Albert Schweitzer's Kingdom introduced eschatologically by God. It took a new lease of life with C.H. Dodd's *Parables of the Kingdom* (London: Nesbit, 1935) proposing realized eschatology, and may be seen in the stark contrast between W. Marxsen, *Mark the Evangelist* (Nashville: Abingdon, 1969 = FRLANT, 67; Göttingen: Vandenhoeck & Ruprecht, 2nd edn, 1959), with a strongly future emphasis, and E. Haenchen, *Der Weg Jesu* (Berlin: Töpelman, 1966). There is a full discussion in N. Perrin, *The Kingdom of God in the Teaching of Jesus* (London: SCM Press, 1963), and J. Schlosser, *Le règne de Dieu* (Paris: Gabalda, 1980); for a recent discussion and bibliography see B.D. Chilton (ed.), *The Kingdom of God* (London: SPCK, 1984). The tendency of modern commentators is to have it both ways; e.g. J. Gnilka, *Das Evangelium nach Markus* (EKKNT, 2; Zürich: Benziger; Neukirchen: Neukirchener Verlag, 3rd edn, 1989), I, pp. 66-67; M.D. Hooker, *The Gospel according to St Mark* (London: A. & C. Black, 1991), pp. 55-58.

23. See my 'A Pauline in a Jacobite Church', in F. van Segbroeck *et al.* (eds.), *The Four Gospels, 1992* (FS F. Neirynck; Leuven: Leuven University Press/ Peeters, 1992), II, pp. 859-76.

24. Hooker, *Mark*, pp. 53-54, 'we are asking questions about Mark's use of language... ἐγγίζειν is generally understood here as referring to the close approach of the kingdom'. R. Gundry, *Mark* (Grand Rapids: Eerdmans, 1993), pp. 64-65, argues that ἐγγίζειν means *has arrived*, and that the formulation goes back to Jesus: this combination of conclusions would also fit my argument, though I do not think it is right! For a history of the discussion cf. Perrin, *Kingdom*, pp. 64-66.

Mk 9.1 perhaps may suggest that the kingdom is here now *in weakness*; and if so Paul would have no objection. There is a similar suggestion in the two parables at 4.26 and 4.30: the kingdom is present *in semine*, but will not be here in fulness until the angel puts in the sickle, or at least until it has become a great shrub.[25] But most often it is clearly in the future. Entering the kingdom is the same as entering/inheriting eternal life (9.43-47); inheriting eternal life means having treasure *in heaven* (10.21), and it is *in the age to come* (10.30). So it is better to enter the kingdom with one eye than to be cast into Gehenna with two (9.47); it is hard for a rich man to enter it (10.23-25); Jesus will drink the fruit of the vine new in the kingdom of God, that is, in the age to come (14.25).

Against this, there are only some ambiguous passages. The disciples are given *the mystery* of the kingdom (4.11); of such as children is the kingdom (10.14); the good scribe is not far from the kingdom (12.34). The nearest to a present reality is 10.15: 'whoever does not receive the kingdom of God like a little child shall not enter it'. We must receive it *now* if we are to enter it; but it may be that we will not enter it till the age to come, as in 9.47 or 10.23-25. Thus Mark's Gospel leaves us with the strong impression that the kingdom is in the future. There are sayings, and the parables of the Seed Growing Secretly and the Mustard Seed, which *imply* something of a present kingdom; and we may perhaps draw encouragement from these for the hypothesis that Jesus saw the kingdom as present in his ministry. But Mark himself seems (as in other matters) to be a solid Pauline: there was no *Already* for him— the kingdom was to come.

Matthew is far more sympathetic to the Jerusalem mission than Mark: he glorifies Peter, he exculpates the Zebedaids and Jesus' brothers, he maintains the validity of the Law and the traditional interpretations of it, sabbath and food-laws and much else that would be abhorrent to Mark. Nevertheless many passages on the kingdom in Matthew show the Markan emphasis: both those taken over from Mark and others. Antinomians *will* be called least in the kingdom (5.19); scribes and Pharisees, and Christian evildoers, and those who do not become like children, *will* not enter it (5.20; 7.21; 18.3); the Lord's Prayer asks that it *may* come (6.10); men *will* come from east and west and sit at table

---

25. Cf. D. Lührmann, *Das Markusevangelium* (HNT, 3; Tübingen: Mohr, 1987), p. 42, *ad* 1.15, '4,1-34 werden zeigen, wie solche Nähe für Mk zu verstehen ist: als Nähe im Wort Jesu'.

with Abraham in it (8.11); Zebedee's wife wanted the best seats in it for her sons (20.21); it will be like the *coming* of the bridegroom (25.1); it is an inheritance *prepared* for the sheep on Judgment Day (25.34). On the other hand, and in contrast to Mark, a number of passages are found with a clear present meaning. 'From the days of John the Baptist until now the kingdom of heaven has been suffering violence' (βιάζεται, 11.12). The context suggests that (in Matthew's understanding) the violence is exemplified by the stream of Pharisaic attacks on Jesus—for claiming to forgive sins (9.1-8), for eating with sinners (9.9-13), for not fasting (9.14-17), for exorcisms (9.32-34)—and finally by Herod's imprisonment of the Baptist (11.2).[26] The kingdom, therefore, is being seen as an earthly institution running since the beginning of Jesus' ministry, as we may say the Christian movement; and violent people, the Pharisees and Herod, have been ravaging it (ἁρπάζουσιν). 'If it is by the Spirit of God that I cast out demons, then the kingdom of God has come upon you' (12.28) is a clear statement of its presence. Peter is given the keys of the kingdom at 16.19, and this means that the decisions he takes for the Church, on *halakha* and on discipline, will be ratified by Christ in heaven.[27] So the kingdom is the Church, and those who submit to his rulings will be 'in' here on earth, and those who defy them will be 'locked out' here on earth. Actually hitherto the kingdom *has been* in charge of Israel. The scribes and Pharisees shut the kingdom against people: they neither enter themselves, nor allow those who would enter to go in (23.13). So the kingdom will be taken away from them and given to a nation producing its fruits, that is the Church (21.43).[28] One can enter the kingdom of heaven here and now,

---

26. Cf. R.H. Gundry, *Matthew: A Commentary on his Literary and Theological Art* (Grand Rapids: Eerdmans, 1982), p. 210: 'the plundering of the kingdom represents the persecution of its members, e.g. the imprisonment of John the Baptist'; U. Luz, *Das Evangelium nach Matthäus* (EKKNT, 1; Zürich: Benziger, 1989; Neukirchen: Neukirchener Verlag, 1990), II, p. 178, 'Die allgemeine Formulierung schliesst ebenso politische Gegner (Herodes Antipas!) wie das religiöse Establishment ein'.

27. Gundry, *Matthew*, p. 334. Luz (*Matthäus*, II, p. 466) denies that the kingdom is here seen as the Church: '[Petrus] soll den Willen Gottes von Jesus her auslegen, um so die Menschen auf denjenigen schmalen Weg führen, an dessen Ende die schmale Pforte zum Himmelreich aufgeschlossen wird (vgl. 7.13f)'. But the picture of 7.13 is not implied here at all; and 23.13, '[the scribes] neither enter themselves...', shows that those with keys can open the door here on earth if they will.

28. Gundry, *Matthew*, p. 430.

and those given authority by God can let one in or exclude one here
and now.

All these passages make it clear that Matthew can think of the
kingdom as a present institution, and this affects our judgment of
otherwise unclear passages. Thus the sons of the kingdom who will be
cast out in 8.12 are the unbelieving Jews, who are presumably therefore
temporary heirs of the Kingdom now, whereas the sons of the kingdom
who constitute the good seed of 13.38 are the Christians, and presumably permanent heirs of the Kingdom, from now on.[29] A scribe can
be made disciple to the kingdom (13.52), just as other scribes make
themselves disciples to Judaism. Similarly, if Jesus' ability to cast out
demons shows that the kingdom *has come* (12.28), it looks as if the
same logic would apply at 10.7-8, for there the disciples are told to cast
out demons, among other healings, while proclaiming, 'The kingdom of
heaven ἤγγικεν'. So ἤγγικεν will mean 'has arrived' to Matthew, and
the same will be true at 3.2 with John Baptist and 4.17 with Jesus—
indeed 11.12, 'from the days of John the Baptist...' virtually guarantees
that Matthew understood 4.17 in this way.[30]

There is often a similar ambiguity with the parables. In the Tares, the
kingdom of heaven is like a man sowing good seed (13.24), and in the
interpretation the Son of Man will send his angels and gather *out of his
kingdom* those who do lawlessness, that is, the sons of the evil one as
opposed to the sons of the kingdom, the Church.[31] So here the kingdom
and the Church are quite distinct: the kingdom is the world once God
has imposed his reign upon it.[32] But alongside the tares, the kingdom is
like a grain of mustard growing into a tree with the birds nesting in its
branches, that is, with Gentiles in the branching communities of the
Church (13.31),[33] like leaven buried in three measures of meal until it

29. So Gundry, *Matthew*, p. 145-46.

30. Against Gundry, *Matthew*, pp. 43-44; but Gundry stresses that the disciples'
message and Jesus' are the same (p. 185).

31. So Gundry, p. 273: the tares are false disciples.

32. It is a commonplace of parable commentary that βασιλεία is a translation of
the Hebrew מלכות and means *reign*, not *kingdom*. This questionable generalization
has been rather easily swallowed. How can one enter a reign, or sit down in a reign, or
be cast out of a reign? Such absurdities are overlooked because of pastoral desire to
preach a reign of God that is here already but not yet. Cf. G.E. Ladd, *The Presence of
the Future Kingdom* (Grand Rapids: Eerdmans, 1974).

33. Cf. Gundry, *Matthew*, p. 267, 'the kingdom includes a large number of
professing disciples, true and false'—and so for the leaven, p. 269.

was all leavened, that is, until the whole world is leavened with the Church's gospel (13.33). It is like treasure in a field, or a pearl of great value, which one will go and sell everything to buy—as the rich man failed to do in ch. 19. So one can gain possession of it here and now (13.44-45). It is like the Church's dragnet which pulls in good Christians and bad, and at the end of the age they will be sorted out (13.47).

With the longer parables we may be in more doubt as to where Matthew saw the stress. The Royal Wedding (22.1-14) seems to provide a conspectus of the whole history of salvation: the first servants are the prophets, the second are the apostles, their maltreatment is the persecution and martyrdom of the Church, the excuses are the failure of the Jewish mission, the burning of the city is the destruction of Jerusalem in 70, the gathering of all sorts into the feast is the Church with its good and bad members, the guest without a wedding garment is a symbol of the judgment to be expected by bad Christians. So it looks as if Matthew saw the kingdom of heaven as a present reality here too, starting in Old Testament times and running on until the End; and the same will be true of the Husbandmen, which precedes the Wedding, with its nearly identical form. But the Workers in the Vineyard (20.1-16) lays the stress entirely on the End, as does the Ten Bridesmaids (25.1-13).

There is nothing surprising about Matthew's ambivalence, for, inevitably, the Jerusalem mission knew from the start that the kingdom was still not quite fulfilled, and one must pray *Marana tha*. It is a mistake to criticize Matthew as debasing the pure Markan doctrine of the kingdom, and turning it into the Church in his zeal for *Frühkatholizismus*. He is merely echoing the Petrine doctrine that we find opposed in 1 Corinthians 4, and which very likely goes back to Jesus himself: that the kingdom is already here. But, as was seen soon after the Lord's death, the Lord needed still to come. The Paulines pushed the kingdom into the future, in horror of the complacency, arrogance and immorality that stemmed from the 'realized' interpretation; and Matthew combined the two doctrines. Paul thought the kingdom of God was to come, and so did Mark and John, his disciples. Matthew speaks for the Petrines as usual, with a main stress on the kingdom as having come, but he builds a bridge to the Paulines with a strong secondary stress on its future fulfilment. It is his bridge-building, the moderation of his Petrine doctrines, that has enabled him to become the first evangelist.

Luke wrote Acts in part to reconcile the two missions, and he does his best for both sides. He sometimes strengthens the Pauline, future emphasis. There are some standing by who will see the kingdom of God *tout court, before they die* (9.27)—no complications about its having come in power, it is a plain future phenomenon. The penitent thief asks to be remembered when Jesus comes into his kingdom (23.42), in time to come. Mark's 'know that he is near' (13.29) becomes 'know that the kingdom of God is near' (21.31). In Lk. 19.11 people thought that the kingdom of God was about to appear, so Jesus told a parable of the nobleman who went into a *far* country to receive a kingdom for himself, and returned in due course to judge his servants and slaughter the rebellious (19.12-27). Here the future stress appears to be polemical: he told the parable 'because they thought that the kingdom of God was about to appear', and the *far* country will stand for the long interval between the ascension and the Lord's coming.[34] Similarly with Acts 1.6: the apostles ask Jesus, 'Lord, are you at this time restoring the kingdom to Israel?', and they are told that it is not for them to know the time of the kingdom. It is not now; it is hidden in the future, at the Parousia.[35] So Luke is a Pauline;[36] he thinks the kingdom is still to come.

But sometimes he strengthens the Petrine, present stress. In Matthew the apostles were to proclaim that the kingdom ἤγγικεν and to heal; at Lk. 10.9 they are to heal and to say, 'The kingdom of God ἤγγικεν *upon you*'—it is clearly here, just as in 11.20, 'If I by the finger of God cast out demons, then the kingdom of God has come upon you'.[37] In 16.16 the kingdom is *preached* from the days of the Baptist, and *everyone forces his way into it*', which implies that it is here to force one's way into.[38] In 17.20 Pharisees ask when the kingdom is coming,

34.   I.H. Marshall, *The Gospel of Luke* (NIGTC; Exeter: Paternoster Press, 1978); J.A. Fitzmyer, *The Gospel according to Luke* (AB, 28; New York: Doubleday, 1981–1985), II, p. 1229; M.D. Goulder, *Luke: A New Paradigm* (JSNTSup, 20; Sheffield: JSOT Press, 1989), II, p. 680.

35.   E. Haenchen, *The Acts of the Apostles* (ET Oxford: Basil Blackwell, 1971), p. 143: after the Gentile mission, in particular.

36.   We do not really need any evidence that Luke is a Pauline, for Paul is the hero of Acts; but he is also sympathetic to Peter, who is regularly whitewashed in the Gospel, and leads the Church in Acts 1–12.

37.   Marshall, *Luke*, p. 421, 'This suggests that the healings are to be regarded as a sign of the presence of the kingdom'; Goulder, *Luke*, pp. 469-70; *contra* Fitzmyer, *Luke*, pp. 848-49.

38.   The meaning of the saying is controverted, and Fitzmyer, *Luke*, II, pp. 1117-

and Jesus replies that it does not come with observation, but is in fact *in their midst* (17.21). So the future idea is wrong, and the present idea is right, for the moment;[39] and Luke is a Petrine. But he is a Pauline again by 19.11. Luke's feeling for fine theological points is not too strong. To put the matter more charitably, we may say that what had been a hot potato in the 50s had become less urgent in the 80s; as the politico's quip goes, if you leave a hot potato alone, in time it will become a cold potato.

The presence, or future coming, of the kingdom is part of the doctrinal field of battle whose scars are left all over our New Testament. What was at issue was the substance of the new faith, and in such struggles there are high aspirations on both sides. To the Jerusalem leaders the transformed world that they had known in Jesus' ministry was still a present reality. They were πνευματικοί, even τέλειοι. They could heal and exorcise; they could speak with the tongues of angels and be carried up to visions of the throne; they could receive messages from spirits and prophesy; they knew the ecstatic joy of shared wealth and shared persecution. To the Paulines this was mostly vacuous self-deception: free-wheeling, unreality, boasting and claims to be above natural desires contrasted with scandalous instances of gross immorality. Christians had, of course, the down-payment of the Spirit; but the kingdom was still to come. Matthew the Petrine and Luke the reconciler do their best to have it both ways and bring the two missions together. But New Testament scholars can recognize the reality of the issue in the earliest history of the Church, and not allow themselves to slip into the trite rhetoric of already-but-not-yet beloved of theological paradox-mongers.

18, renders, 'everyone is pressed to enter it'; but the *presence* of the kingdom on earth is assumed whatever the interpretation. For discussion see my *Luke*, pp. 628-30.

39. Marshall, *Luke*, p. 655, 'more naturally interpreted as referring to the present time'. Fitzmyer, *Luke*, pp. 1159, 1161-62, hesitates between *among you* and *within your grasp*. I had not fully seen the perspective in *Luke*, p. 650.

MIGHTY ACTS AND RULE OF HEAVEN: 'GOD IS WITH US'

Birger Gerhardsson

The evangelist Matthew presents the mighty acts that Jesus performs during his active, public ministry in Israel primarily in three types of text: pericopes about therapeutic miracles, pericopes about non-therapeutic miracles,[1] and a number of summarizing notices. In my study *The Mighty Acts of Jesus according to Matthew*,[2] I analysed these texts, devoting a chapter to each one of the three types. In addition, I examined the material concerning resistance against Jesus' miracles and controversies surrounding them, as well as the christological appellations to be found in Matthew's miracle material. I did not, however, study the relation between Jesus' mighty acts and the basic theme of his proclamation, in spite of the fact that Jesus' therapeutic acts in Israel are expressly connected with *the rule or kingdom of Heaven/God*: 'If it is by the Spirit of God that I cast out demons, then the kingdom/rule of God has come upon you' (12.28).

With this article, I wish to fill this gap in my investigation. I will discuss the relation between Jesus' miracles and *the rule of Heaven*,[3] and, at the same time, the theme *Immanuel*, 'God is with us' (cf. 1.23). In my view, these two motifs are widely synonymous.

It is, of course, not possible here to discuss fully the very complex question of ἡ βασιλεία τῶν οὐρανῶν/τοῦ θεοῦ in Jesus' proclamation and other activity. I shall deal but briefly with some aspects that I find of special interest for our theme. I have tried to clarify some of

---

1. The common term 'nature miracle' should be avoided; see *The Mighty Acts* (next note), p. 52.
2. (Scripta Minora 1978–1979 in memoriam Gustavi Aulén; Scripta Minora Regiae Societatis Humaniorum Litterarum Lundensis 1978–1979, 5; Lund: Gleerup, 1979).
3. I simplify the matter this time and write 'rule of Heaven', without discussing the well-known translation problems.

these matters in more detail elsewhere.

I am not among those who love the word 'eschatology'. I agree with Jean Carmignac[4] that this term brings together too many themes that should be kept apart. This catchword entices us, furthermore, into interpreting the New Testament message—for example, the idea of the rule of Heaven—onesidedly, as something new and future; we forget how deeply Jesus and the Early Church were rooted in Israel's ancient, classic convictions and values, notions and perspectives. The fact that the delay of the Parousia did not shake Early Christianity more than it did has that explanation. The following presentation will, I hope, illustrate my point.

This article about a group of problems in Matthew is dedicated to Robert Gundry who has over the years presented us with 'good fruit' from his thorough studies in this gospel.

The Two Phases in the Ministry of Jesus

The evangelist Matthew regards, as I have tried to show elsewhere, the public ministry of Jesus in Israel as *an activity divided into two phases.*[5]

The first phase is comparatively long (4.12–25.46): Jesus is here overpoweringly successful, completely unstoppable. In the fullest sense, he is under the divine 'blessing', God 'is with him', to use the ancient Jewish terminology.[6] The rabbis could at times also say about a man under the 'blessing' that God deals with him in accordance with his 'good measure' (מדה טובה).[7] This now applies to Jesus—in the highest degree.

---

4. *Le mirage de l'eschatologie* (Paris: Letouzey & Ané, 1978).

5. See my articles, 'Gottes Sohn als Diener Gottes', *ST* 27 (1973), pp. 73-196, and 'Jesus ausgeliefert und verlassen—nach dem Passionsbericht des Matthäusevangeliums', in M. Limbeck (ed.), *Redaktion und Theologie des Passionsberichtes nach den Synoptikern* (WF, 481; Darmstadt: Buchgesellschaft, 1981), pp. 262-91.

6. See, e.g., the comprehensive depiction in Deut. 28, and further my book *The Testing of God's Son*, I (ConBNT, 2:1; Lund: Gleerup, 1966), pp. 36-70. It is said of king Hezekiah in 2 Kgs 18.7: 'The Lord *was with him*; wherever he went, he prospered'. Cf. the words about Jesus in Acts 10.38: 'how he went about doing good and healing all who were oppressed by the devil, for God *was with him*'. And Jn 3.2: 'for no one can do these signs that you do unless God *is with him*'. Cf. on this theme H.D. Preuss, '…Ich will mit dir sein!', *ZAW* 80 (1968), pp. 139-73, and D. Vetter, *Jahves Mit-sein ein Ausdruck des Segens* (AT, 1:45; Stuttgart: Calwer Verlag, 1971). See also next note.

7. See especially *Ber.* 9.5 and ch. 4 in *The Testing*; further my article 'Gottes

The second phase is short (26.1–27.66). Here God is dealing with Jesus in accordance with 'the measure of his punishment, his evil dispensation' (מדת פורענות). Jesus is now under the divine 'curse', God 'is not with him', he has 'delivered him up' to his enemies, he has 'abandoned' him. This is the excruciating part of Jesus' ministry. In this phase, his situation is adequately expressed in his cry to God, 'My God, my God, why have you forsaken me?' (27.46).[8]

In the Gospel of Matthew, Jesus performs all his mighty acts, without exception, during the first phase of his ministry, the time of 'blessing'. Let us now briefly bring the great, overarching perspectives to the fore.

The Ancient Covenant Ideology

The basic idea in Israel's traditional Covenant ideology is that Yahweh is to be Israel's God and Israel Yahweh's people. Yahweh—God—binds himself to 'be with' his people and bestow upon it his 'blessing'; Israel will lack nothing.[9] He promises to provide food and drink for them and all other personal necessities of life, to protect them and save them from diseases, dangers and threats; they will obtain wealth and glory, power and might, happiness and victory—in short, the divine 'blessing' in all its aspects (e.g. Deut. 28).[10]

The conditions of the Covenant—both the 'blessing' and the 'curse'—are set forth in grand, unqualified terms; nuancing is not in order here. The extravagant expressions remind us of the language of the biblical hymns and songs of praise.[11]

Sohn als Diener Gottes', pp. 79-88. The measure symbolism is discussed thoroughly by H. Ljungman in his book *Guds barmhärtighet och dom* (Lund: Gleerup, 1950).

8.　See esp. 'Gottes Sohn als Diener Gottes', pp. 88-106, and 'Jesus ausgeliefert und verlassen', pp. 262-91.

9.　See, e.g., Deut. 2.6-7: 'Surely the Lord your God has blessed you in all your undertakings...the Lord your God has been with you; you have lacked nothing'. See also Deut. 8.9 and Ps. 23.1.

10.　See also, e.g., Deut. 7.12-24, 11.26-28 and Lev. 26. On the 'blessing' motif, cf. further Vetter, *Jahwes Mit-sein ein Ausdruck des Segens*. The classic treatment is J. Pedersen, *Israel: Its Life and Culture*, I-II (London: Cumberlege; Copenhagen: Branner og Korch, 1926), pp. 182-212. Cf. also N. Lohfink *et al.*, *'Ich will euer Gott werden'* (SBS, 100; Stuttgart: Bibelwerk, 1982).

11.　*The Mighty Acts*, p. 24. For other aspects, cf. R. Glöckner, *Neutestamentliche Wundergeschichten und das Lob der Wundertaten Gottes in den Psalmen* (WS,13; Mainz: Matthias–Grünewald, 1983).

The first sentence in Israel's ancient text of confession, the Shema', deals with *God* and his uniqueness: 'Hear, O Israel: The Lord (is) our God, the Lord is one!' Custom dictated already in New Testament times that a blessing was inserted into the Shema' after this sentence: 'Blessed be the name of his glorious rule (kingdom) always and for ever!'[12] Thus the introductory words of the Shema' dealt with the rule of God—the kingdom of Heaven. (It was recited every morning and every evening; in my opinion Jesus took his theme 'the rule of Heaven' primarily from this ever timely text.)

The people of Israel binds itself, for its part, to serve Yahweh and none other: to cleave to him faithfully, listen to his voice, obey him, live according to his will ('do' it) and keep his law, the Torah (see e.g. Exod. 19.3-8, Deut. 6). Or, as the pregnant formulation in the second sentence of the Shema' summarizes the matter, to love him with its whole heart, its whole soul and all its resources.[13]

Israel's dream of the future 'rule of Heaven' appears in a particular light against this background. Israel expected, in hard times, that Yahweh would soon demonstrate—in a new and definitive way—that he is *God*. He would 'arise' and intervene as never before, 'be with' his people, visit it, dwell within it, more fully and completely than ever. His 'blessing' would overflow. The Old Testament books contain numerous passages dealing with a future golden age, the most beautiful ones occurring in the book of Isaiah. It is this comprehensive 'blessing' that is called 'the rule of Heaven' (ἡ βασιλεία τῶν οὐρανῶν); the coming rule will be nothing other than a state of perfect 'blessing'.

It was not always necessary to use explicitly the very term βασιλεία in the narratives of Jesus' mighty deeds (as in Matthew 12.28). The episodes showed by their content clearly enough what the rule of Heaven *is* when it is working on earth, and they illustrated concretely the conditions of the rule (kingdom): divine 'blessing'. Let me now briefly sketch the larger framework.

12. See 'The Parable of the Sower and its Interpretation', in *NTS* 14 (1967–68), pp. 167-69 n. 2.
13. See *The Testing of God's Son*, ch. 4. The rabbis took the phrase 'with all your might (מאד)' in the sense 'with all your mammon (ממון)'. I generally translate it 'with all your resources'. On the translation problem, see my article The 'Shema' in Early Christianity', in *The Four Gospels 1992* (FS F. Neirynck, ed. F. van Segbroeck *et al.*; BETL, 100; Leuven: University Press & Peeters, 1992), p. 277 n. 2.

Immanuel: 'God is with us'

It is said in the brief pericope about the birth of Jesus in Matthew's introductory chapters (1.18-25) that the child would be given the name *Jesus*, and a formula quotation from the prophet Isaiah (7.14) is cited, the first of its kind in the gospel: 'they shall name him Immanuel, which means, "God is with us"'. The child did not get this name. The words from the prophet are here used in order to *interpret* Jesus and his name. In Jesus 'God is with us'. To everyone sharing the faith of Israel and versed in Scripture, the ancient terms of the Covenant as well as the expectations of the Messiah and of the rule of Heaven were here mobilized: it meant 'blessing'.[14] The name Immanuel, which is applied to Jesus, indicates the *content* of the rule of Heaven, that 'God is with us'.

When presenting Jesus' ministry in Israel the evangelists and their predecessors paint their pictures with colours taken from ancient prophetical promises and expectations about a blessed future for Israel. It is only natural for them to derive their words and expressions from these sources. It is said, for example, in Matthew that 'the blind receive their sight and the lame walk, lepers are cleansed and the deaf hear, and the dead are raised, and the poor have good news preached to them' where Jesus is at work (11.4-5). This is *Isaianic* wording (see, e.g., Isa. 26.19; 29.18-19; 35.4-6; 61.1-2), and it paints the situation of a perfect divine 'blessing'.

Immanuel: The Forgiveness of Sin

Matthew uses grand words when, in a number of summaries, he tells his listeners about Jesus' therapeutic activity in Israel: Jesus heals all kinds of sicknesses and all who are sick in Israel. The evangelist could have cited a formula quotation from Isaiah about coming days when the Lord, 'our judge', 'our ruler', 'our king', is going to save Zion:

> No inhabitant will say, 'I am sick'; the people who dwell there will be forgiven their iniquity (Isa. 33.24).[15]

This gives us reason to comment upon the second name connected with Mary's son in the Matthean birth narrative (Mt. 1.18-25), his real,

---

14. 'This expression that Yahweh or God is with one is only another term for the blessing' (Pedersen, *Israel*, p. 194). Cf. Vetter, *Jahves Mit-sein ein Ausdruck des Segens*.

15. Cf. promises such as Zech. 12.8.

proper name: *Jesus*. Joseph gets a message from an angel that the child to be born will have that name (Greek 'Ιησοῦς, recalling Hebrew יֵשׁוּעַ), 'for he will save his people from their sins (ἀμαρτίαι)'. The word-stem in the Hebrew name Yeshua' (יֵשׁוּעַ) means 'rescue', 'deliverance', 'salvation', without any more precise specification. It was most readily taken to mean 'deliverance from enemies and oppressors'. In this text in Matthew, however, the salvation in view is qualified not in this most obvious sense but as a 'saving *from sins*'.[16] This is accordingly a carefully chosen specification and perspective. Obviously Matthew wants his listeners to regard Jesus' ministry *in its entirety* as a divine intervention designed to save God's people from their *sins*.[17] The theme of forgiveness takes also a very important place in the following account of Jesus' teaching.[18]

This aspect is not explicitly articulated in pericope after pericope dealing with Jesus' therapeutic miracles, but it is found with all the more clarity and emphasis in one important text of this category: the narrative about Jesus healing the paralytic in Mt. 9.1-8. This fully explicit example was presumably regarded as enough. The evangelist assumes certainly that his listeners will understand, in the light of this example, that the therapeutic acts of Jesus always include forgiveness of sins. The cured men and women are not only healthy in body after having met Jesus, they have a double reason for bursting out in praise for the blessed fact that now 'God is with us'.[19]

Thus Jesus' therapeutic activity means for Matthew also that the sins of the people are forgiven; the forces of the rule of Heaven manifest

16. Cf. *The Mighty Acts*, p. 77.
17. On the aspect of forgiveness, cf. K. Kjaer-Hansen, *Studier i navnet Jesus* (Aarhus: published by the author, 1982), pp. 285-92, and B. Olsson, 'En textorienterad läsning av bibeln', *Religion och Bibel* 39 (1980), pp. 46-47. On the fact that in Matthew Jesus' ministry in Israel is in its totality regarded as an act of sacrificial service, see my article, 'Sacrificial Service and Atonement in the Gospel of Matthew', in R. Banks (ed.), *Reconciliation and Hope* (FS L.L. Morris; Exeter: Paternoster, 1974), pp. 25-35.
18. *The Mighty Acts of Jesus*, p. 77. See also J.S. Kennard, 'The Reconciliation Tendency in Matthew', *ATR* 28 (1946), pp. 159-63, and W.G. Thompson, *Matthew's Advice to a Divided Community, Mt. 17,22–18,35* (Rome: Biblical Institute, 1970), pp. 22-25.
19. Cf. the reactions of the people in *Luke*, after the raising of the widow's son in Nain. The crowd glorifies God, saying, 'A great prophet has arisen among us', and '*God has visited his people*' (7.16).

themselves in a basic way as forgiveness.

The bestowing of an unconditional forgiveness of sins is explicitly narrated—in fact even commented upon—in this pericope dealing with a discussion with Jewish *opponents* ('some of the scribes'). In another pericope, in which Jesus likewise counters criticism from opponents ('the Pharisees', 12.22-30), he *interprets* his exorcisms: 'If it is by the Spirit of God that I cast out demons, then the rule of God has come upon you'. This is another way of saying that 'God is with us'.

In these texts a characteristic conflict is reflected: Jesus is to the Pharisees and scribes an imposter (πλάνος)[20] and magician, receiving his might from Beelzebul,[21] while he is to the Church *Immanuel*: he embodies the divine 'blessing', God's healing forgiveness to his people—in short, *the rule of Heaven* of which the prophets had spoken.

Immanuel: Other Aspects of the 'Blessing'
The gospel of Matthew contains nine *summary statements* about Jesus' ministry in Israel, what he was doing in different places (4.23-25; 8.16; 9.35; 12.15-16; 14.13-14, 35-36; 15.29-31; 19.1-2; 21.14). The two programmatic ones in 4.23-25 and 9.35 mention both Jesus' preaching/ teaching and his healing, whereas the others mention only his healing. The acts are all of one type, therapeutic acts, they are performed for people beyond the circle of adherents, and Matthew generalizes them and absolutizes them. The intention is obviously to show that now God 'is with' his people, with his 'blessing'. The people around Jesus lack nothing: all sicknesses are healed and all who are sick are made well.[22] The wordings are extravagant—faith and confession have gained the upper hand over historical correctness.[23]

Secondly, Matthew narrates some fourteen specific cases in which Jesus heals one or two *individual sick persons*—in fact, everyone who turns to him, either in person or as represented by another (8.1-4, 5-13, 14-15, 28-34; 9.1-8, 18-19 and 23-26, 20-22, 27-31, 32-34; 12.9-14, 22-29, 15.21-28, 17.14-20, 20.29-34). These narratives about *therapeutic miracles* are uniform and the point is very clear in these texts as well:

---

20. Mt. 27.63. Cf. R. Hummel, *Die Auseinandersetzung zwischen Kirche und Judentum im Matthäusevangelium* (BEvT, 33; Munich: Kaiser, 2nd edn, 1966), pp. 12-22, and S. van Tilborg, *The Jewish Leaders in Matthew* (Leiden: Brill, 1972).
21. Mt. 9.34; 12.24. Cf. Hummel, *Auseinandersetzung*, pp. 109-42.
22. See *The Mighty Acts*, ch. 2.
23. See *The Mighty Acts*, ch. 2, esp. pp. 24 and 34.

where Jesus is at work, God 'is with' his people: he heals, liberates, saves. Life is the subject: the health and life of body and soul.[24]

Deliverance from *hunger* and starvation does not show up in this kind of pericope, but can be found in the treatment of two non-therapeutic acts, the feeding miracles. To be sure, these mighty acts are performed in order to help the *disciples* carry out their commission; but they are also part of the divine action to save the people; in these two cases through deliverance from hunger.

Matthew narrates, thirdly, some six or seven *non-therapeutic* miracles performed by Jesus (8.23-27; 14.13-21, 22-27 and 32-33, 28-31; 15.29-39; 21.18-22, and—presumably—even 17.25-27[25]). These mighty acts are different from each other[26] but they are all of one and the same sort: they are performed for the disciples in order to remove problems that have arisen because of their association with Jesus. They are, in a sense, inner-Church miracles. And they are carried out to show the disciples of Jesus that they can go on safely in their commission, without doubts and deficient faith (ὀλιγοπιστία), because they lack nothing in the company of Jesus. In these episodes the disciples are reminded of their incomparable ἐξουσία: they can feed the people, they are protected from threats and death, safe in every danger, they can count upon the prospect that even their economic problems will solve themselves, in spite of the fact that they have left everything and followed Jesus. The non-therapeutic miracles show that God 'is with' them in the ministry into which Jesus has brought them.[27] And the grand promises from Israel's past history of salvation are now fulfilled.

These pericopes do not describe the situation that arises when God 'delivers up' his beloved children and permits the 'curse' to strike them, but simply the basic 'blessing'. The conditions of the 'curse' are seen during the final phase of Jesus' earthly ministry (26.1—27.66).[28] But until then the 'blessing' prevails and does so to an eminent degree: the rule of Heaven has come near, God visits his people.

---

24. *The Mighty Acts*, ch. 3.

25. It is not narrated in this case that the miracle actually happened—Jesus only promises it—but Matthew means, of course, that Jesus' words never failed.

26. Apart from the fact that two feeding miracles are recorded.

27. See further *The Mighty Acts*, ch. 4.

28. See above n. 8.

The Testing Aspect

In the so-called temptation narrative (Mt. 4.1-11)—the prologue-like text in which he is put to the test at the beginning of his public ministry in Israel—Jesus is verbally attacked by Satan, the Tester (ὁ πειράζων). His inner secret is thus revealed to the listeners of the gospel. The three testing moments are calculated to establish whether Jesus—God's Son—is God's obedient *servant*, or whether he seeks his own good. The test is focused on three points:

In the first act (4.2-4) the question is whether Jesus has a divided *heart*, whether he despairs of God's provision and, yielding to hunger, takes the matter of sustenance into his own hands, thus revealing 'worry' and deficient faith (cf. the warning μὴ μεριμνᾶτε in 6.25-34).

In the second act (4.5-7) the question is whether Jesus despairs of God's protection and wants to put God to the test by forcing him to save his Son's life ('*soul*') from a violent death (cf. the warning for wanting to save one's life at all costs in 16.24-26).

In the third act (4.8-10) the question is whether Jesus desires the power and wealth (*mammon*) of this world so strongly that he is prepared to fall down before Satan in order to gain them (cf. the warning for serving mammon in 6.24).

Jesus stands the test. He shows that he does not despair of God's provision, does not demand that God shall at all costs protect him from violent death, and does not desire the power and wealth of this world.

Taken together these three parts of the introductory picture clarify to the listener that the Jesus who is now beginning his public ministry in Israel is God's Son 'in deed and truth' and ready to act as God's *servant*. He loves God with his whole heart and his whole soul and all his resources, he has 'understood' (cf. 13.23) and 'remembers' what his heavenly Father demands, he is prepared to accept his lot from the Father in faith and obedience, regardless of what that lot may be.[29]

---

29. It belonged to the basic obligations of the Covenant that the people of God should 'not forget' God's mighty deeds for the fathers but 'remember' them (e.g. Deut. 6–8; see in this light Mt. 4.1-11). It was also—in the time of fulfilment—of vital importance to 'understand' the message that is now proclaimed (Mt. 13.1-52, esp. 13.19 and 23). See *The Testing, passim*, and 'Gottes Sohn als Diener Gottes'. I added an observation to ch. 4 of *The Testing* in 'The Hermeneutic Program in Matthew 22.37-40', in R. Hamerton-Kelly and R. Scroggs (eds.), *Jews, Greeks and Christians* (FS W.D. Davies; Leiden: Brill, 1976), p. 148 n. 32.

The evangelist elucidates, by this vivid picture, Jesus' righteousness (δικαιοσύνη) and shows, in a profound and precise way, what kind of a *Messiah* he is.

The three-part pattern in the so-called temptation narrative (4.1-11) is taken from Israel's text of confession, the one which better than any other summarizes the demands of God's law: 'You shall love the Lord your God with your whole *heart* and with your whole *soul* and with all your resources (*mammon*)'. The ancient Shema' gives us the necessary insight into the testing of Jesus[30].

In the account which follows of the two phases in Jesus' ministry, Matthew shows that Jesus manifests throughout his ministry—for better or worse—that he is God's Son acting as God's servant. The double pericope of Jesus' baptism and testing (3.13-17; 4.1-11) is a kind of interpretative prologue to the whole presentation of Jesus' activity and fate in Israel. I have developed this further especially in my article 'Gottes Sohn als Diener Gottes'.[31]

Is There a Testing Aspect in the Miracle Stories?

I have, furthermore, in a series of contributions, tried to show that the command about love for God with heart, soul and material resources (Deut. 6.5) plays a steering role in a considerable number of other important texts in the New Testament, above all in the Gospel of Matthew.[32] In these texts, an examining, a *testing* aspect is normally expressed or implied.[33] In Matthew this is most obvious in the pericopes about Jesus' testing and crucifixion. Now we must ask a new question: Is there a testing aspect even in the Matthean texts about Jesus' *mighty acts*?

1. This aspect is not to be expected in the summary notices and does not in fact appear there.

2. The same is true, on the whole, of the pericopes about the therapeutic miracles, always performed for outsiders, not for the disciples. There the simple, supplicating faith of individual human beings is at work. It is exemplary and is never put to shame. The narrator does not indicate an element of testing in these pericopes, but just describes the

---

30. See *The Testing of God's Son*, ch. 4.
31. See above, n. 2.
32. For a survey, see 'The Shema' in Early Christianity', pp. 275-93.
33. 'The Shema'', pp. 284-86.

way in which a basic, entreating faith gets what it asks for from Jesus: God 'is with' his people.

There are, however, two exceptions. The pericopes about cases in which Jesus sets aside his principles and heals someone from the Gentiles (8.5-13; 15.21-28) include an element of testing. Jesus adopts a negative attitude to the Gentile supplicant, thus testing his or her faith. The test shows in both cases that the person's faith is in full measure, to Israel's shame—and Jesus' great astonishment.[34]

Even in the pericope that bridges the therapeutic and the non-therapeutic miracles (17.14-20), the aspect of testing is apparent. There the disciples play, strikingly, a crucial role, and it is they that are tested. They have attempted to heal an epileptic boy but have failed. Jesus explains this fact by referring to their deficient faith (ὀλιγοπιστία). They have not stood the test; Jesus for his part does.[35]

3. With regard to the pericopes about the non-therapeutic miracles on the other hand, the testing aspect is *pervasive* and obvious, even if the actual expressions are not used. Here the focus is on the situation of believers, the disciples; that is, the situation of those whom God 'is with'. Here faith is—for obvious resons—the center of attention. The faith of the disciples is tested in that problems arise for them.

Of these pericopes, we can—if we wish—connect three with the key word 'the *heart*' (the two narratives about feeding miracles and the one about eating from a fig tree), three with 'the *soul*' or life (the narratives about peril of death at sea) and one with '*mammon*' or material resources (the text about the coin in the mouth of a fish). Let me explain.

a. In the pericopes on the feeding miracles (14.13-21, 15.29-39), a situation of need arises: people hunger and the disciples must give them food. It never occurs to the disciples that God can provide bread for them in the desert, not even when the situation arises a second time. For Jesus there are no problems. It is interesting that the evangelist John has, in his parallel account, an explicit comment that indicates Jesus' aim: 'He said this to test (πειράζειν) him, for he himself knew what he was going to do' (Jn 6.6). The disciples, being put to the test, reveal their deficient faith. They do not understand what it means in this case that

---

34. See further *The Mighty Acts*, pp. 49-51. Cf. below n. 38.

35. The faith motif appears also in the Markan version (9.14-29) but there it is connected with the boy's father. He says to Jesus, 'I believe; help my unbelief!' This is missing in the Matthean version; instead the disciples' '*deficient* faith' is elucidated.

'God is with us'. This occurrence has points of contact with the testing of Jesus in the desert, where, in a situation of hunger, he shows that 'the evil inclination' does not divide his heart, making him uncertain of God's will and disobedient toward God (4.2-4).

In the pericope about the fig tree (21.18-22), the point of departure is that Jesus is hungry. The hunger theme is not developed, however, but merely serves as a starting point for a demonstration of Jesus' miraculous power, followed by an utterance from Jesus about the power of the disciples, provided they 'have faith and do not doubt'. We meet here a testing motif, even if it is presented in a somewhat unfocused form. The faith of the disciples is not so great that they find Jesus' power unlimited, as he himself regards it. They are people of deficient faith, they do not understand what it means that 'God is with us'. Admittedly, the word of 'deficient faith' is not used in this pericope; still, the behaviour of the disciples—their astonishment at Jesus' act—shows that they could not imagine that Jesus could do something like this.

b. In the three texts about distress at sea in Matthew (8.23-27, 14.22-27 and 32-33, 28-31), the activity of Jesus has brought the disciples out on the sea, where the situation becomes grave, their life is in danger. The disciples ought to be secure and calm as Jesus is, confident that 'God is with us', but they become terrified. When Jesus comes to them on the waves, they mistake him for a ghost from the realm of the dead. They are put to the test and reveal nothing but 'deficient faith'. In the inserted episode in which Jesus makes Peter able to walk on the water, all is well in the first half of the episode. Peter starts walking, at Jesus' word, on the water and succeeds in so doing. But then he becomes aware of the danger—'when he saw the wind'—and panics, thus revealing 'deficient faith'. Here the distress is peril of death, here life is threatened, 'the *soul*'. We are again confronted with a test. In this case the testing is akin to that of Jesus on the pinnacle of the temple (4.5-7).

c. In the pericope about the coin in the mouth of a fish (17.25-27), the issue is money. The problem is that Jesus and Peter ought to pay the temple tax but are both without means. This time it is not expressly said that Peter worries, but it is reasonably implicit in the situation, at least in the form of wondering: How are we to pay temple tax when we have left everything and followed Jesus (cf. 19.27)? This is no problem to Jesus. Even with regard to material possessions, he is secure and confident that 'God is with us'. He simply tells Peter what to do.

This pericope has a distinctive character and is, strictly speaking, not a proper miracle narrative; the miracle is merely promised. For my part I suspect that the original form of this pericope has been blurred. However, it is interesting to see that even the problem of *mammon* arises in the Matthean texts about non-therapeutic miracles. Those who love God with all their resources (all their mammon) need not worry about economic problems; the problems solve themselves.[36] The disciples ought to show the same attitude of lofty unconcern about belongings and wealth as Jesus does when he is put to the test on the mountain and spurns the mammon of this world—'all the kingdoms of the world and the glory of them' (4.8-10).

Testing in the Bible concerns the covenant partners, not the enemy; the people of God, not the Gentiles; the son, not the stranger; the righteous, not the godless.[37] It is therefore—in a sense—natural that we do not find this motif in the texts about Jesus' mighty acts on behalf of people outside the Jesus circle but meet them in texts about miracles that Jesus performs for the benefit of his own, the disciples.[38] With the possible exception of one pericope (the borderline case), there is—as we have seen—a testing aspect in all the pericopes about non-therapeutic miracles, indicated more or less clearly. The disciples are put to the test but fall short. Not that they fail completely and turn deserters—they do not demonstrate unbelief (ἀπιστία)—but they show themselves weak with regard to insight and belief, they demonstrate 'deficient faith' (ὀλιγοπιστία).

This very word—characteristic for Matthew, mostly in the adjectival form[39]—reveals that the aspect of testing is in the mind of the evangelist. Faith (πίστις) is in the limelight in all these texts about 'inner-Church' miracles, and it is *assessed and criticized*: it is put to the test. Trial and testing are part of the essense of the life of the believers.

---

36. Cf., e.g., Mt. 6.8, 24-34.

37. See *The Testing*, pp. 25-35, esp. 26 and 31-35.

38. When Jesus tests the Roman centurion (8.5-13) and the Canaanite woman (15.21-28), he treats them as presumptive believers. It belonged to the ritual when a proselyte should be received, that he or she should be tested.

39. The substantive appears in the New Testament only in Mt. 17.20, the adjective in Mt. 6.30, 8.26, 14.31, 16.8; otherwise only in Lk. 12.28. It involves in every case a lack of understanding of the divine 'blessing' or failing confidence in it.

Epilogue

In my study *The Mighty Acts of Jesus according to Matthew*, I tried to show that there is a series of striking differences between Jesus' therapeutic acts and his non-therapeutic miracles. The two types of mighty deeds have been used for two different purposes by those who composed and used these texts.[40] In the present article—which ought to have been included in my book (as chapter seven)—an additional characteristic difference between the texts about the two types of mighty acts has become clear: there is *a testing aspect* in the pericopes about the non-therapeutic miracles of Jesus but not in the pericopes about his therapeutic miracles (apart from three special cases). This observation should be added to those made in my book.[41]

It is remarkable that the traditional material in Matthew has been the object of such a *methodic and consistent reworking* as that reflected in our three types of miracle texts: summary notices, pericopes about therapeutic miracles, and pericopes about non-therapeutic miracles. The First Gospel is a learned and sophisticated gospel; the evangelist reveals scribal learning, and a considerable literary training as well. He knows how to keep different types of text apart, how to profile the content of a text and to give it a clear and neat form, and he works in a purposeful and skilful way, as a rule meticulously.[42] The fact that, still, he adheres to the traditional material and is anxious to preserve it shows, moreover, that he does not just loosely *narrate* for his listeners. He cares both for the traditions and for their historical anchoring. He wants to write salvation history. An interpretation that only takes the Matthean texts as *stories* does not do justice to the character of his presentation.

It belongs to the nature of this kind of history writing that it aims to convey a message for the *present*. The Matthean interpretation of the ministry of Jesus is certainly made by one of those converted 'scribes' who felt that they had 'understood all this' and could—and should—therefore illuminate the Christian community about the meaning of Jesus' work on earth for them (13.51-52). The gospel does not give us a loftily objective history writing, nor does it attempt to preserve a

---

40. See *The Mighty Acts*, chs. 3 and 4, with a summary on pp. 65-67.

41. See *The Mighty Acts*, pp. 65-67.

42. See, e.g., *The Mighty Acts*, pp. 40-41, 53, 57, 75, 78.

distance from the history it relates. The Immanuel aspect—'God is with us'—is certainly crucial for the *evangelist himself* when he narrates the history of Jesus Christ for the listening Christian community some 50 or 60 years after Jesus' ministry in Israel.[43]

43. I thank Stephen Westerholm who polished up my English.

MATTHEW'S ESCHATOLOGY

Donald A. Hagner

The importance of eschatology in the Gospel of Matthew has been recognized especially since G. Bornkamm's seminal essay of 1956, 'Enderwartung und Kirche im Matthäusevangelium'.[1] Bornkamm's essay was concerned with the theological relationship between eschatology and such matters as ecclesiology, law and christology. He showed clearly that Matthew is an interpreter of the traditions he received. Bornkamm did not, however, address the difficult problem of the entire body of eschatological teaching of the Gospel and what in fact the expectation of the evangelist concerning the end might have been. It is to this subject that I turn my attention in this essay.

Any attempt to describe Matthew's eschatology in a comprehensive manner will find its greatest challenge in coping with the variety of materials that must be dealt with. Matthew's eschatological perspective, like that of the other evangelists, includes statements concerning not only the future (near and more distant), but also the present, and even the past (i.e. past from the evangelist's point in time). There are furthermore statements in Matthew concerning the imminence of eschatological events, as well as others that imply a delay of the end, and even an interim period of considerable length, and last but not least, indications of agnosticism concerning the time of the end.

Much, if not most, of the material in question is drawn by the evangelist from his sources. Some of it is the result of his redactional activity and some perhaps is created by him. Given the exceptional complexity—not to say contradictory nature—of the various eschatological statements of

---

1. 'End-Expectation and Church in Matthew', in *idem*, with G. Barth and H.J. Held, *Tradition and Interpretation in Matthew* (trans. P. Scott; Philadelphia: Westminster Press, 1963), pp. 15-51. The essay first appeared in the 1956 Festschrift for C.H. Dodd, *The Background of the New Testament and its Eschatology* (Cambridge: Cambridge University Press).

Matthew, the question is, So far as the evangelist himself is concerned, do these statements cohere in any meaningful way? If we may not properly speak of a 'systematic' view of eschatology in the Gospel, may we at least speak of a 'coherent' view?[2] Or was the evangelist simply content to put traditional materials into his narrative without any concern about their mutual incompatibility?

This essay will explore the problem of Matthew's eschatology with these questions in mind. Our concern is with the eschatology of the Gospel itself and not with the teaching of Jesus.

I. *The Data*

We begin with a brief review of the data before looking at attempts to understand the data as a comprehensive whole. In what follows, there is no hope of being exhaustive—which would be nearly impossible not only because of the sheer amount of material, but also because of the allusive character of much of it, as well as the problem of the exegesis of some of it. I hope only to have touched upon the most significant material.

A. *Realized Eschatology in the Gospel of Matthew*

Matthew's stress on the theme of fulfilment is an obvious characteristic of the Gospel. The evangelist's use of the verb πληρόω in the so-called formula quotations is of course particularly well known.[3] What happens in connection with the birth, ministry and death of Jesus is described with great emphasis by Matthew as the fulfilment of the Scriptures. There is a sense indeed in which the whole of Matthew is eschatological in character.

Regardless of the date one assigns to Matthew, as a primarily historical narrative the Gospel describes a chain of eschatological events—that is, events having eschatological significance—*as already matters of past*

---

2.   The problem in its complexity is quite similar to that of Paul and the Law. E.P. Sanders argues against H. Räisänen that Paul's view of the Law, although not 'systematic', may with some effort at least be seen as being 'coherent' (*Paul, the Law and the Jewish People* [Philadelphia: Fortress Press, 1983], pp. 147-48).

3.   The formulae are found in: 1.22; 2.15, 17, 23; 4.14; 8.17; 12.17; 13.14 (ἀναπληρόω); 13.35; 21.4; and 27.9. Cf. more generally 26.54, 56. See R.H. Gundry, *The Use of the Old Testament in St Matthew's Gospel* (NovTSup, 18; Leiden: Brill, 1967).

history. These past events have somehow a vital connection with the future not only by anticipating or foreshadowing what is yet to occur, that is, what is properly eschatological, but also by constituting the very basis of the eschatological events of the future.

The opening two chapters of Matthew, which serve as prolegomena to the story of Jesus, are nevertheless of great theological significance in establishing the perspective of the evangelist. These chapters of course abound with obviously eschatological motifs. The genealogy (1.1-17), centering on Abraham and David, points to the one who is the fulfilment of the covenantal promises associated with both names, to the one 'who is called Christ (ὁ λεγόμενος Χριστός)'. The child is conceived by the Holy Spirit and is named Jesus, 'for he will save his people from their sins' (1.21). The evangelist adds that 'all this took place to fulfil what the Lord had spoken by the prophet', whereupon follows the first of his fulfilment quotations, drawn in this instance from Isa. 7.14. Chapter 2 continues along the same line, with the motif of fulfilment further strengthened by no less than three formula quotations as well as the quotation in 2.5.

The past events of the birth and the infancy narratives are for the evangelist laden with eschatological significance. They are in themselves eschatological events that inaugurate a new era.

The ministry of Jesus is, of course, marked by the same sense of eschatological fulfilment. Jesus' words and deeds point repeatedly to the coming of the kingdom of God, a phrase used for the long-awaited eschatological reality of God's rule upon the earth.

At the beginning, the words of John the Baptist, 'Repent, for the kingdom of heaven is at hand (ἤγγικεν)' (3.2), are picked up verbatim by Jesus (4.17; it is also the message of the disciples in 10.7). Although the meaning of the verb ἐγγίζω has been extensively debated,[4] it seems to me that its most natural meaning in both instances is that the kingdom has come near, not that it is actually present. What precisely is meant by this nearness is difficult to say. Perhaps it is a way of indicating that the kingdom has come in some sense, but short of the expected apocalyptic consummation. (This is obviously a conclusion that the reader must draw by the end of the Gospel.) On the other hand, it is

---

4.   See W.G. Kümmel, *Promise and Fulfillment* (trans. D.M. Barton; London: SCM Press, 1957), pp. 19–25. Thus Gundry, rightly: 'The verb ἤγγικεν indicates nearness right up to, but not including, the point of arrival' (*Matthew: A Commentary on his Literary and Theological Art* [Grand Rapids: Eerdmans, 1982], p. 43).

possible that the evangelist intends the reader to understand that the
coming of the kingdom, even in its 'realized' sense, depends upon the
completion of the work of Jesus in his death and resurrection. But even
understood as involving nearness, the significance of this statement is
not to be underestimated. A new era, marked by eschatological fulfilment, has begun to dawn.

The ministry of Jesus is summarized by the evangelist as involving the
preaching of 'the gospel of the kingdom' (4.23; cf. 9.35), now with no
mention of nearness, but rather with the presumption of its presence.[5] In
agreement with this conclusion is the remarkable statement of 12.28:
'But if it is by the Spirit of God that I cast out demons, then the
kingdom of God has come (ἔφθασεν) upon you'. There is far less
ambiguity concerning the meaning of the verb φθάνω than concerning
the verb ἐγγίζω. φθάνω clearly asserts the presence of the kingdom.[6]

In relation to the casting out of demons, one further small but
significant indicator of realized eschatology should be noted. In 8.29 the
demons who are about to be exorcized ask plaintively, 'Have you come
here to torment us before the time (πρὸ καιροῦ)?' This motif, unique
to Matthew, points at once to the eschatological character of the
exorcism as well as to the fact that the eschaton proper lies yet in the
future.

In his answer to the question of John the Baptist Jesus implies that he
is the one 'who is to come (ὁ ἐρχόμενος)'. In the words about John
that follow is a statement that again suggests present fulfilment: 'For all
the prophets and the law prophesied until John; and if you are willing to
accept it, he is Elijah who is to come' (11.13-14). Closely related to this
is the statement in 17.12, made in reference to John, that 'Elijah has
already come, and they did not know him, but did to him whatever they
pleased'. Without going into detailed examination of these passages, we
may note that John himself may be classified as an eschatological figure.
In 11.10, where Mal. 3.1 is quoted, John is identified as the one who
precedes the coming of the Lord and prepares his way.[7] This further

5. The same phrase constitutes the message to be proclaimed after Jesus' death
according to 24.14 (cf. 26.13).
6. 'It can therefore be said with certainty that Matt. 12.28 = Luke 11.20 must be
translated "the Kingdom of God has come upon you"' (Kümmel, *Promise and
Fulfillment*, p. 107). See G.E. Ladd, *The Presence of the Future* (Grand Rapids:
Eerdmans, 1974), pp. 139-48.
7. Cf. too Mal. 4.5 [3.23 Heb.] where Elijah is said to come 'before the great

confirms the conclusion that the coming of Jesus is to be understood as an eschatological event.

Referring to his preaching and healing ministry, Jesus makes this quite remarkable assertion in 13.16-17: 'But blessed are your eyes, for they see, and your ears, for they hear. Truly, I say to you, many prophets and righteous people longed to see what you see, and did not see it, and to hear what you hear, and did not hear it.' What was longed for was, of course, eschatological fulfilment, and it is this that Jesus says has now come in and through his work.[8]

The *passion narrative* is also written from the standpoint of fulfilled prophecy. In 26.24 Jesus says, 'The Son of Man goes as it is written of him'. According to 26.54, Jesus will not resist arrest (and the death that will surely follow) because 'How then should the Scriptures be fulfilled, that it must be so (δεῖ γενέσθαι)?' Mt. 26.56 stresses yet again that 'all this has taken place, that the Scriptures of the prophets might be fulfilled'. The evangelist provides a fulfilment formula quotation in 27.9.

It may be questioned whether this stress on the fulfilment of the Scriptures is sufficient to consider the events of the death and resurrection of Jesus as eschatological events. But there are other elements of the narrative that encourage the reader to think of eschatology in these events. A number of unusual occurrences, such as the supernatural darkness that covered the land (27.45), the two earthquakes (27.51 [cf. 27.54] and 28.2), and the descent of the angel from heaven in 28.4 are unmistakably apocalyptic in character. Furthermore, whatever else we make of the narrative, it is clear that the story of the resurrection of 'many bodies of the saints' in 27.51-53 is meant to point to the eschatological significance of the death and resurrection of Jesus.

It is an unusual irony to speak of *eschatological events of the past*. That events of the past can have eschatological meaning is no doubt to be explained by reference to the fact that they are perceived as having an ongoing present and future significance. Realized eschatology for Matthew is therefore not simply a matter of past events. The present significance of these events for the church is probably well known to Matthew's community and it is not the evangelist's immediate purpose to draw this out in his narrative (in the way, for example, that the writer

and terrible day of the Lord comes'.
8. On the other hand, the opponents of Jesus, the Pharisees and Sadducees, who come asking for a 'sign', are apparently unable 'to interpret the signs of the times' (16.3).

of the Fourth Gospel does).[9] There are, however, a few instances in the Gospel where eschatological reality available to the present experience of the readers can easily be seen.

The promise that Jesus 'will baptize you with the Holy Spirit' (3.11) could well have been taken by the readers to refer to a dimension of realized eschatology in their Christian experience. The Beatitudes (5.3-12) speak not only of a blessedness of the indeterminate future, but also of a present blessedness. The present tenses in vv. 3 and 10 ('theirs is [ἐστιν] the kingdom of heaven') are deliberate and point to the present blessedness of those who are receptive of Jesus' message.

Among other items that may be mentioned are freedom from anxiety concerning everyday needs (6.25-34; cf. 7.7-11), and the promise of rest for the heavy laden (11.28-30), both of which have eschatological overtones.

B. *Future Eschatology in the Gospel of Matthew*
It must be admitted that despite the importance of realized eschatology in Matthew, the volume of material devoted to future eschatology is much greater. The bulk of this has to do with the apocalyptic consummation of the age, the day of the Lord when the righteous will receive their reward and the wicked their judgment.[10] The subject is complicated by the fact that Jesus also speaks of other future events that have an eschatological character—in particular, of course, the destruction of Jerusalem. A major challenge of the eschatological discourse of chs. 24–25 is to disentangle what refers to the end of the world and what refers to the destruction of Jerusalem.

What will happen *at the consummation of the age*, according to Matthew, is a complex of events involving the parousia of Jesus and the final judgment wherein the righteous are rewarded and the wicked are sent to their punishment.

9. That the evangelist does to some extent draw out the significance of eschatology for the church is shown by Bornkamm in 'End-Expectation and Church in Matthew'.

10. For a discussion of apocalyptic in Matthew, see D.A. Hagner, 'Apocalyptic Motifs in the Gospel of Matthew: Continuity and Discontinuity', *HBT* 7 (1985), pp. 53–82; O.L. Cope, '"To the Close of the Age": The Role of Apocalyptic Thought in the Gospel of Matthew', in J. Marcus and M.L. Soards (eds.), *Apocalyptic in the New Testament: Essays in Honor of J. Louis Martyn* (JSNTSup, 24; Sheffield: JSOT Press, 1989), pp. 113-24.

Matthew's Gospel is filled with references to *the judgment of the wicked*. The importance of this to Matthew and his Jewish readers seems self-evident. It is already important from the preaching of John the Baptist, who speaks of 'the wrath to come' (3.7), of the trees not bearing good fruit as being 'cut down and thrown into the fire' (3.10), and of the one following him, who will baptize with fire, burning the chaff 'with unquenchable fire' (3.12). Jesus too speaks early and often of the final judgment. In the Sermon on the Mount he speaks of 'the Gehenna of fire' (5.22), again of Gehenna (5.29-30), of 'destruction' in 7.13, and, like John, of the tree not bearing good fruit being 'cut down and thrown into the fire' (7.19). The day of judgment ('that day') is in view in 7.22-23 where the evildoers are told to depart from the presence of Jesus. The sermon closes with the metaphor of a storm symbolizing the eschatological judgment (7.24-27). So too does Matthew stress future judgment in the remaining four discourses.[11] In the missionary discourse Jesus refers to the coming day of judgment which will be more tolerable for Sodom and Gomorrah than for the towns that reject the messengers (10.15). The threat of future judgment appears again in 10.28 and 33. The discourse of the parables of the kingdom alludes repeatedly to the future judgment, sometimes less directly (cf. 13.12-15), but most often in direct and vivid imagery (13.30, 40-42, 49-50), employing the metaphor of the furnace of fire and Matthew's favorite idiom of weeping and the gnashing of teeth (as also in 8.12; 22.13; 24.51; 25.30). What is most remarkable in ch. 13 is of course the stress on the delay of judgment, something we shall investigate below. In the discourse of ch. 18 future judgment is implicit in v. 6, then explicit in vv. 8-9, with mention of 'eternal fire' and again 'the Gehenna of fire', and then parabolically in vv. 34-35.

Before we look at the eschatological discourse itself, the mention of future judgment elsewhere in the Gospel should be noted. In 8.12 the future judgment (being thrown 'into the outer darkness') of unbelieving Israel is mentioned. Mt. 11.22-24 contains reference to 'the day of judgment' for the unrepentant towns of Chorazin and Bethsaida, which are compared unfavorably with Tyre and Sidon, and for Capernaum, which is also compared unfavorably with Sodom (cf. 10.15). Mt. 12.32 is particularly interesting for our purposes since it refers to the

---

11. This is effectively shown by Bornkamm, 'End-Expectation', pp. 16-24.

nonavailability of forgiveness 'either in this age or in the age to come', the latter referring apparently to the final judgment, which is thus clearly distinguished from the present era. Mt. 12.36-37 again speaks of 'the day of judgment'. So too 12.41-42 speaks of the coming 'judgment' for that generation (cf. 12.45). Mt. 16.27 refers to the future judgment to be rendered by the Son of Man, who 'is to come with his angels in the glory of his Father'. Judgment imagery again appears as part of a parable in 22.13, where the one not properly attired for the wedding banquet is to be bound hand and foot and cast 'into the outer darkness', where there will be weeping and the gnashing of teeth. A future sentencing of the scribes and Pharisees to Gehenna is found in 23.33 (cf. v. 35).

We turn finally to the eschatological discourse itself. As is to be expected, much emphasis is given to the judgment to come. The outlook becomes rather complex, however, because of the prophecy of the destruction of Jerusalem. The two items are linked incorrectly—from our point of view at least—if understandably, in the question of the disciples (24.3). Mt. 24.15-26 probably refers to the destruction of Jerusalem. The apocalyptic imagery of 24.29 suggests the coming of the final judgment, as do the parabolic metaphors of 24.39 (flood), 24.43 (unexpected thief), 24.50 (unexpected master), 25.12 (rejected maidens), and 25.30 (worthless servant). In two of these instances Matthew's formulaic judgment language occurs: the 'wicked servant' of 24.48-51 is 'put with the hypocrites' where people will 'weep and gnash their teeth', and the 'worthless servant' of 25.24-30 is cast 'into the outer darkness; there people will weep and gnash their teeth'. Most striking, however, is the final judgment scene with which the discourse closes (25.31-46). Those at the left hand of the King are addressed with the words, 'Depart from me, you cursed, into the eternal fire prepared for the devil and his angels' (25.41; cf. 25.46, 'And they will go away into eternal punishment').[12]

It is obviously important to the Jewish perspective of Matthew's community that there will be a final reckoning in an eschatological judgment to come. If eschatology has somehow already begun, it is clear that one aspect of the eschatological expectation, although delayed for the time being, must yet occur in the future. Like other New Testament

---

12. It may be noted that there is no reference to future judgment in the passion and resurrection narratives (chs. 26–28), except for the indirect allusion in 26.24.

writers, the evangelist uses the coming judgment as a motivation for righteous conduct.

Correlative to the future judgment of the wicked is *the future or eschatological blessing of the righteous*. Although the latter is very important in Matthew, it is referred to rather less often than is the future judgment. It is true that according to the evangelist the followers of Jesus are already blessed; yet that blessing is in the present, even for the righteous, mixed with tribulation, persecution and suffering. Only in the future will the rewards of the righteous be fully experienced.

Future blessings as well as present blessings are in view in the Beatitudes (5.3-12): comfort, the inheriting of the earth, satisfaction, eschatological mercy, the vision of God. In the face of persecution the disciples are to rejoice, 'for your reward is great in heaven'. The petition in the Lord's prayer, 'Thy kingdom come' (6.10), also looks forward to the full experience of eschatological blessing. Future rewards for those who do their righteous deeds in secret are probably in view in 6.4, 6 and 18. Future entry into the kingdom of heaven in connection with the final judgment is found in 7.21. In the second discourse we encounter future salvation in 10.22 and, more allusively, in 10.32. Future rewards for those who receive the message of the disciples are in view in 10.41-42. In the parable discourse future salvation is in view in the image of wheat being gathered into a barn (13.30) as well as the statement that 'then the righteous will shine like the sun in the kingdom of their Father' (13.43). In the fourth discourse future salvation is alluded to only in the final parable (18.27, 32; but cf. 18.13).

We again delay looking at the eschatological discourse in order to review the pertinent material from other parts of the Gospel. In 8.11 we have the remarkable reference to eschatological blessing in the statement that 'many will come from east and west and sit at table with Abraham, Isaac, and Jacob in the kingdom of heaven'. Apart from a few passing allusions (e.g. 12.31-32; 12.37; 16.25; 19.17, 21, 23-25), the next striking passage is in 19.28 where, in response to Peter's specific question concerning future rewards, Jesus states,

> Truly, I say to you, in the new world (ἐν τῇ παλιγγενεσίᾳ), when the Son of Man shall sit on his glorious throne, you who have followed me will also sit on twelve thrones, judging the twelve tribes of Israel. And every one who has left houses or brothers or sisters or father or mother or children or lands, for my name's sake, will receive a hundredfold, and inherit eternal life.

Also notable is the request of the mother of the sons of Zebedee, who in effect asks for special eschatological blessing for her sons in the request, 'Command that these two sons of mine may sit, one at your right hand and one at your left, in your kingdom (ἐν τῇ βασιλείᾳ σου)' (20.21). The reference in 22.28 and 30 to 'the resurrection (τῇ ἀναστάσει)' again indicates the eschatological blessing of the future. The eschatological discourse naturally contains a number of allusions to future eschatological blessing. Salvation is mentioned in 24.13 and the elect are gathered in 24.31. It is the faithful and wise servant who will be blessed (24.46). The wise maidens gain entrance into the marriage feast (25.10); those who have made good use of the talents given them receive the plaudit, 'Well done, good and faithful servant; you have been faithful over a little, I will set you over much; enter into the joy of your master' (25.21 = 25.23). Finally, in the concluding judgment scene, those at the right hand of the King are invited, 'Come, O blessed of my Father, inherit the kingdom prepared for you from the foundation of the world' (25.34), and in 25.46 the righteous enter 'into eternal life'.[13]

It is clear from the above that the evangelist distinguishes between the present blessing of the righteous from a yet-to-come eschatological experience of blessing.

We turn finally in this section to the *predictions of a future coming or return of Jesus*, predictions that to some extent relativize the eschatological import of the events recorded in the narrative of the Gospel. If the ministry of Jesus is somehow to be conceived of as eschatological in character, it is also not absolute or exhaustive so far as the purpose of God is concerned.

Whereas 9.15 speaks (somewhat obscurely) of the bridegroom being taken away from the disciples, there is not yet any indication of a return of the bridegroom. Mt. 10.23 contains the first reference to the future return of the Son of Man (= Jesus), although it has been taken, wrongly on both counts in my view, to mean that Jesus expected the Son of Man (not himself) to come in just a matter of days, that is, before the missionary journey of the disciples was over. Also unlikely, in my view, is the conclusion that this statement simply refers to the fact that Jesus would meet his disciples in a few days or weeks, that is, before they had completed that specific mission.

Since the resurrection is itself a kind of parousia of Christ to the

---

13. Parallel to the observation in the preceding note, there are no direct references to future eschatological blessing in chs. 26–28.

church, I here mention the predictions of the resurrection (16.21; 17.9, 23; 20.19; 26.32), although this resurrection can hardly be thought to satisfy the eschatological expectation of the church.

Important for our purposes is 16.27-28, where it is said that 'the Son of Man is to come (μέλλει...ἔρχεσθαι) with his angels in the glory of his Father', for the purpose of rendering judgment (cf. 13.40-42). This is followed immediately by the famous logion, 'Truly, I say to you, there are some standing here who will not taste death before they see the Son of Man coming in his kingdom'. Allusions to the future coming of Christ are found in 23.39 and 26.29. Then again in 26.64 we encounter an important logion, 'But I tell you, hereafter (ἀπ' ἄρτι) you will see the Son of Man seated at the right hand of Power, and coming on the clouds of heaven'.

The eschatological discourse takes its point of departure from the disciples' question in 24.3, who ask about the time of the destruction of the temple and 'what will be the sign of your coming (παρουσίας) and of the close of the age (συντελείας τοῦ αἰῶνος)?' Jesus responds by describing what must happen before his coming and by noting that his coming will be as unmistakable as lightning in the sky (24.27). The event itself is referred to in 24.30: 'then will appear the sign of the Son of Man in heaven...and they will see the Son of Man coming on the clouds of heaven with power and great glory'. That the time of the parousia of the Son of Man may be unexpected (implying delay), and thus the importance of being ready, is the point of the material that follows (24.37-44; 24.50; 25.1-12). The final judgment scene begins with the last logion concerning the coming of the Son of Man: 'When the Son of Man comes in his glory, and all the angels with him, then he will sit on his glorious throne. Before him will be gathered all the nations, and he will separate them from one another as a shepherd separates the sheep from the goats' (25.31-32).

C. *Passages that Presuppose an Interim Period before the End*

There can be no doubt that the presence of the eschatological kingdom proclaimed by Jesus through his words and deeds is clearly distinguished by the evangelist from the eschatological denouement at the end of the present age. Further evidence of this can be seen in those passages that imply an interim period, whether of shorter or longer duration.

Jesus' *calling, training and commissioning of disciples* obviously implies an interim period of some length. When Jesus first calls disciples in 4.19 he says, 'Follow me, and I will make you fishers of people'. This could of course be regarded as being fulfilled in the sending out of the twelve in 10.5-42, yet the content of 10.16-25 obviously points to a time much later than the journey for which the disciples are being instructed in 10.5-15. Indeed, that material points beyond the disciples (as does much, if not most, of the material addressed to the disciples) to the later church. Similarly, 23.34 refers to an indeterminate future, when Christian prophets, wise men and scribes will be rejected and persecuted. Of the greatest importance, of course, is 16.18-19, where Jesus talks of building his church. That church during its existence will withstand the 'gates of Hades'. The disciples will have an ongoing responsibility in the community (16.19; 18.18) and Jesus promises in the future to be in their midst (18.20).

In the giving of the great commission with which the Gospel ends (28.20), the disciples (and the church) are told to evangelize, to baptize and to teach, and again the promise is given, 'lo, I am with you always, to the close of the age (ἕως τῆς συντελείας τοῦ αἰῶνος)'.

Another element, related to the preceding, but deserving of special mention, is *the necessity of the preaching of the gospel*. Over against the temporary limitation of his and his disciples' mission to Israel (10.5-6; 15.24), a future time is also in view when the gospel of the kingdom will be preached to the whole world, including the Gentiles. With the mission to Israel, or perhaps eventually to the Gentiles, Jesus tells the disciples to pray for more laborers to be sent into the harvest (9.37-38). The Gentile mission adumbrated in 10.18 (and more allusively in 2.1-12; 4.15; 8.11) and 12.18, 21 comes to explicit expression in 24.14, where it is linked with the end of the age: 'And this gospel of the kingdom will be preached throughout the whole world (ἐν ὅλῃ τῇ οἰκουμένῃ), as a testimony to all nations (πᾶσιν τοῖς ἔθνεσιν), and then the end (τὸ τέλος) will come'. A universal mission is also in view in 26.13: 'wherever this gospel is preached in the whole world'. It is preeminently in view in 28.19, where the disciples are told to 'go and make disciples of all nations (πάντα τὰ ἔθνη)'.

The amount of space given to *ethical teaching* in the Gospel itself (e.g. chs. 5–7; 9.15b; 12.33-37; 16.21-27; 18.21-22; 22.15-21; 23.8-11) also suggests an interim period in which the righteousness of the kingdom is to be manifested. If this is an 'interim ethics', it need not be for only a short interim, despite its radical idealism. Note should be taken too of the disciplinary procedure of 18.15-17, and also the statement

'For you always have the poor with you, but you will not always have me' (26.11).

Promises made by Jesus seem also to presuppose an interim period. Among others, and in addition to the promises of Jesus' presence already mentioned (e.g. 18.20; 28.20), we may point to the assurance of 6.33 and 7.11, the comfort of 10.19, 28-30, the invitation of 11.28-30, and the promise of 17.20 and 21.21-22.

A final and important aspect pointing to the interim period, especially in the eschatological discourse, is *the necessity for certain things to happen* before the end. This includes such things as various tribulations (24.6-8), persecution (24.9-10; see also 10.17-31), the deceitful claims of false prophets and christs (24.5, 23-26), and the destruction of Jerusalem (24.15-22).

D. *Logia Concerning Imminence*

We begin to approach the difficulty of our problem when we now review those logia that indicate, or at least seem to indicate, imminent judgment or an imminent parousia (and hence, end of the age), that is, not necessarily at any moment, but to be experienced by that very generation. The evangelist has apparently found no problem in including these logia together with the material just reviewed that implies an interim period.

Two of these statements have to do with *the imminence of the parousia*, or at least with some kind of 'coming' of the Son of Man.

Toward the end of the missionary instructions given to the twelve, Jesus asserts, 'When they persecute you in one town, flee to the next; for truly, I say to you, you will not have gone through all the towns of Israel, before the Son of Man comes' (10.23). Some interpretative options are: (1) the parousia is expected before the immediate mission at hand is completed, that is, within a matter of days or weeks; (2) the mission in view is that carried on in Israel until the fall of Jerusalem, with the coming of the Son of Man understood as a coming in judgment upon the city; (3) the mission to Israel to be carried on by the church will continue until the parousia at the end of the age and thus the time of the parousia is not delimited by the statement. I favor the second explanation of this difficult passage,[14] but without taking it to mean the

---

14. Gundry understands the passage as referring to the parousia (*Matthew*, pp. 194-95). D.A. Carson also interprets 10.23 as referring to the fall of Jerusalem

end of the evangelizing of the Jews in 70 CE.

The logion found in 16.28 is of key importance to our problem: 'Truly, I say to you, there are some standing here who will not taste death before they see the Son of Man coming in his kingdom'. Although it is theoretically an option to attempt to understand 'some standing here who will not taste death' in some way other than in the natural or plain sense of the words, this seems to me an arbitrary and unsatisfactory solution to an awkward problem. Some may think the same of any similar attempt to understand the coming of the Son of Man as meaning anything other than the parousia. To my mind, however, this is at least a possibility worth considering. The most obvious options, other than the parousia itself,[15] are: (1) the resurrection, (2) pentecost (yet Matthew shows no awareness of this) and (3) the destruction of Jerusalem. Again I favor the conclusion that this, like 10.23, may be a reference to the coming of the Son of Man in judgment (cf. v. 27) in the destruction of Jerusalem.[16] Because of the typological connection between the destruction of Jerusalem and the final judgment, the latter is also in view through the foreshadowing provided by the former.

Two of the imminence logia have to do with *judgment*, and do not mention the parousia directly.

According to 23.35, the guilt of the Jews in having murdered the prophets and having persecuted the Christians—the latest of God's emissaries—will come upon them in the form of some kind of judgment. Upon them will come 'all the righteous blood shed on earth', to which is added in 23.36, 'Truly, I say to you, all this will come upon this generation'. This very probably refers to the destruction of Jerusalem, understood as a vindictive judgment upon unbelieving Israel.

The second and last logion is the most general of all. At the end of the short parable of the budding fig tree (24.32-35) comes the statement, 'So also, when you see all these things, you know that he (it) is near (ἐγγύς ἐστιν), at the very gates'. This is followed by the words, 'Truly,

---

('Matthew' in *The Expositor's Bible Commentary* [Grand Rapids: Zondervan, 1984], VIII, pp. 250-53).

15. Gundry, with many commentators, favors the parousia here (*Matthew*, pp. 341-42).

16. For me the decisive point in the exegesis of this passage is the reference to 'some standing here who will not taste death' (i.e. die), for which only the fall of Jerusalem makes sense.

I say to you, this generation will not pass away till all these things (πάντα παῦτα) take place' (24.35). Since this parable follows, as in Mark, not the material of 24.15-28, but that of 24.29-31, which refers to the parousia of the Son of Man, it may well be that the evangelist means to include the parousia. On the other hand, the words themselves do not refer to the coming of the Son of Man; the ἐγγύς ἐστιν is vague and could easily be understood as referring to something else, such as the fall of Jerusalem.[17]

E. *Statements Referring to a Delay of the Parousia*
In our survey of the data we look next at a few passages that contain a specific reference to delay. The material in view here is found mainly in passing references in parables, all in the eschatological discourse, but it may for that reason be even more significant. These references stand in some tension with the imminence logia just reviewed. They are related to and indirectly support the material that implies an interim period, but are distinctive in the employment of the notion of delay.

In the parable of the faithful or unfaithful servant (24.45-51), the wicked servant says to himself, 'My master is delayed (χρονίζει)' (24.48). He uses this delay as an excuse to act unrighteously.

The very next parable, that of the ten maidens (25.1-14), contains the words, 'As the bridegroom was delayed'. The parable of course depends on the idea of a long wait, and stresses the idea of preparedness.

In the third parable, that of the talents (25.14-30), which follows immediately upon those just mentioned, the master is introduced as a man 'going on a journey (ἀποδημῶν)' (25.14). After he distributed the talents, it is said that 'he went away' (25.15). His return to settle accounts is described as being 'after a long time (μετὰ πολύν χρόνον)' (25.19).[18]

F. *Agnosticism concerning the Time of the End*
The final data to be reviewed here are the statements that the time of the end cannot be known. Like the references to delay in the previous section, these are found only in the apocalyptic discourse. There is,

17. Cf. Lk. 21.31, which supplies ἡ βασιλεία τοῦ θεοῦ as the subject. Gundry argues for a double fulfilment, one in AD 70 and the other at the parousia (*Matthew*, p. 491).
18. A delay of the parousia may also be possibly hinted at in 24.6: 'the end is not yet'; and in 24.8: 'all this is but the beginning of birthpangs'.

indeed, a close connection between the delay and the motif of agnosticism.

Most remarkable of all is the logion of 24.36. 'But of that day and hour no one knows, not even the angels of heaven, nor the Son, but the Father only.' It is little surprise that copyists, with christological concerns in mind, were inclined to omit the reference to the Son's ignorance of the time of the end. This is clearly a saying that the early church could not have created. It stands in considerable tension with the imminence sayings, unless one concludes that what is in view is not the general time, but only the particular hour and day—a highly unlikely interpretation, in my opinion.

Further references to the fact that the time of the end is unknown are found in the exhortatory material that follows the passage just mentioned. As those in the days of Noah did not know of the approaching disaster, those of the last day will not know the time of the coming of the Son of Man. Thus Jesus exhorts, 'Watch, therefore, for you do not know on what day your Lord is coming' (24.42). And again, 'Therefore you also must be ready, for the Son of Man is coming at an hour you do not expect' (24.44).

The same emphasis is found in the two parables that follow this passage. Thus, with reference to the wicked servant: 'the master of that servant will come on a day when he does not expect him and at an hour he does not know' (24.50). The parable of the ten maidens concludes with the exhortation, 'Watch, therefore, for you know neither the day nor the hour' (25.13).

These exhortatory references to the time being unknown point to an undetermined future, to an unexpected time, when people apparently have no reason whatever to expect the end.

II. *Theses concerning Matthew's Eschatology*

The material we have surveyed is filled with tensions, some of which appear to involve quite contradictory assertions. It is of course arguable that the evangelist has simply collected disparate traditions that were available to him and blithely ignored the fact that they were incompatible. On the other hand, it is equally possible that in the evangelist's mind the various eschatological elements we have noted did fit together in some larger, comprehensive whole. It is at least worth investigating this possibility before throwing up our hands in dismay at the challenge of an integrated understanding Matthew's eschatology.

A. *The Present–Future Tension*

The fundamental tension in the eschatology of the New Testament and of Matthew is that between presently realized eschatology and the eschatology of the future. If we sometimes call the latter 'eschatology proper', we thereby indicate the central oddity of the New Testament affirmation that what lies properly in the future has somehow already entered the present in and through the work of Jesus Christ.

This particular tension has of course been thoroughly explored in our century.[19] The significance of the breakthrough of Weiss and Schweitzer in establishing the fundamental importance of the apocalyptic perspective for Jesus can hardly be exaggerated. This viewpoint of 'consistent eschatology' stressed only one side of the tension. Dodd stressed the other side of the tension in his emphasis on realized eschatology. It was clear that a strong case could be made for each side of the tension. Kümmel, Jeremias, Cullmann, Schnackenburg and others effectively showed that it was not a matter of either/or, but of both/and. Something like a consensus seems to have emerged, although there have continued to be dissenters.[20] Little more needs to be said here about this tension, except to indicate its importance to the other problems to be discussed.

The tension between present and future eschatology constitutes the foundational complexity giving rise to the specific problems discussed below. If eschatology is a single fabric of reality, a divided eschatology, with some present and some future, becomes problematic. The reality of present eschatology that is short of consummation itself implies not only a necessary future eschatology, but even its imminence. Where the end

---

19. For a review of the discussion, see G. Lundström, *The Kingdom of God in the Teaching of Jesus* (trans. J. Bulman; Richmond: John Knox, 1963); G.E. Ladd, *The Presence of the Future* (Grand Rapids: Eerdmans, 1974), pp. 3-42. See also the symposium, *The Kingdom of God in 20th-Century Interpretation* (ed. W. Willis; Peabody, MA: Hendrickson, 1987) and the collection of essays, *The Kingdom of God* (ed. B. Chilton; Philadelphia: Fortress Press; London: SPCK, 1984).

20. E.g. R.H. Hiers (*Jesus and the Future* [Atlanta: John Knox, 1981]) and C. Sullivan (*Rethinking Realized Eschatology* [Macon, GA: Mercer University Press, 1988]), who continue to espouse the consistent eschatology viewpoint; T.F. Glasson (*The Second Advent* [London: Epworth, 3rd edn, 1963]) and J.A.T. Robinson (*Jesus and his Coming* [London: SCM Press, 1957]) deny that Jesus ever spoke of his parousia. See most recently the stimulating article of C.C. Caragounis, 'Kingdom of God, Son of Man and Jesus' Self-Understanding', *TynBul* 40 (1989), pp. 3-23; 223-38.

is announced as having begun, its final aspect cannot easily be thought of as distantly future.

B. *The Imminence–Delay Tension*

A further complicating factor is found in the expectation of two distinct events in the future: the fall of Jerusalem and the coming of the Son of Man. The fall of Jerusalem is described in quasi-eschatological language and in the same discourse that describes the coming of the Son of Man. The two events are obviously linked in the minds of the disciples (as their question implies, 24.3) and very probably also in the mind of the evangelist.

The fall of Jerusalem is obviously the most natural referent of the imminence sayings. So far as length of time is concerned, it fits best language such as 'there are some standing here who will not taste death before they see...' (16.28, which of course refers to 'the Son of Man coming in his kingdom'), and the references to 'this generation' (23.36; 24.35).

It seems possible that all the imminence sayings spoken by Jesus originally referred to the fall of Jerusalem. Then, if we may speculate further, since those who heard Jesus speak of the fall of Jerusalem could not in their minds dissociate such a catastrophic event from the end of the age, it may be that the idea of imminence became attached to sayings about the coming of the Son of Man. If the destruction of Jerusalem was imminent, so too must the coming of the Son of Man be imminent.

There is a theological relationship between the fall of Jerusalem and the end of the age, since both involve judgment. If the two are thought of as happening independently, the former may be regarded as a prefiguration of the latter. As the length of time between the two increases, the theological connection replaces the apparent earlier, though wrongly conceived, chronological association.

The logia concerning the coming of the Son of Man can be quite vague so far as the time is concerned (cf. 16.27 [where the μέλλει need not imply imminence];[21] 24.27; 25.31; 26.64 [where the ἀπ' ἄρτι, lit. 'from now on', is difficult to understand[22]]; as well as the allusions in

---

21. BAGD, p. 501a.

22. Gundry regards it as a referring to 'a mental seeing of the Son of man sitting at God's right hand', a seeing that begins immediately with the events of 27.51b-53 (*Matthew*, p. 545).

23.39 and 26.29). Even 10.23 with its reference to the evangelizing of Israel is indeterminate, since it could mean up until the destruction of Jerusalem or until the parousia itself. So too, the *locus classicus*, 24.30, remains vague despite the εὐθέως of 24.29, since it is not altogether clear which tribulation is in view in the phrase, 'after the tribulation of those days.'[23]

Mt. 16.28 is the least ambiguous of the imminence logia so far as time reference is concerned. It is arguable that the expression 'the Son of Man coming in his kingdom' could refer to the destruction of Jerusalem.[24] Many argue, however, that the most natural interpretation of this verse is that it refers to the parousia. If this conclusion is correct, then the author of Matthew probably regarded the parousia as imminent because he regarded the destruction of Jerusalem as imminent.

Further to be noted is the fact that the delay motif is applied not to the destruction of Jerusalem, but is restricted to allusions to the parousia (see section II.E., above).

Similarly, the agnosticism motif, with its accompanying exhortation to 'watch', occurs only in reference to the time of the parousia (see section II.E., above).

Thus we may conclude that the references to the destruction of

23. In Gundry's view, from 24.15 Matthew is writing about the tribulation of the end time, i.e., something yet future, and thus the problem of the 'immediately' disappears (*Matthew*, pp. 481-89). Blomberg regards 24.15-20 as referring to the fall of Jerusalem, but 24.21-28 to the yet future tribulation, thereby avoiding the problem (*Matthew*, pp. 357-61; cf. L. Morris, *The Gospel according to Matthew* [Grand Rapids: Eerdmans, 1992], pp. 605-10). R.T. France, on the other hand, takes the entirety of 24.5-35 as referring to the destruction of Jerusalem, again thereby avoiding the problematic 'immediately' (*Matthew*, pp. 335-47). F.D. Bruner regards the material throughout as having 'a double reference', i.e., both to the destruction of Jerusalem and the parousia of the Son of Man (*Matthew*, II, pp. 860-69). Without denying the typological connection between the events, I regard Bruner's approach as too easily bypassing the exegetical difficulties of the passage.

24. There are, as we have noted above, many possible interpretations of this clause. I mention a coming in judgment upon Jerusalem here because it fits best the time span referred to in the words 'some standing here who will not taste death before they see'. Among other popular interpretations are the transfiguration (which seems too soon to suit the time reference), the resurrection (e.g. 28.16-20, as a 'coming to the church in an anticipated "parousia"' [J.P. Meier, *Matthew* (NTM; Wilmington: Glazier, 1980), p. 188]) or pentecost, but these too do not fit the time reference. For a history of the widely varying interpretations of the logion, see M. Künzi, *Das Naherwartungslogion Markus 9,1 par* (BGBE, 21; Tübingen: Mohr, 1977).

Jerusalem are, as one might expect, much more delimited by the emphasis on imminence. By contrast, references to the coming of the Son of Man are less delimited, being also conditioned by indications of delay and lack of knowledge. The idea of imminence, however, by cross-over influence, may well have become attached to a few logia concerning the coming of the Son of Man.

C. *The Length of the Implied Interim Period*
The material reviewed in section II.C. above shows that the evangelist must have considered an interim period as necessary between the ministry of Jesus and the end of the age. Can anything be said about the length requirements for that interim period?

Of greatest interest is whether the forty years between the death of Jesus and the destruction of Jerusalem in 70 CE may be thought to be a sufficiently long interim period for the accomplishment of all that is expected. If so, this material need not be regarded as incompatible with the imminence motif, taken as referring to events of 70.

Forty years is enough time for extensive evangelization, for the building of a church, for the practice of kingdom ethics, for the experience of the presence of the risen Jesus, and so forth.

The Gentile mission, especially through the work of Paul, had been quite successful by the year 70. Already more than a decade earlier Paul could speak of the gospel as having been preached throughout the world (Rom. 10.18), meaning of course the Roman world, and he had to plan to work in Spain in order not to build on the work of another.

The experience of various trials and tribulations, famine, persecution, false prophets and christs, during the forty-year period prior to 70, also seems sufficient to correspond to what was prophesied as coming before the end.

At the same time, it may be admitted that an interim period of this kind is by nature not delimited, but open-ended. From our late perspective the centuries that followed continue to fulfil the promises and expectations of the interim period.

D. *Conclusion: The Eschatological Expectation of the Evangelist*
We may now attempt on the basis of the preceding discussion to draw together some concluding theses concerning Matthew's expectation concerning the future. At a few points more than one option may be given. The bearing of these concluding remarks on the dating of the

Gospel will also be given some attention.

1. Matthew views the ministry of Jesus as the inauguration of eschatology. A new era has dawned in fulfilment of some, though not all, promises of the Scriptures.

2. By its very nature, present or realized eschatology brings with it the promise of a future wrap-up of an apocalyptic character, that is, involving the judgment of the wicked, the reward of the righteous, and the establishment of a new world.

3. The future consummation, brought about by the coming of the Son of Man, will not occur immediately, but only after an interim period. (The consummation can nevertheless be described as imminent, i.e., as occurring within that generation.)

4. As promised by Jesus, that generation was to see the destruction of the temple and the fall of Jerusalem.

5. It was virtually unthinkable that the events just mentioned could happen without bringing with them the coming of the Son of Man and the end of the age. Therefore the coming of the Son of Man is, like the fall of Jerusalem, also regarded as imminent, that is, as to occur within that generation. They are part of the same complex of events; as the evangelist's added εὐθέως in 24.29 may indicate, the destruction of Jerusalem was to be followed 'immediately' by the parousia of the Son of Man.

If the statements of the preceding paragraph are true, it would be most natural to date Matthew before 70 (despite 22.7, which has often been made to bear more weight than it can).[25] The evangelist would then not have known of the failure of the parousia to occur in connection with or immediately after the fall of Jerusalem.

At least two other possibilities, each concerning a post-70 date, should be mentioned. The first is the least attractive: The evangelist, writing say a decade later, may have felt the necessity to be faithful to traditions he received, and hence preserved them even though the events themselves did not bear out the predictions. A second possibility is that the

---

25. On the language of 22.7, see B. Reicke, 'Synoptic Prophecies on the Destruction of Jerusalem', in D. Aune (ed.), *Studies in New Testament and Early Christian Literature* (Leiden: Brill, 1972), pp. 121–34 (123). For a recent impressive argument for a pre-70 date (65–67), see R.H. Gundry, *Matthew* (Grand Rapids: Eerdmans, 1982), pp. 599–609. See also J.A.T. Robinson's comments on the date of Matthew in *Redating the New Testament* (Philadelphia: Westminster Press, 1976), pp. 102-107.

evangelist had witnessed the fall of Jerusalem and now consequently awaited a parousia that might occur at any moment (but how long can such an extended expectation reasonably be thought to last?).

6. The interim period of some forty years, already experienced by the evangelist, was regarded by him as sufficient time in which to fulfil the prerequisites to be accomplished before the end.

7. It is, in my opinion, less plausible to believe that the evangelist really did separate the fall of Jerusalem, which was obviously imminent, from the parousia of the Son of Man, which he then put forward into the indeterminate future. In order to sustain such a view one has to put an unusual twist on the imminent parousia logia, especially 16.28 (preceded by 16.27, which clearly refers to the coming of the Son of Man), unless it be taken as referring to the fall of Jerusalem.[26]

III. *Postscript*

The conclusions drawn above, if correct, mean that the evangelist, apparently in good company with others in the early church, may have been wrong about the time of the parousia. Although it has not been the concern of this paper to deal with the teaching of Jesus, insofar as it can be known, it may well be the case that he too associated the fall of Jerusalem with the end of the age and the coming of the Son of Man. This possibility would be consonant with his own admission of ignorance concerning the time of the consummation (24.36). On the other hand, it may well be that Jesus spoke of imminence (cf. the expressions 'this generation', 'those standing here') only in connection with the fall of Jerusalem, speaking of the parousia only in indeterminate language.[27] In that case, the disciples would be responsible for confusing the imminence of the fall of Jerusalem with the coming of the end of the age.

It is intriguing that the data examined above are capable of such

---

26. It is possible that the logia of vv. 27 and 28 refer to different events. Cf. the note in the New Jerusalem Bible: 'In vv. 27-28 two sayings of Jesus, each dealing with a different event, have been joined together because they have a common reference to the coming of the kingdom of God: v. 27, the kingdom of the Father; v. 28, the kingdom of Christ'.

27. B.S. Crawford, in a stimulating article, argues that the imminence sayings concerning the parousia 'are community formulations reflecting the eschatological outlook of the early church as expressed in the utterances of its prophets'. 'Near Expectation in the Sayings of Jesus', *JBL* 101 (1982), pp. 225-44 (244).

different possible interpretations. Whether or not the evangelist (or his contemporaries) was able in his mind to separate the fall of Jerusalem from the apocalyptic coming of the Son of Man, his later interpreters have been able to do so, even if under necessity. The data are actually, for the most part, remarkably amenable to such an interpretation. As we have seen, the time of the coming of the Son of Man and the concomitant end of the age is usually left vague and indeterminate; it is furthermore the case that the time of the end is conditioned by the delay motif, which can be understood as open-ended, as well as the ignorance motif, which is regularly accompanied by the exhortation to faithful watching. The one really difficult statement in Matthew for this view is 16.28, which, however, as we have seen, *can* be understood as referring to something other than the parousia.

Luke, one of the earliest interpreters of the difficult Markan logion, has already 'de-eschatologized' it: 'there are some standing here who will not taste death before they see the kingdom of God' (Lk. 9.27). Many in the church have since done likewise.

It is a pleasure for me to dedicate this essay to Robert H. Gundry, whose friendship I have valued over the years and whose scholarship I have always admired, not only for its obvious, uncompromising respect for the text of Scripture, but also for its inimitable freshness and fairness.

THE SYNOPTIC 'SON OF MAN' SAYINGS
IN THE LIGHT OF LINGUISTIC STUDY

I. Howard Marshall

The topic of the Son of man continues to be one of the most important in contemporary study of the Gospels. At least three reasons may be mentioned:

1. 'Son of man' is one of the most frequent theological terms to appear in the Synoptic Gospels, and it also plays an important part in John, although we shall not be considering the Johannine usage in this context. When due allowance is made for parallel versions of the same sayings, there are about 40 different Son of man texts in the Synoptic Gospels. The term 'kingdom of God' occurs more frequently, but there is no other term, except 'God' or the various other names for God, which is found so often.

2. Scholars are agreed that, if Jesus used any phrases as self-designations, then this one, or whatever Aramaic equivalent may lie behind it, was one of them. There is strong dispute whether Jesus ever referred to himself as the Son (sc. of God) or as the Messiah, and it is clear that if he used these terms at all it was seldom and hardly ever in his more public utterances as opposed to private teaching to his disciples. But the authenticity of at least some occurrences of the term Son of man is granted by most scholars, although, as we shall see, (a) there are some scholars who argue that Jesus used it purely as an Aramaic idiom and not in any sense as a 'christological' title, and (b) there are others who would argue that Jesus used it not to refer to himself but rather to somebody else. In any case, it is clear that the term is of great significance in attempting to penetrate the mystery of the person of Jesus. Even if the use of the term should stem from the early church and not from Jesus, it would still be of immense importance in charting the earliest developments in Christology.

3. Finally, the question is an important one simply because it remains

unsolved and there are wide differences of opinion regarding the meaning and usage of the term. There continues in fact to be a vast output of literature on this problem. Since 1974, when I last attempted to survey the debate,[1] the question has continued to be hotly debated, and there have been several major monographs together with many articles on the topic.[2] I cannot pretend even to have read all this literature, but I should like to try to consider some of the contributions made in the English-speaking world since 1974 and to see whether any progress has been made towards a consensus of opinion. It is particularly congenial to undertake this task in the context of a volume honouring Robert H. Gundry, who has made such highly significant contributions to the understanding of the Synoptic Gospels and especially to the use of the Old Testament in them.[3]

The Position in 1974

I begin by summarizing the position as it appeared in 1974. The main areas of discussion then were:

1. The linguistic background to the phrase ὁ υἱὸς τοῦ ἀνθρώπου as used in the Gospels.
2. The conceptual background to the phrase 'Son of man'.
3. The authenticity of the sayings attributed to Jesus in the Gospels.
4. The meaning and significance of the sayings in the Gospels.

---

1. 'The Synoptic Son of Man Sayings in Recent Discussion', *NTS* 12 (1965–66), pp. 327-51; 'The Son of Man in Contemporary Debate', *EvQ* 42 (1970), pp. 67-87; there is a brief overview of the contents of these articles in my book, *The Origins of New Testament Christology* (Leicester: Inter-Varsity Press, 1976), which took account of the discussion up to 1974; in the revised edition (1990) there is a very brief updating (pp. 132-34). See further 'The Son of Man and the Incarnation', *Ex Auditu* 7 (1992), pp. 29-43.

2. For other surveys of the position, see G. Vermes, 'The Present State of the "Son of Man" Debate', *JJS* 29 (1978), pp. 123-34 (this is a slightly longer form of his essay, 'The "Son of Man" Debate', *JSNT* 1 (1978), pp. 19-32); W.O. Walker, 'The Son of Man: Some Recent Developments', *CBQ* 45 (1983), pp. 584-607; J.R. Donahue, 'Recent Studies on the Origin of "Son of Man" in the Gospels', *CBQ* 48 (1986), pp. 484-98.

3. See most recently *Mark: A Commentary on his Apology for the Cross*, (Grand Rapids: Eerdmans, 1993).

There was no consensus of opinion on any of these areas of discussion. However, it was at least possible to analyse the state of scholarship by concentrating on the different answers given to the third question: which sayings, if any, in the Gospels are authentic? The answer to this question could be most easily given in terms of an analysis of the sayings into three groups:

Group A: sayings about the earthly activity of the Son of man, such as Mk 2.10, 28; Lk. 7.34; 9.58; 12.10; 19.10 (with parallels where appropriate).

Group B: sayings about the suffering, death and resurrection of the Son of man, such as Mk 8.31; 9.31; 10.33-34, 45.

Group C: sayings about the future coming and glory of the Son of man, such as Mt. 10.23; Mk 8.38 (cf. Lk. 12.8-9); 13.26; 14.62; Lk. 17.24, 26.

In the light of this analysis four main approaches to the problem of authenticity can be noted:

1. Such scholars as O. Cullmann, F.H. Borsch, M.D. Hooker and O. Michel[4] held that at least some sayings in all three groups are genuine utterances of Jesus, spanning the whole of his earthly and future career. On this view Jesus was principally inspired by Daniel 7 where the Son of man is a figure of authority and glory, but he linked this figure to suffering and rejection, either by interpreting it in the light of Isaiah 53 or by the identification of the Son of man with the persecuted saints of the Most High in Daniel 7 itself. This type of approach has been given fresh support by C. Caragounis.[5]

2. The view of such scholars as P. Vielhauer and N. Perrin was that none of the sayings is genuine, and all of them represent the thinking of the early church.[6] In particular Perrin argued that the Son of man concept arose from creative exegesis of Daniel 7 and was especially

4.   O. Cullmann, *The Christology of the New Testament* (London: SCM Press, 1959); F.H. Borsch, *The Son of Man in Myth and History* (London: SCM Press, 1967); M.D. Hooker, *The Son of Man in Mark* (London: SPCK, 1967); O. Michel, 'ὁ υἱὸς τοῦ ἀνθρώπου', in *NIDNTT*, III, pp. 613-34.

5.   C. Caragounis, *The Son of Man* (WUNT, 38; Tübingen: Mohr, 1986). Cf. R.H. Gundry, *Mark*, pp. 118-19.

6.   P. Vielhauer, *Aufsätze zum Neuen Testament* (Munich: Kaiser, 1965), pp. 55-91, 92-140; N. Perrin, *Rediscovering the Teaching of Jesus* (London: SCM Press), 1967.

developed by Mark to express the authority of Jesus.[7]

3. The hypothesis against which Vielhauer and Perrin were reacting (and which they tended to assume was the only viable alternative to their own) was the one associated with (among others) R. Bultmann, H.E. Tödt and A.J.B. Higgins.[8] This view is that only the future sayings in Group C are authentic, and that in them Jesus was looking forward to the coming of a Son of man other than himself. Something like this view was also held by J. Jeremias and C. Colpe[9] but with the important qualification that they saw some kind of self-identification being made by Jesus with this future actor. Both of these scholars also allowed that in certain other texts Jesus might have used the Aramaic equivalent of the Greek phrase as a self-designation of a particular kind.

4. Finally, there was the theory of E. Schweizer that only sayings in Group A about the earthly Jesus have strong claims to authenticity, and that the background to them is to be found in Ezekiel rather than in Daniel.[10] Here Son of man is less of a title denoting authority and more of a humble self-designation of Jesus.

A brief summary of some of the earlier critical discussion of these views is now necessary in order that we may see where the points of debate emerge.

The proponents of View 2 can be seen to be open to criticism at four points: a. They argued that, since the kingdom of God and the Son of man are never linked in Judaism or in the Gospels, but are rather alternative, parallel expressions, then one or other of them cannot be authentic on the lips of Jesus. However, in both Dan. 7.13-14 and *1 En.* 69.26-28 the Son of man is given dominion, and it seems

---

7. See further W.O. Walker, 'The Son of Man Question and the Synoptic Problem', *NTS* 28 (1982), pp. 374-88, with the rebuttal by M.D. Hooker, 'The Son of Man and the Synoptic Problem', in F. van Segbroeck *et al.* (eds.), *The Four Gospels 1992* [*Festschrift Frans Neirynck*] (Leuven: Leuven University Press, 1992), I, pp. 189-201.

8. R. Bultmann, *Theology of the New Testament* (London: SCM Press, 1952), I, pp. 28-32; H.E. Tödt, *The Son of Man in the Synoptic Tradition* (London: SCM Press, 1965); A.J.B. Higgins, *Jesus and the Son of Man* (London: Lutterworth, 1964). See further A.J.B. Higgins, *The Son of Man in the Teaching of Jesus* (Cambridge: Cambridge University Press, 1980).

9. J. Jeremias, 'Die älteste Schicht der Menschensohn-Logien', *ZNW* 58 (1967), pp. 159-72; C. Colpe, 'ὁ υἱὸς τοῦ ἀνθρώπου', *TDNT*, VIII, pp. 400-77.

10. E. Schweizer, *Neotestamentica* (Zürich: Zwingli Verlag, 1963), pp. 56-84, 85-92.

impossible to separate the Son of man from the thought of kingly rule.[11]
So far as the Gospels are concerned, the actual phrases 'kingdom of
God' and 'the Son of man' do appear in different contexts, but it may
be significant that, while both occur in sayings addressed by Jesus to all
kinds of audiences, 'Son of man' (especially with future reference) tends
to be more restricted to sayings addressed in private to the disciples.[12]
Further, if Jesus did use the term Son of man in some other way than as
an overt title of dignity, then there would be no conceptual tension
between the two phrases.

b. It was argued that Jesus displayed no messianic consciousness such
as would be necessary to explain his claiming the status of the Son of
man. Again, this is a dubious argument. In the view of E. Käsemann
Jesus did display the characteristics of the Messiah, although Käsemann
then went on to argue that Jesus did not make any kind of overt
messianic claims or use any messianic titles.[13] This is a very odd position
to adopt, and I would claim that, if the first half of what Käsemann says
is correct, then the possibility that Jesus used messianic concepts in his
teaching is highly probable.[14]

It should be added that some scholars think that the concepts of
Messiah (which is associated with the kingdom of God) and Son of man
are so different that Jesus could not have joined them together. This is a
false antithesis. There is a good case that the Son of man in Daniel 7
must represent the leader of the saints of the Most High, or at the very
least be a symbol for them, in which case he is clearly associated with
the kingdom of God, and later writers certainly interpreted the Danielic
Son of man as a messianic figure.[15]

c. It was argued especially by Perrin that there was no Son of man
concept or tradition in Judaism for Jesus to pick up. What we have
instead is a series of pieces of creative exegesis of Daniel 7 in *4 Ezra*,
1 Enoch and the Christian tradition. I would agree that the contents of

11. For the messianic, including kingly, character of the Son of man, see
W. Horbury, 'The Messianic Associations of "The Son of Man"', *JTS* NS 36
(1985), pp. 34-55.

12. T.W. Manson, *The Teaching of Jesus* (Cambridge: Cambridge University
Press, 2nd edn, 1935), pp. 211-36, provides the basic analysis.

13. E. Käsemann, *Essays on New Testament Themes* (London: SCM Press,
1964), pp. 43-44.

14. Marshall, *Origins of New Testament Christology*, pp. 54-57.

15. See Horbury, 'Messianic Associations'.

4 Ezra and *1 Enoch* may be explicable simply in terms of the use of Daniel 7, and to this extent Perrin's view is justified. But the fact that both writers took up Daniel 7 may well suggest that there was a tradition of turning to Daniel 7, and of course the New Testament also testifies to this taking place. There are sufficient similarities between the three sources to suggest that a common tradition of interpretation existed. It can of course be argued that both *4 Ezra* and *1 Enoch* represent a Jewish reaction to Christian use of Daniel 7 and therefore have no independent value as evidence, but I fail to see evidence for anti-Christian polemic in either source.

d. Finally, it is argued that the type of use made of Daniel 7 is typical of the early church and not of Jesus himself. This argument seems to me to be simply a begging of the question, and the approach of R.T. France[16] offers a better picture in my view.

These points are sufficient in my opinion to show that the basis for this view is unsound, and that the case that Jesus could not have referred to himself as the Son of man of Daniel 7 simply does not stand up, at least so far as the arguments of the Vielhauer–Perrin school with reference to the content of the sayings are concerned. This point must be borne in mind when we come later to discuss the contemporary *linguistic* argument that Jesus could not have been referring to the Danielic Son of man.

As far as View 3 is concerned, here the crucial point is that its proponents observed that in Greek a person who uses the phrase Son of man would appear to be referring to another person besides himself. This observation was then applied to the future sayings in Group C where Jesus could be speaking about somebody other than himself. To be sure, in the sayings in Groups A and B, as they stand, the reference is manifestly to Jesus himself, but it could be argued that this could be traceable to the creation of these sayings by the early church or to the insertion of the phrase Son of man in them once the early church had proceeded to identify Jesus as the Son of man. The question is then whether there is real evidence that in the Group C sayings Jesus was referring to another person besides himself. The primary evidence for this was discovered in Lk. 12.8-9 (and parallels) where Jesus says that if anybody acknowledges him (sc. Jesus) before human beings, the Son of man will acknowledge him before the angels of God. Here, it is said, is

---

16. R.T. France, *Jesus and the Old Testament* (London: Tyndale Press, 1970).

evidence that the present attitude of people to Jesus will be upheld by
the Son of man as the independent vindicator of Jesus in the presence of
God. It is argued that the early church would not have created a saying
in which Jesus and the Son of man were contrasted as two separate
persons in this way, and therefore this must be the most primitive type
of saying. A similar type of contrast could also be found in Mt. 19.28
and Mk 14.62.

This view faces some fatal objections. First, it puts the whole weight of
the argument on one text which has strong claims to authenticity,
namely Lk. 12.8-9 and parallels, and on the basis of this one authentic
text the authenticity of a score or more others is denied. But, granted
that the text is in fact authentic, it will not bear this weight of proof
because the interpretation given to it in support of this theory is highly
dubious. J.D.G. Dunn observes that, if scholars had noted that the saying
is expressed in Hebrew parallelism, they would never have gone astray
by thinking that it refers to Jesus and another person, and he suggests
that the difficulty of the text is traceable to the attempt to incorporate a
reference to Daniel 7 in it.[17] Rather, the text refers to one person in two
different ways, as an earthly figure and in terms of his heavenly role.
Secondly, there is no other evidence in the Gospels that Jesus expected
the future appearance of another eschatological figure distinct from
himself.[18] Thirdly, it can be argued that, so far as their general content is
concerned, the other Son of man sayings in Groups A and B have
strong claims to genuineness; it is really only the presence of the phrase
'Son of man' as a self-reference that calls their authenticity into
question. But, if so, it seems much more likely that the phrase is an
authentic usage by Jesus, in other words that the term was not added to
a whole series of authentic sayings in Groups A and B, rather than that a
dubious interpretation of a single text should lead to the assignment of a
large set of sayings to the early church. It follows that View 3 is very
weakly based.

I need not comment at this point on the arguments for and against
Views 1 and 4. We shall now see how a view very similar to View 4 has

17. J.D.G. Dunn, *Christology in the Making* (London: SCM Press, 2nd edn,
1989), pp. 87.

18. See, however, B.D. Chilton, 'The Son of Man: Human and Heavenly', in van
Segbroek *et al.* (eds.), *The Four Gospels*, pp. 203-18, who argues that one use of the
phrase in the Gospels is with reference to 'an angel of advocacy in the heavenly
court'.

been reached by a different (linguistic) approach to the material. For the moment it is important to note that we have established, on the one hand, that (linguistic arguments apart) the case that Jesus could not have referred to himself as the Danielic Son of man (i.e. sayings in Group C) is implausible, and, on the other hand, that the authenticity of the sayings in Groups A and B is inherently probable, whatever be our verdict about the sayings in Group C. But could Jesus have referred linguistically to the Danielic Son of man by using the phrase (א)בר אנש, and, if he used this phrase, did it have the force that has been traditionally assigned to it? We must now turn to the dominant question in the scholarship of the last twenty years, the linguistic problem raised by (א)בר אנש.

2. *The Linguistic Approach*

The main factor in discussion of the Son of man in the English-speaking world subsequent to 1974 has undoubtedly been this linguistic problem.[19] The point had already been raised in a most powerful manner earlier, but it had certainly not made the impact that it should have made, particularly outside the UK. Three scholars in particular have made contributions along somewhat similar lines in this area.

The first was G. Vermes. Already in 1967 he had drawn attention to the fact that the Aramaic phrase (א)בר אנש could be used as a self-designation.[20] This was not of course a new discovery, but Vermes's contribution was to find evidence for its use in rabbinic sources and to argue that it was used in situations of modesty or where there was reference to situations of humiliation, danger and death. Vermes argued that the speaker used it to make statements that were true of his own particular situation rather than general truths. Such statements could have a double entendre in that the hearers might hear them as general truths and not realize that the speaker was referring specifically and

---

19. This point has been surprisingly ignored in German-speaking scholarship. The massive volume of essays by R. Pesch *et al.*, *Jesus und der Menschensohn: Für Anton Vögtle* (Freiburg: Herder, 1975), is virtually unaware of the problem. For the new approach, however, see M. Müller, *Der Ausdruck 'Menschensohn' in den Evangelien: Voraussetzungen und Bedeutung* (Leiden: Brill, 1984).

20. In an appendix contributed to M. Black's book, *An Aramaic Approach to the Gospels and Acts* (Oxford: Clarendon Press, 3rd edn, 1967), pp. 310-28. Cf. *Jesus the Jew* (London: Collins, 1973).

indeed only to himself.[21] A position similar to that of Vermes has been adopted by D.R.A. Hare who holds that the phrase 'was capable of functioning in some contexts as a modesty idiom, whereby a speaker referred to himself exclusively'.[22]

The second scholar is P.M. Casey, who has built on the work of Vermes and developed it in the course of a thorough study of Daniel 7 and its subsequent influence in his book, *Son of Man*.[23] Casey follows the interpretation of the linguistic material offered earlier by J. Jeremias. Their view is that in the Rabbinic texts the speakers made statements that were true of mankind in general and therefore true of themselves also.

A more nuanced approach was offered by B. Lindars.[24] Like Casey he argues that the use of the phrase in Aramaic is generic, but whereas Casey argued that the Son of man texts are true of mankind in general, Lindars states that they are true of the individual who utters them and also of any person who is in the same class as the speaker, such as, for example, would be the case with Jesus and his group of disciples.

In subsequent publications[25] Casey has drawn close to the position of Lindars and now agrees that there are many cases in the use of language where the phrase 'everybody' is in fact limited in application by the context. This is a welcome clarification and shows that we can safely discuss the views of Lindars and Casey together.

For all three of these scholars there is an important corollary. In Aramaic the phrase was purely a way of making statements about oneself expressed in a peculiar idiom, and therefore it could not have been used in Aramaic as a title. In fact there was no christological title

---

21. Cf. *Jesus the Jew*, pp. 164-65.

22. D.R.A. Hare, *The Son of Man Tradition* (Minneapolis: Fortress Press, 1990).

23. P.M. Casey, *Son of Man: The Interpretation and Influence of Daniel 7* (London: SPCK, 1979); *From Jewish Prophet to Gentile God* (Cambridge: J. Clarke, 1991).

24. B. Lindars, *Jesus Son of Man* (London: SPCK, 1983).

25. Casey, *Jewish Prophet*; cf. 'The Use of the Term "Son of Man" in the Similitudes of Enoch', *JSJ* 7 (1976), pp. 11-29; 'The Jackals and the Son of Man (Matt. 8.20 // Luke 9.58)', *JSNT* 23 (1985), pp. 3-22; 'Aramaic Idiom and the Son of Man Sayings', *ExpTim* 96.8 (May, 1985), pp. 233-36; 'General, Generic and Indefinite: The Use of the Term "Son of Man" in Aramaic Sources and in the Teaching of Jesus', *JSNT* 29 (1987), pp. 21-56; 'Method in our Madness, and Madness in their Methods: Some Approaches to the Son of Man Problem in Recent Scholarship', *JSNT* 42 (1991), pp. 17-43.

sitting around and waiting to be picked up by Jesus and the early church. (א)בר אנש was nothing more than a way of referring to oneself in certain types of context.

This corollary was then linked with the view that we have already mentioned in discussing the work of Perrin, namely that there was in fact no 'Son of man' figure in Judaism that could have been referred to by this Aramaic phrase. Thus according to Casey there was no Son of man as a concept or a figure in Daniel 7. He argues that after we have had the foreign empires represented by animals in the vision in Daniel 7 it was natural to use a figure like a man to represent the people of God, and this figure is used purely as a symbol; it undergoes no experiences at all other than the symbolical experiences in vv. 13-14. There is no mythological background from which the figure has been drawn; it is purely a symbol for a collective entity, the saints of the Most High.

How, then, is the Gospel evidence to be explained in terms of this linguistic background? Both Vermes and Casey divide up the sayings into categories. Vermes is content to offer two categories: sayings where Son of man could represent an Aramaic self-designation, and sayings where it is a term based on, or alluding to, the figure in Daniel 7. Casey offers a more precise analysis into four categories:

1. Possible examples of Aramaic idiom (cf. Group. A)
2. Predictions about the suffering of the Son of man (cf. Group. B)
3. Sayings showing the influence of Daniel 7 (cf. Group. C)
4. Sayings with a more complex background (cf. Groups A and C).

This is a different analysis from that which I used earlier in comparing the views of the pre-1974 group of scholars. Very broadly it could be said that Casey's Category 1 is equivalent to Group A; Category 2 is equivalent to Group B (but a number of Group B sayings fall into his Category 1); Category 3 corresponds to Group C; and Category 4 contains sayings from Groups A and C.

Vermes argues that the sayings that use the phrase 'Son of man' as a self-designation can generally be regarded as authentic sayings by Jesus in which he was simply referring to himself in the specific kinds of context already mentioned, and he is able to compile a list of some 20 sayings of this kind. However, where sayings reflect the influence of Daniel 7, he argues that they come from the early church and not from

Jesus. What happened was that Jesus used the phrase in Aramaic as a self-designation. Once it was translated into Greek it looked like a title and the similarity of the Greek phrase to the corresponding phrase in Daniel 7 was recognized, and hence the early church began to use the phrase as a title of dignity for Jesus and to elaborate its significance with features taken from Daniel 7. Where 'Son of man' had originally been simply a translation of a self-designation into Greek, it now began to be understood even in these sayings as though it were a title. The sayings based on Daniel 7 reflect a consciousness that Jesus is the Messiah which was not historically present in Jesus himself.

Casey adopts a position that is very similar. He isolates a smaller group of nine sayings in which he claims that the original Aramaic phrase could be understood generically, that is, as true of Jesus because it is also true of people in general. He adds three more sayings that were later individualized and arrives at a total of twelve sayings that can be ascribed to Jesus (Mk. 2.10, 28; 8.38; 9.12; 10.45; 14.21 *bis*; Mt. 8.20 // Lk. 9.58; Mt. 11.19 // Lk. 7.34; Mt. 12.32 // Lk. 12.10; Lk. 12.8; and Lk. 22.48). Then, as a result of its belief in the return of Jesus, the early church proceeded to apply Dan. 7.13 to Jesus and so the process of creating further Son of man sayings developed. Casey claims that this theory solves various problems raised by the phrase: (1) The impression that Jesus was speaking of a person different from himself (View 3 above) arises from the literal translation of the Aramaic idiom into Greek. (2) The association of the Son of man with humiliation and suffering is traceable to the context in which it was used in Aramaic: it was used in referring to the fact that all people must die and was linked to the contemporary theology of martyrdom. (3) Since Jesus' relation to the kingdom of God was not that of other human beings, it could not be expressed in terms of (א)בר אנש which is generic. Consequently, we do not find the phrases 'Kingdom of God' and 'the Son of man' in the same sayings. (4) The term Son of man appears only on the lips of Jesus because only he talks about himself in the Gospels. (5) Equally the term does not appear outside the Gospels for the same reason. (6) The apparent 'corporate' reference of the term in some sayings, which was especially focused on by T.W. Manson, is traceable to their originally generic character. (7) The Greek term translates the Aramaic term, and exegetes in the early church who knew that Jesus had used it, and secondly, that the coming of a Son of man was predicted in Daniel 7, proceeded to create sayings that expressed the fact that Jesus would come again. For examples of such created sayings Casey refers to Mt. 16.28; 25.31 and Lk. 18.8.

The position Casey reaches is thus very similar to that of R. Leivestad who argued that the apocalyptic figure 'the Son of man' was a phantom, and that Jesus used the term simply as a self-designation, which explains why nobody else used it of him.[26] He did not, however, provide the philological backing for his view, which the English-speaking scholars have now done. It is also, of course, somewhat similar to that of E. Schweizer (View 4 above), who also recognized the authenticity of sayings where Jesus speaks as a humble human being.

Finally, we must outline the position of Lindars, the third scholar to follow more or less the same line. He argues for the authenticity of only six Son of man sayings. The first is Mt. 8.20 // Lk. 9.58, which gains in force if Jesus is associating the disciples with him. The second is Mt. 11.16-19 // Lk. 7.31-35 where Jesus compares himself with John the Baptist and avoids making an open claim by comparing himself with anybody else who comes eating and drinking. The third is Mt. 12.32 // Lk. 12.10 where speaking against the Son of man means speaking against anybody like Jesus. The fourth is Lk. 11.30 where Jesus says that there is a person who will be a sign to the present generation. The fifth is Mk 2.10-11, which says that a human being may have authority to forgive sins. And the sixth is Mt. 10.32-33 // Lk. 12.8-9 where Jesus says that if somebody confesses him before people, there will be somebody to speak for that person before God, namely his own response. Next he examines the passion sayings and argues for three authentic underlying sayings that in effect state the fate of humankind as being to die. After this the sayings began to be taken as self-references and for the rest of the development Lindars' account is not too different from the others.

3. *An Assessment of Recent Study*

We must now attempt some kind of assessment of this new solution to the problem. It has the merits of offering a total solution which tries to account for the whole process of the generation of Son of man sayings. Nevertheless, it seems to me to have some significant weaknesses, and I now want to explore these before looking at yet another contribution to the problem.

26. R. Leivestad, 'Exit the Apocalyptic Son of Man', *NTS* 18 (1971–72), pp. 243-67.

Texts with an Aramaic Background

If we accept Casey and Lindars's view of the Aramaic background, then it follows that all the genuine sayings in the Gospels must have a generic character in the sense that they will all be true not only of Jesus but also of 'everybody', whether we take 'everybody' to refer to 'all humankind' or 'everybody in the sort of position that I, the speaker, am in'. Now earlier C. Colpe had argued that a similar sort of explanation would fit three of the sayings: Mk 2.10; Mt. 11.18-19 // Lk. 7.33-34; and Mt. 8.20 // Lk. 9.58. But there is an important dif- ference in that according to Colpe the usage in these statements is *not* generic in the sense that 'Son of man' can refer to people in general.

Thus in Mk 2.10 the point, as Colpe sees it, is not that people in general can forgive; rather it is that not only God may forgive but also in the case of Jesus a man may forgive. Lindars, however, tries to secure a generic sense by arguing that there is a class of people who have God's mandate to heal and forgive, and he instances the Jewish exorcist mentioned in the *Prayer of Nabonidus* (4QPrNab). Casey uses the same evidence and comments, 'The small quantity of the evidence is due to the fact that we have so little evidence of popular religion in this period';[27] he adds that Mt. 9.8 shows that Matthew took the saying in a general sense of authority given by God to humans. However, it must be observed that the Jewish exorcist in question is presumably Daniel,[28] who is a revered prophet belonging to the past and not an example of 'man in general', and that Matthew's comment is concerned with the way in which the people thought of Jesus as a man and does not necessarily reflect Matthew's own mind.

The second example is Mt. 11.18-19. Here again Colpe takes the Aramaic idiom to mean simply 'somebody', namely Jesus, and stresses that the phrase is not a reference to any ordinary person. Lindars tries to take the phrase to mean 'somebody else' and to argue that the reference is to anybody else who came as a preacher with the same message as John but without his asceticism. This seems to me to be quite forced. Casey simply takes over the view of Colpe without apparently realizing that it is not the same as his own. He paraphrases: 'If anybody comes eating and drinking, they say...' and assumes that there was a general

---

27. *Son of Man*, p. 229.

28. A. Dupont-Sommer, *The Essene Writings from Qumran* (Oxford: Basil Blackwell, 1961), p. 322 n.

class of people who ate and drank with tax-collectors and sinners and who were normally condemned by the Pharisees. But it seems much more likely that Jesus is here referring specifically to himself, and the existence of this class of people like him seems dubious. Further, the contrast with the specific reference to John in the first half of the saying suggests that a definite reference is required in the second half also.[29]

The third example is Mt. 8.20 // Lk. 9.58. This seems at first sight to have some plausibility. Colpe takes it to mean, 'Even animals have dens but a man such as I, Jesus, has nowhere to lay his head'. But Jesus is not talking about something that happens to him simply because he is a man as opposed to an animal. Much more plausibly Lindars says that Jesus means that anybody who shares his missionary vocation will have nowhere to lay his head. Casey discusses the statement at some length. He tries to justify the view that the statement is true of mankind in general who have to build their homes whereas the animals do not have to make their holes or their perches. But he recognizes that Jesus is really speaking about himself and the disciples. Inasmuch as he had no home himself, he could not provide his followers with homes. This second way of taking the saying is surely much more probable than the more general way, which I find to be quite unlikely. But the logic is surely the wrong way round. The saying is one that appears to be true of the disciples because it is true of Jesus, as opposed to Jesus applying a saying true of homeless people or travelling preachers in general to himself.

Other sayings of the same character which may be more plausible as examples include Lk. 12.10 where a contrast is said to be drawn between speaking against people in general and against the Holy Spirit. However, none of the sayings demands an explanation of this kind, and in several of them this explanation is much less likely and in some cases quite unconvincing.[30] It is very dubious whether statements

---

29. Casey (*Jewish Prophet*, p. 48) argues that in *Gen. R.* 79.6 ('A bird is not caught without the will of heaven; how much less the soul of a son of man'), since the first part of the statement is general, the second part must also be general. He evidently does not accept the converse, that where the first part of a statement is specific, the second part is the more likely to be specific as well.

30. Casey's argument that if Mk 2.28 follows on logically from Mk 2.27, the reference in 'Son of man' must be to human beings having authority over the sabbath has some plausibility. It is, however, equally plausible that the (א)אנש בר as man's representative and lord has authority over the sabbath to decree how it is to be used for human good.

The interpretation of Lk. 12.8-9 to mean that, if anybody confesses Jesus before

about a class of people are here being used by Jesus to refer specifically
to himself.

The Nature of the Aramaic Idiom

A second point is concerned with the Aramaic idiom that may be present in these sayings. So far as the extant Aramaic evidence from the rabbinic materials is concerned, Casey and Lindars have a better case than Vermes. The view that in the Aramaic materials (as opposed to the Gospel sayings) there is a generic use of the phrase, referring to people in general or a class of people and hence including the individual who makes the statement, appears to be sound; there is no case apparently where the phrase must refer purely to the speaker. And yet we have seen that the generic sense simply does not fit the Gospel sayings without some extraordinary contortions of meaning.

Here, however, a further point must be taken into consideration. According to R.J. Bauckham[31] there is a distinction between the

men, there will be people who will confess them before the angels of God, is quite unpersuasive, since no such class of people is defined in the context. The point of the saying is that Jesus will confess them; the concept of people in general bearing witness at the last judgment is odd—nobody else besides Jesus comes into the picture.

The interpretation of Mk 14.21a to mean 'People (including me) go their death, as it is written of them' is implausible, (a) because the 'it is written' clause suggests a specific application of a prophecy, and (b) because Jesus does not mean 'all men, me included, die sooner or later', but 'I am on my way to a specific and imminent death'. The interpretation of Mk 14.21b to mean 'Woe to the person who betrays people (including me)' might be plausible if this were an isolated remark, but the close link with Mk 14.21a excludes this possibility.

To interpret the basic 'passion prediction' as 'people (including me) will die, and after three days rise' produces an improbable statement. A general resurrection of all people 'after three days' (i.e. 'in a short time') was not expected.

Mk 10.45 is perhaps plausible in its first half ('People (including me) came not to be served but to serve') as a statement of an ideal (but it is not so formulated), and the second half ('that is, to give their lives as a ransom for many') is certainly not universally true or applicable even as an ideal.

Lk 22.48 could be taken as a general statement (Would you betray a fellow human being with a kiss?), but it does not need to be so taken, and it is hard to see why so specific a question should be put in a general form.

31. R.J. Bauckham, 'The Son of Man: "A man in my position" or "Someone"', *JSNT* 23 (1985), pp. 23-33; see also the reply by B. Lindars, 'Response to Richard Bauckham: The Idiomatic Use of Bar Enasha', *JSNT* 23 (1985), pp. 35-41.

indefinite and the generic uses of the Aramaic phrase. In the former use the phrase means 'somebody', 'a person', and in the latter 'every person' or 'every one in my position'. I suggested above that Colpe understood certain texts in the former sense, but Casey seems to have thought that he was defending the latter position. Bauckham then goes on to suggest that Jesus could have used the indefinite sense as an oblique self-reference. This possibility is denied by Lindars, who asserts that we are dealing with cases where the Aramaic phrase has the emphatic form (hence the Greek translation 'the Son of man') and is generic rather than indefinite. However, according to Colpe,[32] the determinate and indeterminate forms can all have the same range of meanings. Similarly, Chilton observes that 'there was an increasing tendency for the determined state to be used with an indefinite sense as the language developed'.[33]

The problem is at present in a state of stalemate. On the one hand, Casey, who remained active in discussion while Lindars and Vermes were more or less silent, has continued to insist that in Aramaic the various forms of the phrase, emphatic or non-emphatic, have all the same force, namely to refer to a general class of people including the speaker. On the other hand, D.R.A. Hare, who has just entered the fray, has argued that we know insufficient about Aramaic usage in the first century to rule out the possibility of an exclusive self-reference in the idiom, and that it seems probable that at the stage of Aramaic transmission of the tradition the sayings of Jesus were so understood.[34]

I cannot claim any expertise whatever in Aramaic, but there are one or two points that a non-Aramaicist may perhaps be allowed to make with due caution. The first is that there is in any case an unfinished debate over the date and relevance of the Aramaic materials used to reconstruct the Aramaic idioms current in the first century.[35] This

---

32. *TDNT*, VIII, p. 403.

33. Chilton, 'Son of Man', p. 204. By contrast Casey argues that in fact all the forms would be definite rather than indefinite.

34. Hare, *Son of Man Tradition*, pp. 241-56.

35. J.A. Fitzmyer, *A Wandering Aramaean: Collected Aramaic Essays* (Missoula, MT: Scholars Press, 1979), pp. 143-60; in *The Gospel according to Luke I–IX* (AB; New York: Doubleday), 1981, pp. 208-11, he appears to support the indefinite use, although he calls it 'generic'. B. Witherington, III, *The Christology of Jesus* (Minneapolis: Fortress Press, 1990), pp. 236-38, claims that the emphatic state had not yet become weak in the New Testament period and hence that a titular or

suggests that any conclusions should be regarded as tentative.

The second point is that in the Gospels the presence of a large number of texts that do not make good sense when taken generically but which do make sense when taken to refer to a specific individual suggests that perhaps there was an Aramaic idiom in which (א)אנש בר could be taken to refer specifically to the speaker. In other words, although Vermes failed to produce early Aramaic evidence for an exclusive use of the idiom, the Gospel texts themselves may provide the missing link to prove the case.

The third point is that some of the Aramaic evidence cited by Vermes is ambiguous: although it can be taken generically, it is not necessary that it should be so understood, and it may be that in certain cases the term should be taken as an indefinite reference to the speaker. These are the cases where Vermes says that, even if the phrase has a generic meaning, the equivocal phrase may be used by an individual to refer specifically and only to himself. According to Witherington, a 'titular or semi-titular sense' was also possible with the form אנשא בר. In this case the phrase would have referred to the figure in Daniel 7 and subsequent literature.[36] I am, therefore, not persuaded that Casey is right in arguing that the phrase is always and only used in the genuine sayings of Jesus with a general application which is also true of him in particular.

The Interpretation of Daniel 7

We must turn our attention next to Daniel 7. Here it seems to me that Casey's treatment is very much open to question. First, he does not do justice to the fact that many subsequent interpretations of the vision took the Son of man to be an individual. To be sure, the individual is associated with a community, and he is not explicitly identified either with the group or with their leader.

Secondly, this raises the question whether the writer of Daniel did not need to make an explicit identification of the figure in the vision because the readers were already familiar with the intended identification. I find it most plausible that a messianic figure is in mind, that is, a future ruler of God's people appointed by God.[37]

definite use of the phrase by Jesus was possible. See further the discussion by Casey, 'Method in our Madness'.

36. Witherington, *Christology of Jesus*.

37. See G. R. Beasley-Murray, 'The Interpretation of Daniel 7', *CBQ* 45 (1983), pp. 44-58. J.J. Collins, 'The Son of Man in First-Century Judaism', *NTS* 38 (1992),

Thirdly, it must be observed that not all the traits of the Son of man in the Gospels can be derived directly from Daniel 7. It is in fact surprising that it is only the Son of man sayings that come comparatively late in the Gospels that have a clear background in Daniel 7. (The first clear references in each Gospel with a Danielic background are in fact Mt. 10.23; Mk 8.38 and Lk. 9.26 respectively.) This suggests that at least some of the Son of man sayings must have been intelligible without a flag indicating that in order to understand the phrase it was necessary to recognize that it was derived from Daniel 7. And this in turn reopens the question as to whether 'Son of man' was a phrase more generally known than is sometimes allowed in the time of Jesus. I agree with the view that the usage in *4 Ezra* and *1 Enoch* does not demand a background or source other than exegesis of Daniel 7; but the fact that both of these books—and the early Christians (or Jesus, if you will)—go back to Daniel to draw inspiration brings us back to the suggestion made above that there was at least a tradition of doing so, in other words that speculation about the role of the Son of man in Daniel 7 was current at the time, and that, therefore, use of the phrase could have been intelligible. As C.F.D. Moule has observed, a reference to 'the Son of man' could be taken to be a reference to 'the (well-known, Danielic) Son of Man' who was 'the Man par excellence'.[38] We must also take into account the evidence produced by W. Horbury to show that 'Son of man' had messianic associations by the first century.[39]

The Relation of the Gospel Sayings to Daniel 7

This leads us to the question of the origin of allusions to Daniel 7 in the Son of man sayings. There are two obvious difficulties about ascribing the origin of these allusions to the early church.

First, this theory does not explain why the phrase, even with a Danielic background, is found only on the lips of Jesus as a self-designation, and why it is never used confessionally by the early church.[40] It is puzzling that, although according to this theory the early church proceeded to develop the use of the term far beyond the bland

---

pp. 448-66, argues that the Son of man in Dan. 7 is a heavenly figure who was interpreted messianically in *4 Ezra* and *1 Enoch*.

38. C.F.D. Moule, *The Origin of Christology* (Cambridge: Cambridge University Press, 1977), p. 14.

39. Horbury, 'Messianic Associations', pp. 34-55.

40. The few exceptions to this rule can be satisfactorily explained as exceptions.

use as an Aramaic idiom by Jesus and to make it a key term in its Christology, it somehow respected the fact that Jesus used it as a self-designation when there was nothing in the Greek phrase to indicate that this was the only way in which it could be used. But if the early church was controlled by the memory that the phrase was a self-designation, then one might perhaps have expected a reticence to create fresh Son of man sayings. This objection might be rebutted by appeal to the existence of early Christian prophets speaking in the first person in the name of Jesus and so using 'Son of man' as he was believed to have done, but this explanation is very difficult to accept on other grounds. The recent attempt by M.E. Boring[41] to defend the case for extensive activity by Christian prophets does not convince me, and in any case it should be remembered that he expressly says that his theory should be applied only to sayings that are to be considered inauthentic on other grounds.[42]

The second objection is that it is not evident why it is the early church that should be regarded as capable of using Daniel 7 but not apparently Jesus himself. If one denies any kind of 'messianic consciousness' to Jesus, then it is improbable that he would have found a role of this kind in the Old Testament that he was called to fulfil, but I have already discussed this point earlier and claimed that Jesus was conscious of a messianic function. If the difficulty is that the detection of an allusion to Daniel 7 in the phrase 'Son of man' could occur only when the sayings were translated into Greek, then it must be noted that Casey himself admits that the allusion could have been detected at the Aramaic stage.[43] It would seem that the possibility of creative exegetical activity by the early church should be invoked only if the sayings cannot be attributed to Jesus.

The real problem is that we have two types of sayings in the Gospels. On the one hand, we have sayings where 'Son of man' appears to be no more than some kind of self-reference and no allusion to the kind of figure in Daniel 7 is either visible or necessary in order to understand the saying. On the other hand, we have sayings that clearly refer to the figure in Daniel 7 and where the possibility of a generic use is ruled out

---

41. M.E. Boring, *Sayings of the Risen Jesus: Christian Prophecy in the Synoptic Tradition* (Cambridge: Cambridge University Press, 1982). Cf. *The Continuing Voice of Jesus: Christian Prophecy and the Gospel Tradition* (Louisville: Westminster/ John Knox, 1991).

42. *Sayings*, p. 57 = *Continuing Voice*, pp. 189-90.

43. *Son of Man*, p. 235.

since the reference is clearly to Jesus alone. Some scholars would argue that the one usage refers to a human figure, and the other to an angelic type of figure. There are two ways in which one might try to account for these two types of material.

First, one might try to develop a theory on the basis that derivation from Daniel 7 was primary. On this view Jesus (or the early church) used the term Son of man primarily and originally to refer to a figure possessing authority and dominion who at present is humiliated but who will one day be exalted and return in glory. It can then be argued that the theme of authority, or more correctly, of rejected authority, runs through the sayings, including those that make no direct allusion to Daniel 7.[44]

The difficulty is that this view is not easy to apply to those sayings recorded early in the Gospels where there is nothing to suggest that it is the Danielic figure which is in view, although of course the Evangelists may have assumed that their readers were familiar with the early church's christological identification of Jesus with the Danielic Son of man and would have applied this identification right from the outset.

The second view is that Jesus started with the use of an Aramaic idiom that was some kind of self-designation, and he then moved from it to a self-identification with the figure spoken of in Daniel 7. J.D.G. Dunn has argued for this possibility. He argues that Jesus came to the conclusion at some point that his ministry would end in disaster, but that God would vindicate him.

> Somewhere within this train of thinking it is entirely plausible that his speech mannerism (the son of man) should have triggered off the recognition that Daniel 7.13 is a reference to that vindication. The apparent distinction between Jesus and the Son of Man in a saying like Luke 12.8f. would then simply be the effect of Jesus' own adaptation of his regular speech usage to incorporate an allusion to Daniel 7.13.[45]

This suggestion would give a smooth transition between the two types of saying. And once Jesus had taken this step, then it is understandable how the thought of authority could come into the picture without the need for an explicit allusion to the actual coming of the Son of man in power and glory in Daniel 7.

44. Cf. R. Maddox, 'The Function of the Son of Man according to the Synoptic Gospels', *NTS* 15 (1968–69), pp. 45-74.

45. Dunn, *Christology in the Making*, p. 87. Cf. Bauckham, 'Son of Man', pp. 29-30.

If such a view as this is adopted, then it follows that there will be some sayings where Son of man need be no more than a self-designation based on Aramaic idiom, other sayings which are fairly clearly based on an identification with the authoritative figure in Daniel 7, and yet other sayings where there is some ambiguity. Such a theory is, of course, similar to that of Vermes, Casey and Lindars, but where these scholars assign the jump from the Aramaic idiom to the early church and deny that Jesus saw himself as the Danielic figure, Dunn's view is that it can plausibly be assigned to Jesus himself.

A version of the former view is upheld by R.H. Gundry in his most recent contribution to the study of the Gospels. He holds that Jesus identified himself with the figure in Daniel 7, and 'this self-identification led him to use בר אנשא or a similar phrase often and only in referring exclusively to himself'. In this way he could use the phrase 'for himself as a human being without regard to any further identity'.[46]

It is difficult to tell whether Jesus first came upon בר אנש(א) with whatever idiomatic force it may have had in the first century and then saw the possible reference to Daniel 7 or whether he started from Daniel 7 and made use of a phrase that could be taken in a neutral way or as reference to 'the Son of man par excellence'. As I have suggested elsewhere, it may have been partly because of his consciousness of the other roles devolved on him by the Father that Jesus came to see himself as the Danielic בר אנש(א).[47]

A theory along these lines seems to me to have considerable merits. If we may compare it with Casey's theory we can make the following points:

a. Since it accepts that Jesus used an Aramaic expression by which he could have appeared to be merely talking about himself in an indirect and even modest way or perhaps speaking about somebody else or incorporating an allusion to the figure in Daniel 7 into his statements, we can see why the theory that he was talking about somebody other than himself could have arisen. At the same time we do justice to the great majority of the statements where the reference is clearly to Jesus himself. Further, we do not have to regard a whole series of texts as inauthentic when there are really no grounds in their actual content to compel us to do so other than the view that a reference to the Danielic Son of man cannot stem from Jesus himself.

46. Gundry, *Mark*, pp. 118-19.
47. Marshall, 'Son of Man and the Incarnation', pp. 37-38.

b. The references to humiliation and suffering arise from the association of the Son of man with the role of the Servant in Isaiah 53, an association that has been strongly defended by P. Stuhlmacher in his discussion of Mk 10.45.[48] Son of man is used appropriately in these sayings in terms of later Aramaic idiomatic usage.

c. The lack of association between the Son of man and the kingdom of God is traceable to the fact that Jesus does not generally discuss the question of who 'rules' in the kingdom. The connection is, of course, made in Mt. 19.28 // Lk. 22.29-30 where the Son of man and the disciples are associated with judgment.[49]

d. Clearly Son of man appears on the lips of Jesus exclusively because it was his chosen way of speaking, and the tradition respected his usage. Nor does it appear outside the Gospels for the same reason. This of course is not to deny that the term was added to and subtracted from sayings, as a study of the synoptic parallels indicates.

e. The corporate reference found by a number of scholars in some of the sayings may be traceable to the fact that in Daniel 7 the Son of man symbolizes the saints of the Most High.

f. The difficulty that needs to be faced squarely is the objection that 'a [son of] man' could not be taken as an allusion to the figure in Daniel 7 since it was too vague and since such a phrase could hardly become a title; as Casey says, there would need to be unambiguous reference to Daniel 7 in the context to make such an allusion possible.

It is true that 'Son of man' as a title is not attested in the literature of the time. But the phrase did not need to be a 'title' in order to allow an allusion to the human figure in Daniel 7, just as it is used in *4 Ezra* 13.3. Further, there are places where the Gospel texts refer to the (א)אנש בר as a figure active in the future without any direct allusion to Daniel 7 (e.g. Lk. 12.8; 17.22, 26). The mistake is to think that an explicit reference to Daniel 7 is necessary every time that Jesus refers to the Danielic figure; but this is quite unnecessary, since it is sufficient that Jesus should make clear allusions sufficiently often to create a context in which less explicit references would be naturally understood. This in fact is what he does in Mk 13.26 and 14.62 where the language demands such an allusion.

---

48. P. Stuhlmacher, *Versöhnung, Gesetz und Gerechtigkeit: Aufsätze zur biblischen Theologie* (Göttingen: Vandenhoeck & Ruprecht, 1981), pp. 27-42.

49. 'Son of man' may be an addition in the Matthaean form of the saying, but the imagery reflects Daniel 7.

Casey's objections, therefore, do not hold.[50]

My conclusion, then, is that Jesus could and did use the phrase בר אנש(א) to refer to himself as the Danielic Son of man but in such a way that the phrase could also function as a form of self-reference that would not necessarily carry this full connotation every time he used it and to all his hearers. In this way we can claim that View 1, outlined earlier, still stands firm despite the linguistic arguments that have been brought against it.

---

50. See further D.C. Allison, *The End of the Ages Has Come* (Edinburgh: T. & T. Clark, 1985), pp. 128-37; W.D. Davies and D.C. Allison, *The Gospel according to Saint Matthew* (ICC; Edinburgh: T. & T. Clark, 1992), II, pp. 43-53.

MALE AND FEMALE IN CREATION AND NEW CREATION:
INTERPRETATIONS OF GALATIANS 3.28C IN 1 CORINTHIANS 7

Judith M. Gundry-Volf

Form-critical analyses have led to the conclusion that Paul incorporates early Christian baptismal paraenesis or liturgy from a Hellenistic Jewish-Christian milieu into Gal. 3.26-28.[1] Part of that early tradition recorded there is the eschatological declaration, 'There is no male and female'. The meaning of this bold but 'strange' statement[2] has been hotly disputed. And the dispute began long ago. We shall look at two of the earliest interpretations of the formula, which are accessible to us in 1 Corinthians 7. One is Paul's. The other, as I will suggest, is the Corinthian sexual ascetics'.[3] In this study I will attempt to show that we can deduce from Paul's argument in 1 Corinthians 7 the Corinthians' use of the declaration 'There is no male and female', and that this slogan served them as a theological basis for sexual asceticism. Paul's own interpretation of the tradition in 1 Corinthians 7 must be read as a response to their interpretation in support of sexual asceticism. I will try to give both the Corinthians' and Paul's interpretations. Others have already suggested that 1 Corinthians 7 shows how Paul understands Gal. 3.28,[4] and a few have assumed that the Corinthian sexual ascetics

1. See W. Meeks, 'The Image of the Androgyne: Some Uses of a Symbol in Earliest Christianity', *HR* 13 (1974), pp. 165-208 (180-82); R. Scroggs, 'Paul and the Eschatological Woman', *JAAR* 40 (1972), pp. 283-303 (291-92); H.D. Betz, *Galatians. A Commentary on Paul's Letter to the Churches in Galatia* (Hermeneia; Philadelphia: Fortress Press, 1979), pp. 181-84.

2. Betz, *Galatians*, p. 195.

3. The Corinthians would have been familiar with the tradition through the baptismal paraenesis or Paul's teaching in general.

4. S.S. Bartchy (*First-Century Slavery and 1 Corinthians 7:21* [SBLDS, 11; Missoula, MT: Scholars Press, 1973], pp. 163-64) was apparently the first to note Paul's dependence on the tradition of Gal. 3.28 in 1 Cor. 7. Scroggs ('Eschatological Woman', p. 293) has called 1 Cor. 7.17-27 Paul's 'explicit commentary on Gal. 3.28'.

appealed to this tradition.[5] This essay tries to bring the discussion further along by using 1 Corinthians 7 as a basis for investigating how the Corinthians used the tradition 'no male and female' (hereafter referred to as Gal. 3.28) and by making Paul's debate with the Corinthian ascetics the framework for his interpretation of the tradition in this chapter. The question to what extent Paul in 1 Corinthians 7 drew social implications from the eschatological vision of Gal. 3.28c, and what those implications were, must be asked within this framework. I will also address that question.

The discussion between Paul and the Corinthians on the meaning and implications of Gal. 3.28c is about the relationship of the eschaton or the redeemed order to the created order. For, as I will show, both parties are interpreting the eschatological declaration, 'There is no male and female', in the light of biblical creation theology, and in particular, Gen. 1.27, 'male and female he created them'. The allusion to Gen. 1.27 in Gal. 3.28c has received some attention but has not yet been discussed in terms of a debate between Paul and the Corinthian ascetics about the validity of the created order for new life in the body of Christ. Thus the broad framework of the present investigation is Corinthian and Pauline eschatology and the relationship between creation and eschatology or redemption.

The majority of interpreters today think that Paul's discussion of sexual asceticism in 1 Corinthians 7 presupposes that some Corinthians were themselves sexual ascetics and were promoting continence in the Corinthian church.[6] It is their slogan which Paul quotes in 7.1: 'It is good for a man not to touch a woman'. Some married people were withdrawing from conjugal relations, even against their spouse's will (7.3-5). Others were divorcing as a way out of relationships with unbelievers (7.10-16). The single or betrothed were deciding against marriage or being pressured to do so (esp. 7.36-40). Paul's own preference for celibacy is also clear from this chapter (7.7-8, 26, 28b-35, 40). But he will not accept the Corinthian trend to withdraw from marital and thus also sexual commitments *already made* in order to practice celibacy. His instruction to 'remain in the condition in which you were

    5. Bartchy, *Slavery*, pp. 131-32; E.H. Pagels, 'Paul and Women: A Response to Recent Discussion', *JAAR* 42 (1974), pp. 538-49 (540); apparently also G. Fee, *The First Epistle to the Corinthians* (NICNT; Grand Rapids: Eerdmans, 1987), p. 270.
    6. E.g., Fee, *1 Corinthians*, 269-70; W. Schrage, 'Zur Frontstellung der paulinischen Ehebewertung in 1 Kor 7,1-7', *ZNW* 67 (1976), pp. 214-34.

called' (7.20) has the effect of requiring people with prior commitments not to opt out of them.

Paul incorporates two other arguments for 'remaining' into his argument that married people should stay married and not adopt celibacy: the person called while circumcised or uncircumcised should remain so, and the person called while a slave or a free person should remain so (7.18-22). There is no evidence that circumcision or slavery was under debate in Corinth. Rather Paul can count on his readers' agreement with his point of view in these parallel examples of 'remaining', and thus uses them illustratively to support his exhortation in the disputed matter of marriage and celibacy. In choosing these illustrations he is prompted by their association in the tradition of Gal. 3.28, which has the three contrasting pairs Jew–Greek, slave–free, male–female.[7] The terminology employed for these pairs in 1 Corinthians 7 does not always replicate that of the tradition. The correspondence is exact in the case of the pair 'slave–free' (δοῦλος–ἐλεύθερος). But 'Jew–Greek' ('Ιουδαῖος–Ἕλλην) from Gal. 3.28 becomes 'circumcision–uncircumcision' (περιτομή–ἀκροβυστία, 7.18-19, as in Col. 3.11). And the biological terms 'male–female' from Gal. 3.28 (ἄρσεν–θῆλυ) are substituted by the social terms 'man' (ἀνήρ, also ἄνθρωπος) and 'woman' (γυνή) in 1 Corinthians 7. Man and woman are here considered as sexual beings, thus the allusion to the tradition in Gal. 3.28c is clear, despite the change in terminology.[8]

Strangely, however, no one seems to find it odd that Paul employs the tradition from Gal. 3.28 in 1 Corinthians 7. But it should come as a surprise that Paul alludes to the eschatological declaration, 'There is neither Jew nor Greek, there is neither slave nor free, there is no male and female', when he is instructing the Corinthians to 'remain in the

---

7.   Bartchy, *Slavery*, pp. 162-63. It is likely that Gal. 3.28 represents an earlier form of the tradition than that in 1 Cor. 12.13 and Col. 3.11. Those texts essentially repeat the first two pairs of Gal. 3.28 with variations in terminology and, in the case of Col. 3.11, elaborations ('barbarian and Scythian'). Rom. 10.12 may also reflect the tradition but has only the first pair. The presence of 'male and female' in Gal. 3.28 alone—where it is foreign to the context—suggests that it was eliminated from later Pauline versions of the tradition as 'problematic' in the light of sexual behavior and gender roles which early Christians had taken up (see Scroggs, 'Eschatological Woman', pp. 291-92).

8.   Cf. Rom. 1.26-27 for the use of the biological terms as substantives, rather than the social terms, when the focus is on sexual activity. See BAGD, *s.v.* θῆλυς; *s.v.* ἄρσην.

condition in which you were called'. For this formula is said to have played an important part in engendering *new* behavior and a *new* self-consciousness especially among early Christian women and slaves.[9] Corinth's 'eschatological women' are the parade example. They disregarded customs, stepped outside of traditional roles and exercised uncommon leadership in the early church (cf. esp. 1 Cor. 11.2-16). For justification, they looked to the tradition recorded in Gal. 3.28, it is often claimed.[10]

Wayne Meeks has called attention to the power of the liturgical declaration to alter behavior when reinforced by the dramatic gestures associated with baptism (disrobing, immersion, robing) and by the community's accepted norms of order. Under these conditions the declaration 'does what it says'. It creates a new symbolic universe in which an 'objective' change in reality has come about that modifies social roles. A modern philosopher might call it a 'performative utterance'.[11] '*There is no* Jew *nor* Greek, *there is no* slave *nor* free, *there is no* male and female' (Gal. 3.28; cf. Col. 3.11). These are statements of 'fact'. The repeated negations οὐκ ἔνι...οὐδέ emphasize the radical break with past reality and norms. This is elaborated in the baptismal motif of 'putting off' the former identity and 'putting on' the new: 'You who have have been baptized into Christ have put on Christ...For you all are one in Christ Jesus' (Gal. 3.27, 28b). The break with the former identity and assumption of the new identity is the basis for new ethical behavior in Col. 3.9-11:

> You have stripped off the old self with its practices and clothed yourselves with the new self, which is being renewed in knowledge according to the image of its creator. In that renewal there is no longer Greek and Jew,

---

9. E. Schüssler Fiorenza takes the baptismal declaration to explain 'at least' women's exercise of leadership roles in the house churches and mission of the early Christian movement (*In Memory of Her: A Feminist Theological Reconstruction of Christian Origins* [New York: Crossroad, 1985], p. 209). On the effect of Gal. 3.28 on early Christian slaves' behavior, see J.E. Crouch, *The Origin and Intention of the Colossian Haustafel* (FRLANT, 109; Göttingen: Vandenhoeck & Ruprecht), pp. 126-27.

10. The Corinthian women's behavior and their use of the tradition in Gal. 3.28c has been subjected to much critique. For a critique of the critique, see L. Schottroff, 'Frauensünde', in C. Schaumberger and L. Schottroff, *Schuld und Macht: Studien zu einer feministischen Befreiungstheologie* (Munich: Christian Kaiser Verlag, 1988), pp. 56-87.

11. Meeks, 'Image', pp. 182-83.

circumcised and uncircumcised, barbarian, Scythian, slave and free; but Christ is all and in all.

In Colossians the vision for social change is limited, however: the household code (3.18-25) requires slaves' obedience to their masters. The declaration that 'there is no male and female' drops out of the tradition completely; instead we find the household code's requirement that wives 'submit to their husbands...' That requirement only goes to show, however, what forces for change in gender roles were put in motion at baptism which the household code was trying to keep in check.[12]

If the tradition did have such tumultuous effects on early Christians' perception of their social and sexual identity, why does Paul not steer clear of it here? After all, he is trying to convince the Corinthians that divine calling to faith and conversion do *not* necessitate a change in one's status: 'Let each of you remain in the condition in which you were called' (7.20; see also v. 24). 'Was anyone at the time of his call already circumcised? Let him not seek to remove the marks of circumcision! Was anyone at the time of his call uncircumcised? Let him not seek circumcision!' (7.18-19). 'Were you a slave when called? Do not be concerned about it!' (7.21). 'Whoever was free when called is a slave of Christ... Do not become slaves of human masters!' (7.22-23) 'Are you bound to a wife? Do not seek to be free! Are you free from a wife? Do not seek a wife!' (7.27). True, Paul makes exceptions in 7.9, 11, 15, 28, 36, 38, 39 and arguably in 21b. But he allows a change of status only when the opportunity presents itself, or to avoid immorality or strife with an unbeliever, or to reconstitute the marriage bond. The thrust of his argument is *against* change, in marital status in particular, and *for* living one's Christian life under the outward conditions in which one finds oneself.[13]

Moreover, Paul seems to know that the Corinthians take the formula, 'There is no male and female', in a way with which he disagrees. For when he uses the baptismal tradition again in 1 Cor. 12.13, he drops the pair 'male and female'. He also gets rid of the strong multiple negations 'neither...nor' and substitutes them with harmless 'whether...or's: 'All were baptized into one body, whether Jews or Greeks, whether slaves or

12. Cf. Crouch, *Origin*, pp. 130-44.
13. Differently, Bartchy, *Slavery*, p. 153. But it must also be said that in his insistence on 'remaining' Paul is not blind to at least some relative advantages and disadvantages of different types of alternate statuses (see, e.g., 7.7-8, 22-23, 25-26, 35, 40).

free'. Would it not then have been easier for Paul to avoid the tradition entirely in his discussion of sexual relations in 1 Corinthians 7? Incorporating it into his argument only makes his task harder. Why then does he do it? The answer must be that he cannot *avoid* using the tradition because it was such a powerful element in the Corinthian sexual ascetics' theology that he had to address it and try to reinterpret it in a way compatible with his response to the ascetics. *We can conclude from Paul's unexpected use of the tradition from Gal. 3.28 in 1 Corinthians 7 that the Corinthians themselves were using it as a theological basis for their sexual asceticism.* 1 Corinthians 7 is thus a 'commentary' on the baptismal tradition chiefly in the sense that Paul gives here a polemical reinterpretation of it.[14]

This way of explaining the Corinthians' justification of their asceticism can make a strong appeal to the text, as we have seen, and it is corroborated by the undisputed assumption that the Corinthians knew the tradition of Gal. 3.28. To be sure, other Christian traditions have been proposed as the source of the Corinthians' celibacy, but the connections have been difficult to prove. David L. Balch[15] argued that the Corinthians based their sexual asceticism on ascetic words of the Lord (e.g. Lk. 20.34-35) and on Moses traditions that Paul's opponents had introduced representing Moses an an ascetic 'divine man'. Wolfgang Schrage, however, in a detailed interaction with Balch,[16] remains unconvinced that such words of the Lord were current in Corinth or that the Corinthians even could have known them, since most of the ascetic material comes from Lukan redaction rather than Q. Further, he judges Balch's methodology of deducing the influence of ascetic Moses traditions through the Jewish opponents and their Moses typology in 2 Corinthians 3 to be problematic. John C. Hurd thinks that the Corinthian ascetics were inspired by Paul's own earlier teaching, which included the slogan in 1 Cor. 7.1b, 'It is best for a man not to touch a woman'.

---

14. By contrast, the baptismal tradition suits Paul's argument in Galatians well. There too Paul wants the readers to 'remain'. The words 'There is neither Jew nor Greek...' do not conflict with this aim, since in this context they do not encourage new behavior. The Gentile Christians will not profit by becoming Jews; rather, they will lose their freedom, he argues (5.1-2). Paul applies the tradition to the Galatian situation because it was likely to reinforce the (already new) status quo.

15. 'Backgrounds of I Cor. VII: Sayings of the Lord in Q; Moses as an Ascetic ΘΕΙΟΣ ANHP in II Cor. III', *NTS* 18 (1972), pp. 351-64.

16. 'Frontstellung ', pp. 224-28.

Combined with Corinthian 'enthusiasm', this teaching accounts for their strenuous sexual asceticism.[17] Against Hurd, most interpreters today take 7.1b not as Paul's formulation or view, but the Corinthians'.[18] Thus there is no evidence that Paul taught sexual asceticism early on, and that in 1 Corinthians 7 he is modifying his former position, as Hurd thinks. Further, as C.K. Barrett has argued, the shortness of time between the end of Paul's initial stay in Corinth and the writing of 1 Corinthians (between fifteen and twenty-seven months) speaks against the violent swings in Paul's teaching that Hurd's reconstruction presupposes.[19] My suggestion that the Corinthian sexual ascetics appealed to the tradition of Gal. 3.28 need not rule out complementary explanations of their behavior, and we can certainly point to various probable motivations on the basis of Paul's comments in 1 Corinthians 7 especially, yet no solid evidence for the Corinthians' recourse to other *Christian traditions* has yet been put forward.

Gal. 3.28 is therefore a tradition which not only *Paul* applies to the discussion of sexual asceticism, but one whose implications in this respect are a matter of dispute between Paul and the Corinthians. In studying 1 Corinthians 7, therefore, we need to ask how the Corinthians used the tradition to support sexually ascetic behavior, and how Paul reinterpreted it in response to such behavior. We will be looking at Gal. 3.28 in a new way here by asking not simply how it fueled social and gender emancipation in early Christianity, which many have done before,[20] but how such emancipation might be conceived in terms of sexual asceticism. It also follows that we must analyze Paul's interpretation of the tradition in 1 Corinthians 7 not simply in terms of the broad question of how much social or gender emancipation Paul finds room for here. Rather we must see this chapter as Paul's answer to the more specific question, how valid is it to argue for the freedom of the ascetic on the basis of Gal. 3.28c?

---

17. J.C. Hurd, *The Origin of 1 Corinthians* (London: SPCK, 1965), pp. 274-78.

18. E.g. Fee, *1 Corinthians*, pp. 274-76.

19. C.K. Barrett, *A Commentary on the First Epistle to the Corinthians* (London: Black, 1968), pp. 7-8. For the view that the Corinthians derived their ascetic position from Paul's teaching in a different way, namely, on the basis of his strong warning against immorality, see O.L. Yarbrough, *Not Like the Gentiles: Marriage Rules in the Letters of Paul* (SBLDS, 80; Atlanta, GA: Scholars Press, 1985), pp. 121-22. Firm evidence is lacking for this view too, however.

20. E.g. Schüssler Fiorenza, *Memory*, 205-41; Betz, *Galatians*, 189ff.

How did the Corinthians see Gal. 3.28c to ground their sexual asceticism? Can we explain how they could have drawn this implication from the claim that in Christ 'there is no longer male and female'? Dicussions of the meaning of this statement in the early Christian baptismal formula often proceed from the important observation that it contains an allusion to Gen. 1.27 LXX: 'male and female he created them'.[21] This allusion is fairly certain since Gal. 3.28c follows the wording of the LXX of Gen. 1.27, ἄρσεν καὶ θῆλυ. This precise phrase occurs in the LXX only one other time, at Gen. 5.2, which is an exact parallel to 1.27, 'male and female he created them'. Gal. 3.28c follows the wording of the LXX despite the fact that doing so requires sacrificing parallelism between the members in the traditional formula: the copulative conjunction καί in 'no male *and* female' matches that in Gen. 1.27 LXX and displaces the disjunctive conjunction οὐδέ used to connect the other two pairs in 'neither Jew *nor* Greek, neither slave *nor* free'.[22] We are therefore justified in asking how the allusion to Gen. 1.27 affects the meaning of the traditional formula and whether the implication of sexual asceticism could be drawn from the resulting interpretation of Gal. 3.28c.

First we will consider the interpretation of the baptismal formula in terms of the androgynous ideal. In Wayne Meeks's view[23] an interpretation of Gen. 1.27 in terms of the Adam-Androgyne myth lies behind Gal. 3.28. The early Christians who formulated the baptismal tradition took Gen. 1.27 to mean that God created humanity originally androgynous: '"male and female" he created them' means 'masculo-feminine he created "him"'.[24] This androgynous humanity is restored somehow

---

21. E.g. K. Stendahl, *The Bible and the Role of Women: A Case Study in Hermeneutics* (trans. E.T. Sander; Philadelphia: Fortress Press, 1966), p. 32; Schüssler Fiorenza, *Memory*, p. 211.

22. Meeks ('Image', p. 181 n. 77) rejects the possibility that καί is simply stylistic variation, since the allusion to Genesis in the baptismal tradition is also clear in Col. 3.10. There the baptismal tradition borrows the theme and language of creation in the image of God from Gen. 1.26 LXX (κατ' εἰκόνα).

23. Meeks, 'Image', p. 185 with n. 88. Followed by Betz, *Galatians*, pp. 196-200; B.H. Brinsmead, *Galatians—Dialogical Response to Opponents* (Chico, CA: Scholars Press, 1982).

24. Meeks ('Image', p. 185 n. 88) appeals to the following LXX translation of Gen. 1.27 known to rabbis in early talmudic times: 'A male with corresponding female parts created he him' (*b. Meg.* 9a; Mekilta, *Pisha* 14, translation by Lauterbach). He conjectures that the text reflects the influence of the common myth of a bisexual

in the act of Christian initiation. The baptismal tradition thus employs a 'reunification formula' which takes up the *Urzeit–Endzeit* pattern to interpret eschatological salvation as return to the original androgyne.

To this one can reply, if the baptismal tradition did understand Gen. 1.27 in this way and wanted to communicate that the androgynous image is restored in baptism, it would not have *negated* the phrase 'male and female = masculo-feminine' of Gen. 1.27. As a matter of fact, however, the tradition draws on Gen. 1.27 to make a denial about what that text says: '*There is no* "male and female"'. The only way to read this early Christian declaration as an affirmation of androgyne is to say that it sees *already in Gen. 1.27* the 'fateful division' of humanity narrated in Gen. 2.21-22, which is now overcome in Christ. But to say this is to saw off the limb on which one is sitting, for then Gen. 1.27 no longer expresses the ideal of an originally androgynous humanity which could have inspired the early Christians who were seeking to define *Endzeit* in terms of *Urzeit*. The whole interpretation of Gal. 3.28c as expressing the androgynous ideal falters once we take seriously 'There is no "male and female"' as an allusion to Gen. 1.27 *and, in some sense, its negation.*[25] And because the interpretation of Gal. 3.28c in terms of androgyne falters, the evidence from gnostic and encratite Christian sources (dating from the second century on)[26] that the putative return to original

progenitor of the human race, such as the widely known version of Plato (*Symposium* 189 D–193 D).

25. B. Witherington ('Rite and Rights for Women—Galatians 3.28', *NTS* 27 [1981], pp. 593-604) argues against Meeks that Paul interprets reunification to mean that 'we are becoming part of one male person—εἷς (3.28)', not 'being reunited into a new singular male–female identity' (p. 597). But Meeks can escape this criticism by dissociating Paul's view from the supposed original meaning of the tradition: 'Paul himself did not—or did not always—accept the androgynous interpretation of Genesis 1:27 which...lay behind the baptismal language of Galatians 3:28—further reason for regarding that tradition as not of Paul's coinage' ('Image', p. 203 n. 153). Schüssler Fiorenza (*Memory*, p. 205; cf. p. 211) argues more cogently against Meeks that his argument is heavily dependent on later gnostic texts.

26. See Meeks, 'Image', pp. 193-97; D.R. MacDonald, *There is no Male and Female: The Fate of a Dominical Saying in Paul and Gnosticism* (Philadelphia: Fortress Press, 1987), pp. 30-63. Not only the late date of these sources but their description of the sexual ascetic makes a genuine parallel with the Corinthian ascetics unlikely. The asocial isolation of the *monachos* in the *Gospel of Thomas* and the itinerant life of the ascetic in the *Encratite Acts* (e.g. Thecla in *Acts of Paul and Thecla*) contrast with the social integration of the Corinthian ascetics in the Christian community.

androgyne could foster sexual asceticism is not relevant to the Corinthians' sexual asceticism. For, as I have argued, they appealed to Gal. 3.28c, but it does not affirm the androgynous ideal.

Dennis R. MacDonald[27] thinks that the Corinthians were influenced by a soteriology of androgyne such as that found in the dominical saying quoted in *Gospel of the Egyptians* (second century CE), quoted by Clement of Alexandria, *Strom*. 3.13.92, and in *2 Clem.* 12.2 (early second or late first century CE, probably from Corinth), and in *Gospel of Thomas* 37, 22b (prior to 200 CE, possibly second half of the first century). Its most well-known form is in *Gos. Thom.* 22b:

> Jesus said to them: 'When you make the two one, and you make the inside as the outside, and the outside as the inside, and the above as the below, and when you make the male with the female into a single one, so that the male will not be male and the female not be female. When you make eyes in the place of an eye, and a hand in the place of a hand, and a foot in the place of a foot—an image in the place of an image—then you shall enter the Kingdom.'

MacDonald claims this saying pre-dates the one in Gal. 3.28c, despite the date of our sources for it, and that Paul has modified it away from androgyne and social equality in Galatians. But much of MacDonald's argumentation is highly speculative and his formulations hypothetical. He will not go so far as to say that the Corinthians knew the saying itself. And he does not attempt to attribute the Corinthians' sexual asceticism to the influence of this soteriology.[28] For lack of evidence to the contrary, then, it seems best to assume that the Corinthians were operating with the same baptismal tradition Paul knew and used in Gal. 3.28, not an earlier (androgynous) version, and that this tradition did not picture baptism as return to primordial androgyne.[29]

27. *No Male and Female*, pp. 14ff., 65-111.

28. Rather he follows David Balch, who argues that the Corinthians' sexual asceticism was partly based on sayings of Jesus such as Mk 12.25; Lk. 20.34-35, according to which the life of the resurrection excludes marriage (*No Male and Female*, pp. 70-71). For a description and critique of this view, see above, pp. 100-101.

29. Against the androgynous interpretation, see also P. Trible, *God and the Rhetoric of Sexuality* (Philadelphia: Fortress Press, 1978), p. 18; W. Schrage and E. Gerstenberger, *Woman and Man* (trans. D.W. Stott; Nashville: Abingdon, 1981), p. 150; K.R. Snodgrass, 'Galatians 3.28: Conundrum or Solution?', in A. Mickelsen (ed.), *Women, Authority & the Bible* (Downers Grove, IL: Intervarsity Press, 1986), p. 171; A.C. Wire, *The Corinthian Women Prophets* (Minneapolis: Fortress Press, 1991), p. 125.

In conclusion, we can state that Gal. 3.28c negates the creation of humanity as 'male and female' according to Gen. 1.27 from some other perspective than the androgynous ideal. What other perspective might the Corinthian ascetics have adopted so as to claim the baptismal tradition in support of sexual asceticism? Elizabeth Schüssler Fiorenza suggests that Gal. 3.28c presupposes the interpretation of Gen. 1.27 'primarily in terms of marriage and family', and that the tradition can be interpreted to support sexual asceticism.[30] Two questions will guide us in the following discussion: What evidence is there for the interpretation of Gen. 1.27 in terms of marriage and family? In this light, how could the Corinthians have justified their sexually ascetic practices—including remaining virgins, withdrawing from conjugal relations, divorcing and remaining unmarried if widowed—with the claim 'There is no longer "male and female"'?

An early Christian interpretation of Gen. 1.27 in terms of marriage and sexual union appears in Mk 10.6-9 (par. Mt. 19.4-9).[31] Here Jesus makes Gen. 1.27 the basis for marriage and sexual union in Gen. 2.24, as his citation of both texts shows: 'From the beginning of creation "male and female he created them". "For this reason a man shall leave his father and mother [and be joined to his wife], and the two shall be one flesh." So they are no longer two but one flesh.' The point Jesus wants to make is that the marriage bond is indissoluble. This is his answer to the Pharisees' question about Moses' allowance of divorce: 'Therefore what God has joined together, let no one separate'.[32] God's

---

30. *Memory*, p. 219.

31. Schüssler Fiorenza notes Mk 10.6 (*Memory*, p. 211).

32. D. Daube (*The New Testament and Rabbinic Judaism* [London: Athlone, 1956], pp. 71ff.) tries to suggest that Gen. 1.27, 'male and female he created them', can make sense as an argument against divorce only if it refers to the creation of an original androgynous human being in which the sexes were united. He finds the androgynous interpretation in the rabbis (*Gen. R.* on Gen. 1.26-27, *Mek.* on Exod. 12.40) and says it goes back to New Testament times, namely, Philo (*Op. Mund.* 24.76). Daube regards Jesus' second quotation, Gen. 2.24, as an insertion (by Mark or an earlier interpolator) which makes no sense in the argument. Against Daube, Jesus cites Gen. 1.27 (creation of sexually dimorphic humanity) to prepare for Gen. 2.24, which pictures the marriage of man and woman as the joining of the two in a one-flesh union for which their creation as male and female has prepared. 'What God has joined together (viz. in marriage, συνέζευξεν)' refers not to God the Creator (Gen. 1.27) but God the Matchmaker (Gen. 2.24); cf. E. Lohmeyer, *Das Evangelium des Markus* (MeyerK, I/2; Göttingen: Vandenhoeck & Ruprecht, 1967), p. 201.

original intention for marriage is seen not in the Law but in creation. Not that this point itself is important for our discussion, but the Scripture interpretations that Jesus uses to establish it are. Jesus intends his citations of Genesis to show that marriage and sexual union are based on God's creation of humanity as 'male and female'. The one-flesh union of man and woman in marriage fulfils the Creator's intention in creating humanity sexually dimorphic.[33]

While Jesus used the first creation account to support the indissolubility of marriage, in Jewish tradition it supplied the obligation itself of marriage and procreation. The rabbis appealed in particular to the command in Gen. 1.28: 'be fruitful and multiply and fill the earth!' Gen. 1.27, 'male and female he created them', was introduced as a 'help to a more exact understanding of this *halakha*'.[34] The rabbis grasped the intention of the Priestly writer correctly here, if we follow Phyllis Bird's exegesis of Gen. 1.27.[35] She argues that P's description of humanity as 'male and female' by creation supplies the logical prerequisite for the blessing of fertility and the command to procreate which follows in the narrative. Her exegesis of Gen. 1.27 is not frequently encountered so I will state it briefly here.

According to Gen. 1.27 *'ādām* was created 'male and female'. The terms *zākār* and *n^eqēbâ* (LXX: ἄρσεν and θῆλυ[36]) are biological terms referring to the biological sex distinction in the human species. Humanity is *sexually dimorphic* by creation. The purpose of this description of humanity is to make comprehensible the immediately following blessing, 'Be fruitful and multiply and fill the earth!' (Gen. 1.28). For the blessing presupposes the human ability to procreate, which depends on sexual differentiation and sexual union. But the immediately preceding description of humanity as created 'in the image of God' makes the ability to procreate doubtful and the blessing of fertility thus unjustified. For

---

33. E. Gould, *Critical and Exegetical Commentary on the Gospel according to St Mark* (ICC; Edinburgh: T. & T. Clark, 1896), p. 184.

34. Daube, *Rabbinic Judaism*, pp. 76-78. He refers to *m. Yeb.* 6.6, *t. Yeb.* 8.4, *b. Yeb.* 62a.

35. P.A. Bird, '"Male and Female He Created Them": Gen. 1.27b in the Context of the Priestly Account of Creation', *HTR* 74 (1981), pp. 129-59. See also her similar 'Genesis I–III as a Source for a Contemporary Theology of Sexuality', *Ex Auditu* 3 (1987), pp. 31-44; 'Sexual Differentiation and Divine Image in the Genesis Creation Texts', in K.E. Børresen (ed.), *Image of God and Gender Models in Judaeo-Christian Tradition* (Oslo: Solum, 1991), pp. 11-34.

36. See A. Oepke, 'ἀνήρ', *TDNT*, I, p. 362.

the idea that God might possess any form of sexuality, or any differentiation analogous to it, would have been for P an utterly foreign and repugnant notion. Consequently, the word that identifies *'ādām* by reference to divine likeness must be supplemented or qualified before the blessing of fertility can be pronounced.

'Male and female he created them' thus provides the necessary statement of humanity's sexual constitution (viz. sexual differentiation) which is the presupposition of the blessing of increase. The description of humanity as 'male and female' thus fits P's overarching interest in describing all creatures as able to reproduce and thus to fill an empty earth, and to do it without recourse to the fertility cult, since God alone is the source of life, both its creation and its sustenance.[37]

To summarize, in the intention of the Priestly writer, and in the apologetic use of Jesus according to early Christian tradition, as well as in rabbinic teaching, the creation of humanity as 'male and female' has roughly the same sense: sexual dimorphism implies marriage, sexual union and procreation. *Early Christians familiar with the biblical creation account or with early Christian or Jewish interpretation of it could have thus understood the words of the baptismal tradition, 'There is no "male and female"', to alter or abolish the implications of the created sexual distinctions 'male' and 'female' for marriage, sexual union and procreation.[38] In the hands of sexual ascetics such as those in Corinth, the eschatological formula could be taken to justify sexual asceticism.* The Corinthians might have played the baptismal tradition off against Jesus' interpretation of Gen. 1.27 supporting the indissolubility of marriage (assuming they knew this tradition): 'there is no "male and female"' meant freedom from marriage, both future and existing marriage, and freedom from sexual union, both for the celibate and for the married. 1 Corinthians 7 makes it clear that they argued for both types of freedom.[39] Paul's reinforcement of Jesus' prohibition of

37. Bird, 'Male and Female', 146-50.

38. The fact that the early Christians used the LXX translation in Gal. 3.28c does not pose a problem for making comparisons with the MT and its interpretation, since the LXX follows the MT quite closely in its translation of Gen. 1.26-28.

39. 1 Cor. 7 shows that Gal. 3.28c was being interpreted to have social consequences in the area of sexual behavior. It thus does not follow, against L. Fatum ('Image of God and Glory of Man: Women in the Pauline Congregations', in K.E. Børresen [ed.], *Image of God and Gender Models*, pp. 67-68), that because the formula uses sexual rather than social terminology—'male and female'—it does not make a statement about social behavior but only about reproduction. Fatum is trying

divorce in 1 Cor. 7.10 is one way in which Paul indicates that he does not agree with the Corinthians' interpretation of Gal. 3.28c.[40] A fuller discussion of Paul's interaction with the Corinthians over the implications of Gal. 3.28c for marriage, sexual union and procreation is necessary, and will follow below. But first some comments must be made on the relation of this understanding of Gal. 3.28c to two trends in the exegesis of the biblical creation narratives.

Two mutually compatible exegetical trends have obscured the meaning of Gen. 1.27 which, I have argued, stands behind the allusion to this verse in the baptismal tradition of Gal. 3.28c. First, Karl Barth's interpretation of the 'image of God' in terms of 'male and female' in Gen. 1.27 has had great influence and has drawn attention away from the link between the statement 'male and female he created them' and the following blessing and command to 'be fruitful and multiply' in that same verse. Secondly, this trend to interpret 'male and female' in terms of the 'image of God' fits into the larger program of many feminist biblical exegetes to uncover egalitarian readings of Genesis 1–2 and thus recover the creation narratives as liberating texts for women.[41] The exegetical contributions of Phyllis Trible are the prime example.[42]

Briefly, Trible argues that 'male and female' in Gen. 1.27 (also 5.1b-2) defines *'ādām*, humankind, as two sexually distinct creatures who are equal, not created to stand in a hierarchical relationship to one another.

to invalidate the interpretation of Gal. 3.28c as a socially liberating tradition of the primitive church (*contra* Schüssler Fiorenza *et al.*). In fact, the tradition is just the opposite, she claims. By negating sexual duality and thus reproduction, it re-establishes the original, sexually undifferentiated image of God, but understands that asexual image as male/man according to Gen. 1.27a. Fatum's argumentation, however, is based on two faulty assumptions: (1) that the allusion to Gen. 1.27, 'male and female he created them', in Gal. 3.28c is to be understood in terms of 'the image of God' (see further below); (2) that Paul repudiates sexuality from a dualistic ascetic attitude toward life. 1 Cor. 7 may once have been read in this way, but it certainly is no longer.

40. Paul allows an exception to this prohibition—if the unbeliever is not willing to live with the believer, the brother or sister is not bound (7.15). But this exception is not based on Gal. 3.28c, 'there is no male and female', but on the fact that 'God has called you in peace' (7.15).

41. For a radical critique of all attempts to ground a feminist theology of liberation of women in the biblical texts, see e.g. Fatum, 'Image of God and Glory of Man', pp. 56-129.

42. Trible, *God*, pp. 12-30, 72-143; 'Depatriarchalizing in Biblical Interpretation', *JAAR* 71 (1973), pp. 30-48 (35-42).

They are given equal power in Gen. 1.26, where God gives the responsibility for dominion over the earth to both equally: 'let *them* have dominion...' (similarly, 1.28). 'Male and female' interprets the 'image of God' in which humankind is created, thus there is an 'equality in the image of God male *and* female'. Woman too bears the divine image.[43] Trible explicitly disputes that the creation of humanity as 'male and female' pertains to procreation.[44]

Then Genesis 2 undergoes a process of depatriarchalization: the creation of woman after man and from the rib of the man does not signify inferiority or subordination, rather she is the splendid culmination of creation and the man's equal in solidarity with him. The creation of woman to be man's 'helper' does not imply her subordination since even God is called 'helper'. The man does not name woman in an act of power over her, but recognizes her sexuality as *'iššâ*. Even Genesis 3 is depatriarchalized. The narrative of the fall does not identify woman with temptation nor present her as the morally weaker sex but as more intelligent, aggressive, and aware than the man. The woman's subordination under the rule of her husband is not her created role but a consequence of the fall.

Certainly it is important for contempory Christians to re-examine their reading of Genesis 1–3. Nevertheless, some of the specific interpretations above can be challenged on exegetical grounds, and scepticism is growing about *intentional* egalitarianism in these texts.[45] Such criticisms aside, however, the interpretation of Gen. 1.27 by Karl Barth, which feminist exegesis has also made its own, cannot make sense of the use of

---

43. By contrast, many interpreters read Paul in 1 Cor. 11.7 to say that only the man is the image of God.

44. Trible, *God*, pp. 15, 19.

45. For the purposes of this discussion, a criticism of Trible's interpretation of Gen. 1.27 is especially significant. She argues on the basis of *formal parallelism* between 'in the image of God created he him' and 'male and female created he them' for *semantic correspondence* between 'image of God' and 'male and female' (*God*, p. 17). But this interpretation (insofar as it is meant to give P's intended meaning) does not stand up against Bird's explanation of this verse in terms of the structure of the priestly writer's argument and his overarching theological concerns. For this and further criticisms, see Bird's 'Image', pp. 135-55; 'Sexual Differentiation', pp. 11-31; F. Watson, 'Strategies of Recovery and Resistance: Hermeneutical Reflections on Genesis 1–3 and its Pauline Reception', *JSNT* 45 (1992), pp. 79-103; D.J.A. Clines, *What Does Eve Do to Help? and Other Readerly Questions to the Old Testament* (JSOTSup, 94; Sheffield: JSOT Press, 1990), pp. 25-48.

this verse in the early Christian baptismal formula. The eschatological declaration, 'There is no "male and female"', puts out of force the primordial description, 'male and female he created them'. Gen. 1.27 is not the solution here. Rather the early Christians were trying to get beyond it.[46]

The fact that Gal. 3.28c is formulated in explicit contrast to Gen. 1.27, however, has been taken seriously by very few scholars, doubtless because the dominant exegetical treatments of Gen. 1.27 do not favor such a reading, as well as because of the theological difficulties it might imply for a doctrine of creation. Krister Stendahl is one of the few who does face the issue head on: 'This statement [Gal. 3.28c] is directed against what we call the order of creation...In Christ... something has happened which transcends...even the order of creation.'[47] It seems that we ought to conclude that the early Christians who formulated the baptismal tradition and those who used it after them were struck negatively instead of positively by what they read in Genesis 1. Perhaps modern biblical scholarship, by disjoining Gen. 1.1–2.4a and 2.4–3.24 into separately authored accounts with distinct language, dynamics and intentions, has blocked the way to the ancients' view of creation and fall as interwoven, mutually interpreting biblical narratives. In the eager attempt to 'recover' biblical texts from patriarchal interpretations feminist exegesis seems to have largely missed the pessimism of the first

---

46. M. de Merode ('Une théologie primitive de la femme', *RTL* 9 [1978], pp. 176-89 [181-86]) fails to recognize that the baptismal tradition makes a negation of Gen. 1.27. Here the trail of mistakes in her argument begins. She proposes that the primitive community saw in this verse the basis of woman's being in the image of God. Gal. 3.28c thus expresses a pre-pauline theology of woman, which Paul then tries to correct along the lines of Jewish theology.

47. *The Bible and the Role of Women*, pp. 32, 34; followed by Scroggs, 'Eschatological Woman', p. 292 n. 29. Cf. W. Schrage's comment on Gal. 3.28: 'In the one body of Christ all secular categories are transcended, even distinctions inherent in the created order' (*The Ethics of the New Testament* [trans. D.E. Green; Philadelphia: Fortress Press, 1988], p. 223 see also 225). According to Wire (*Women Prophets*, pp. 125-26, 185-86), the reversal of the first creation by the new creation is a crucial insight of the Corinthian women prophets which Paul is unable to follow. Contrast to Stendahl's statement the views of K. Snodgrass, 'Galatians 3:28', p. 177; M. Hayter, *The New Eve in Christ: The Use and Abuse of the Bible in the Debate about Women in the Church* (London: SPCK, 1987), p. 137; A. Feuillet, 'La dignité et le rôle de la femme d'après quelques textes pauliniens', *NTS* 21 (1975), pp. 157-91 (158).

Christians about those texts—from the perspective of the new creation. May the reader indulge my speculations about those first century readers' thinking.

Ignorant of higher critical theories of authorship of the Pentateuch, the early Christians read Genesis 1, 2 and 3 together. These chapters left them with the impression of a creation marred by the effects of sin. The bright vision 'in the beginning' of man and woman's future—he shall leave his father and mother and cleave blissfully to his wife, and together they shall fill the earth in God's good creation and exercise caretakership over it—did not come to pass. The man's initial praise of the one who is 'bone of my bones and flesh of my flesh' gave way to his accusation against 'the woman you [God] gave me to be with me—she gave me fruit from the tree and I ate it'. God's blessing upon male and female, 'be fruitful and multiply and fill the earth', turned bitter through the curse: 'I will greatly increase your pangs in childbearing; in pain you shall bring forth children'. The childbearer must now suffer in the very fulfilment of the blessing. The mechanism of heterosexual attraction which 'guarantees' the population of the earth remains in place, however, and thus makes this curse 'inescapable': 'Yet your desire shall be for your husband'. The sublime 'one-flesh' union of man and woman in marriage contrasts to their post-fall hierarchical division into subordinate and ruler: 'And he [your husband] shall rule over you'. In the beginning God said, 'Let *them* fill the earth and subdue it'. But the woman's partner in subduing the earth became a master who subdues her. This, in short, is what it means to be created male and female *in human experience*, or so the early Christian readers of Genesis 1–3 could have thought.

But now 'there is no "male and female"'. Rather, 'if anyone is in Christ, there is a new creation. Everything old has passed away, see, everything has become new' (2 Cor. 5.17). Gal. 3.28c with its critique of the created order is formulated from the perspective of the redeemed order. It is now inaugurated. And it is a new creation. The Corinthians doubtless shared this perspective, given their highly realized eschatology and their sense of living according to new norms in the power of the eschatological gift of the Spirit as those already resurrected to new life (cf. esp. 1 Cor. 4.8-10; 15.12). This understanding of present Christian existence lent itself well to a rejection of the first creation's implications for marriage, sexual relations and procreation.[48]

---

48. Thus Schrage is wrong when he claims, 'Umgekehrt is von einer eschatologischen Begründung der asketischen Parole in Korinth nichts zu erkennen'

According to Elizabeth Schüssler Fiorenza and Antoinette Wire, the point of Gal. 3.28c as a statement about marriage and family in the new creation as opposed to the first creation is freedom from patriarchy and male privilege.[49]

> Sexual dimorphism and strictly defined gender roles are products of a patriarchal culture, which maintain and legitimize structures of control and domination—the exploitation of women by men. Gal. 3.28...advocates the abolition...of domination based on sexual divisions.[50]

Freedom from such domination is to be attained especially through sexual asceticism, for women who live celibate lives can escape subordination to a husband and the biological determination of their roles as wives and mothers in a patriarchal culture which oppressed them in various ways.[51]

But it would be wrong to limit the significance of Gal. 3.28 to freedom from patriarchal structures, as Schüssler Fiorenza's and Wire's investigations tend to do. The eschatological declaration clearly had a wider meaning for the Corinthians. We can hardly think that the *male* ascetics in Corinth welcomed the abolition of patriarchy through the formula 'there is no "male and female"'. And there *is* clear evidence for male sexual ascetics in Corinth (e.g. 1 Cor. 7.1-4, 11-16, 36-38), despite Wire's ingenius but exegetically indefensible construal of Paul's rhetoric to make it address only female ascetics.[52] Sexual asceticism attracted men too in a Hellenistic milieu, who found various reasons to escape the burdens of marriage and family.[53] Thus male celibates in Corinth also could have appealed to the eschatological reversal of Gen. 1.27 to justify their behavior. So it would be more accurate to say that Gal. 3.28c functioned as a justification for sexual asceticism as such

---

('Frontstellung', p. 228; here he is responding to Balch's thesis that the Corinthian ascetics appealed to a dominical saying like that in Mt. 19.12).

49. Schüssler Fiorenza, *Memory*, pp. 211-18; Wire, *Women Prophets*, p. 126.

50. Schüssler Fiorenza, *Memory*, p. 213.

51. Wire, *Women Prophets*, pp. 64-66; Schüssler Fiorenza, *Memory*, pp. 224-26; cf. R. Kraemer, *Ecstatics and Ascetics Studies in Functions of Religious Activities for Women* (Ann Arbor, MI: University Microfilms International, 1976), pp. 131-32.

52. Wire, *Women Prophets*, pp. 78ff.

53. Cf. 1 Cor. 7.32-33. On the Epicureans' rejection of marriage and the duty to produce children, see Diogenes Laertius 10.118-19 (noted by Meeks, 'Image', p. 173 n. 48). Cf. Epictetus, *Dis.* 3.22.69-72, who discourages the Cynic from marrying because of the resulting familial obligations.

in Corinth, and leave room for a variety of motivations, including freedom from patriarchy and from the burdens of marriage and family under the conditions of the fallen creation.

I cannot discuss here all the possible reasons why the Corinthians had adopted sexual asceticism. In 1 Corinthians 7 we find some evidence related to their motivations. The Corinthians rejected marriage as 'sin' (cf. 7.28, 36, 38). They associated sexual asceticism with inspiration.[54] They understood celibacy as devotion to the Lord and the Lord's service (implied in 7.33-34). My point here, however, is simply that the Corinthian ascetics could appeal to the formula in Gal. 3.28c as a fundamental Christian tradition that can be taken to support sexual asceticism.

Earlier we observed that Paul gives a 'commentary' on Gal. 3.28 in 1 Corinthians 7. This commentary, moreover, is written in the light of the Corinthians' understanding and use of Gal. 3.28c. Now we are in a position to ask how Paul interprets the declaration, 'There is no "male and female"', in his polemical response to the Corinthian ascetics. In the following discussion of his interpretation I will show how he addresses the items on their agenda and takes a position on the relation between creation and redemption/eschaton with respect to gender roles and relations.

Paul neither completely agrees nor completely disagrees with the Corinthian ascetics. First let us take up the matter of marriage and conjugal relations. In 1 Cor. 7.9 Paul commands those who burn with passion to 'marry' (similarly 7.36), and in 7.3-5 he tells those who are married to 'fulfil the obligation' of conjugal relations to their spouse. The command 'Let each husband have his own wife and let each wife have her own husband!' (7.2) also refers to marital relations.[55] Marriage is a guard against immorality ('on account of immoralities...', 7.2).[56] Paul's argument in favor of marriage and conjugal relations is thus based on the reality of sexual desire and the view that it finds its proper expression in the marriage relationship and not outside.

---

54. See my forthcoming article on celibacy and inspiration in 1 Corinthians 7.

55. ἔχειν can mean 'to have sexually' (e.g. Exod. 2.1; Deut. 28.30; Isa. 13.16 LXX) or simply to be in the state of marriage in which sexual intercourse habitually takes place (e.g. 1 Cor. 5.1; 7.12, 13, 29). On this usage in biblical Greek, see Fee, *1 Corinthians*, p. 278 with notes.

56. This is not an exhaustive description of the purpose of marriage in Paul's view; he does not try to give a rounded view of marriage in 1 Cor. 7. See further Schrage, *Ethics*, p. 226.

Paul's thinking here corresponds to Genesis 2 and 3 where sexual desire is a basis for marriage and its consummation in one-flesh union. Phyllis Bird has drawn attention to this erotic emphasis of the Yahwist's account of creation.[57] The man was alone in the garden, and this was 'not good'. So the Lord made various creatures and brought them to the man, none of which elicited any excitement from him until finally the woman appeared. This time the man burst forth in praise showing sexual delight and desire. The chemistry was there! They promptly elope, which the narrator turns into a generalization about all couples in love: 'For a man shall leave his father and mother and be joined to his wife, and they shall become one flesh' (Gen. 2.23-24). Eve's sexual desire is not mentioned until after the fall (Gen. 3.16), but there desire binds her to a husband, even though he rules over her and their union makes her give birth in great pain.

With respect to sexual passion, the Corinthian men and women correspond to their prototypes Adam and Eve. There is enough sexual activity in Corinth for Paul to draw that conclusion, despite the ascetics' protestations. Therefore marriage and conjugal relations are also in order for the Corinthians. Unless they have the *charisma* that Paul has (7.8), which enables him to live a celibate life, they have not yet transcended the created order with respect to sexual desire. Therefore, marriage still serves its purpose according to the created order, providing a context for expression and fulfilment of sexual passion. Paul wishes that all did have the *charisma* of celibacy, but recognizes that not all do (7.7), and that these should follow the example of Adam and Eve. In Paul's view, then, the declaration, 'There is no "male and female"', does not do away with or invalidate sexual desire and its fulfilment in conjugal relations. Here there is continuity with the first creation.

The reason for Christians to marry is thus passion. Procreation is not a reason to marry, however. Paul sees the *lovers* Adam and Eve as Christians' prototypes, but not *father* Adam and *mother* Eve.[58] Here

---

57. She comments that 'the attraction of the sexes is the author's primary interest, the sexual drive whose consummation is conceived as a re-union' ('Sexual Differentiation', p. 20).

58. The distinction between 'lovers' and 'parents' is not an anachronistic one, since contraception was practiced in antiquity (see A. Rousselle, *Porneia: On Desire and the Body in Antiquity* [trans. F. Pheasant; Oxford: Basil Blackwell, 1988], p. 45). Further, the distinction makes sense in the case of childless couples or barren women and sterile men. Freedom from the obligation of procreation would

Paul abandons the point of sexual dimorphism in Gen. 1.27-28, that since the human species is created 'male and female', it can 'be fruitful and multiply and fill the earth'. He does not turn this biblical text into an argument against the Corinthian sexual ascetics.[59] The terminology he uses in 1 Corinthians 7 also suggests his view. When he speaks of woman here he calls her not 'mother' but 'sister' (ἀδελφή, in the sense of female fellow believer, 7.15)—though she be a woman with children (7.14)—or he calls her 'wife' (γυνή, 7.2-4, etc.), or 'widow' (χήρα, 7.8). He does not speak in derogatory terms of the 'virgin' (παρθένος, 7.34, etc.) or 'unmarried woman' (ἡ γυνὴ ἡ ἄγαμος, 7.34) who is consecrated to the Lord 'in body and in spirit', as if her proper role was mother. Likewise, Paul shows no interest in the man's ability to father children.

Paul's silence about procreation as the purpose of Christian marriage is telling, given the Jewish view of marriage as an obligation for the sake of producing children,[60] a view we might expect Paul to espouse. Women and men in a Greco-Roman environment also lived under that obligation owing to political considerations. Imperial policy penalized bachelors and rewarded the married and mothers.[61] Interpreters often attribute Paul's lack of interest in procreation to his conviction that the end is near (cf. 7.29-31).[62] But it is likely that the theological statement in Gal. 3.28c played an important role in his thinking also. Through its negation of Gen. 1.27 the early Christian baptismal formula can be taken to dissociate procreative *capacity* from procreative *duty* or *purpose*. Christian women and men were thus free to devote their time and resources to the 'things of the Lord' (7.33-34) rather than to producing children. Here he is also doubtless in agreement with the Corinthian ascetics.

have positive implications for such persons.

59. Contrast 1 Tim. 2.15, where the author sees childbearing to be the woman's lot, and alludes to Gen. 3.16. The statement that the Christian woman 'will be saved διὰ τῆς τεκνογονίας' does not call into question this lot, regardless of whether we take the verse to refer to salvation (1) by means of childbearing, or (2) from the risks of childbearing.

60. See above, pp. 106-107.

61. See P. Csillag, *The Augustan Laws on Family Relation* (Budapest: Collets, 1976); Rousselle, *Porneia*, p. 364.

62. E.g. J.M. Bassler, '1 Corinthians', in C.A. Newsom and S.H. Ringe (eds.), *The Women's Bible Commentary* (London: SPCK; Louisville, KY: Westminster/John Knox, 1992), pp. 321-329 (324).

Besides the omission of procreation as the purpose of marriage and sexual dimorphism, the other striking thing about Paul's characterization of Christian marriage in 1 Corinthians 7, which many have noted, is the equality of husband and wife in the sexual relationship. This equality comes to expression both in the content and the structure of the passage. Paul asserts the wife's 'authority' over the body of her husband (7.4). He obligates the husband to give her her conjugal rights as 'what is due' (ὀφειλή, 7.3). Of course, the husband has these rights too. But the point is the complete mutuality between them, as Paul's repetitious formulations indicate, alternately making the wife, then the husband, the subject of his injunctions (7.2-5, 10-16, 32-35).[63] To be sure, we should not overestimate the egalitarianism of this passage. Equality here is applied to a single sphere: sex in marriage.[64] And one cannot miss the androcentrism of the chapter (e.g. 7.27, 28, 36-38). Nevertheless, this limited egalitarianism remains striking because it is stated emphatically and because the area of the sexual relationship in marriage is a very significant one.

Since Paul is engaged in a reinterpretation of Gal. 3.28 in 1 Corinthians 7 it is likely that he has been inspired by the tradition when he speaks of the equality of wife and husband as sexual partners. The formula, 'There is no longer "male and female"', negates sexual differentiation as a basis for a hierarchical and oppressive role differentiation at least in the sexual relationship in marriage here. *Mutual* subordination in conjugal relations replaces the sex-determined subordination of the wife: 'Let the husband fulfil his obligation to the wife, and likewise the wife to the husband!' (7.3; cf. 7.4-5). It is unlikely that Paul would have adopted such a forcefully egalitarian view of sexual rights as he does here simply to ensure that women's sexual desire find

63. Paul's statements here can be compared with some of the Stoics' comments on marriage which also support sexual equality, at least in theory, if not in practice, e.g., Antipater EE VII 1245a 30; NE IX 1170b 6; Musonius, frag. 3; 38,26-40,2; frag. 4; 46,32 Lutz; Epictetus *Dis.* 3.22.63, 68, 76; cf. 2.22.2, 36. These and other passages are discussed by D.L. Balch, '1 Cor 7:32-35 and Stoic Debates about Marriage, Anxiety, and Distraction', *JBL* 102 (1983), pp. 429-39 (436-39).

64. The husband's 'authority over the body' of his wife (and vice versa) does not entail authority over the whole person, as if σῶμα meant more than the physical body and were interchangeable with 'man, his person as a whole' (see R.H. Gundry, *Sōma in Biblical Theology with Emphasis on Pauline Anthropology* [SNTSMS, 29; Cambridge: Cambridge University Press, 1976], p. 34, *contra* R. Bultmann, *Theology of the New Testament* [New York: Scribners, 1951]), I, p. 195.

an outlet in marriage. Not only his fear of immorality (7.1), but also a vision of Christian marriage enlarged by Gal. 3.28 accounts for his stress on equal rights and responsibilities. I do not want to claim that Paul concluded from the formula in Gal. 3.28c that Christian marriage or the relationship between the sexes in general should be egalitarian in every way.[65] Other passages come to mind that suggest he did not (1 Cor. 11.2-16; 14.34-35 if authentic[66]), even apart from later developments in the Ephesian and Colossian household codes (Eph. 5.21-33; Col. 3.18-19) and in the Pastorals' paraenesis (1 Tim. 2.11-15). On the other hand, Paul recognized two *married* women as exceptional leaders in the early church: Junia, who, along with her husband Andronicus, was 'outstanding among the apostles' (Rom. 16.7),[67] and Priscilla, a Christian teacher and Paul's co-worker who even instructed Apollos and whose reputation surpassed that of her husband (Acts 18.26; Rom. 16.3). There were also doubtless married women among the prophetesses in Corinth, whose ministry Paul implicitly affirms in 11.2-16, though he requires them to cover their heads and thereby conform to prevailing customs for women of their status.[68] Thus it is possible that Paul also took the early Christian formula in Gal. 3.28c to imply a degree of freedom from sex-determined subordination in the body of Christ for women ministers.

In his interpretation of the baptismal formula's implications for

65. Cf. Scroggs's overstatement: 'Chapter 7 is in complete consonance with Paul's theological stance of liberation. In the home as well as at work in the church, woman is equal to man' ('Eschatological Woman', p. 295).

66. See Fee, *1 Corinthians*, pp. 705-708, for the argument that 1 Cor. 14.34-35 are a later interpolation.

67. See B.J. Brooten, '"Junia...Outstanding among the Apostles' (Romans 16:7)', in L. Swidler and A. Swidler (eds.), *Women Priests: A Catholic Commentary on the Vatican Declaration* (New York: Paulist Press, 1977), pp. 141-44.

68. How Paul could affirm the prophetesses' ministries and at the same time insist on customary headcoverings is a thorny question and has received various answers in the vast amount of literature on 1 Cor. 11.2-16. On the one hand, it is unlikely that Paul presupposes an egalitarian view of marriage here, but on the other hand, one should not resort too quickly to the interpretation that the woman's head-covering symbolizes subordination to her husband, since no clear evidence has been offered in support of this claim, and it is difficult even to know what type of head-covering Paul has in mind. See A. Jaubert, 'La voile des femmes (1 Cor. xi. 2-16)', *NTS* 18 (1971–72), pp. 419-30 (425); E.-B. Allo, *Saint Paul: Première Epitre aux Corinthiens* (Paris: Lecoffre, 1956), pp. 260-61.

patriarchal marriage, Paul surely differed from the Corinthian ascetics. Ascetic women would have used the formula to justify escaping subordination (among other things) in marriage through divorce. The fact that Paul's discussion of divorce in 1 Cor. 7.10-16 pays special attention to ascetic women (see 7.10-11a) suggests that they had a stronger motivation to divorce than did ascetic men, and that motivation could easily have been freedom from patriarchal marriage. But Paul, referring to the Lord's command, does not allow divorce, except at the unbeliever's wish (7.15).[69] And egalitarianism in the sexual relationship of husband and wife, which Paul affirms, may not have taken the implications of Gal. 3.28c for patriarchal marriage far enough in the eyes of the Corinthian ascetic women. Paul's interpretation of the tradition would have pleased most the *unmarried* women ascetics, whom he does not hinder in their freedom from patriarchal marriage, insofar as they can remain continent.[70]

This investigation began by asking why Paul takes up a Christian tradition that engendered radically new behavior in order to argue that the Corinthians should 'remain in the calling in which [they were] called'. It was proposed that the Corinthians' use of the tradition to support sexual asceticism forced Paul to try to reinterpret it for them and either to affirm or deny various social implications which they had drawn from it. What social implications then does Paul see Gal. 3.28c to have in 1 Corinthians 7? On the one hand, he does not think that the sexual differentiation of 'male and female', which goes back to creation, obligates Christians to procreate, thus marriage is not mandatory for this reason. Further, he restricts one-sided subordination of women on the basis of their sex by advancing mutual subordination in conjugal relations. His affirmation of the leadership of various women, including married women, in the early church may also have a basis in Gal. 3.28c. On the other hand, Paul requires the sexual ascetics who are hankering for

69. Schüssler Fiorenza's comment (*Memory*, p. 222) that 'wives...still have the possibility of freeing themselves from the bondage of patriarchal marriage, in order to live a marriage-free life' misrepresents Paul's words in 1 Cor. 7.10, where he instructs the woman who has *already* become divorced (χωρισθῇ) to remain unmarried or be reconciled to her husband.

70. Contrast the thesis of Wire, *Women Prophets*, who thinks Paul is trying to persuade the Corinthian ascetic women to give up celibacy so that men can marry them and avoid sexual immorality. The evidence for male sexual ascetics in Corinth (see above, pp. 112-13) makes this part of her thesis unpersuasive.

emancipation from marriage and conjugal relations not to desert the family hearth, and not to shun the bedroom. They may not seek divorce as an alternative, except when an unbelieving spouse wants it. Only when the opportunity to live a celibate life arises of itself through widowhood or divorce does Paul make room for a change in marital status (7.8, 11, 15, 27, 40). Finally, his admonition to 'remain in the calling in which one was called' cuts both ways: it can support the unmarried celibate in her or his decision not to marry, over against the pressures of society, as well as limit the freedom of the already married. Thus Paul in 1 Corinthians 7 neither develops from Gal. 3.28 a radical program for social reform, nor simply legitimizes the institutional structures that inhibit such change.[71] He neither abolishes patriarchal marriage as such for Christians,[72] nor leaves it untouched by the eschatological freedom of the believer.[73] His views here are more nuanced and more complex

71. His interpretation of the traditional formula, 'There is neither slave nor free', in 1 Cor. 7.21-24 can be described in much the same way. The slave and free person ought to remain so, for they derive thereby no disadvantage or advantage in Christ. Yet Paul seems to make a parenthetical exception in 7.21b by recommending taking advantage of the opportunity to become free: 'Were you called as a slave, don't be bothered by it. But if you can even become free, make use [of it]. For the one in the Lord called as a slave is a freedperson of the Lord, likewise the free person who is called is a slave of Christ' (7.21-22). Although the meaning of μᾶλλον χρῆσαι is disputed, there are good reasons to take these words as a command to use the chance to become free, not to maintain one's present condition of slavery. Bartchy (*Slavery*, pp. 87-120) has shown that the opportunity to refuse manumission did not exist for a slave, therefore Paul could not have given the command to preserve one's position as a slave. Moreover, the context clearly supports the other interpretation. Paul obviously thinks freedom is preferable to slavery, since he tells Christians not to sell themselves into slavery: 'Do not become slaves of human beings!' (7.23). We ought to take this command in a literal (not merely metaphorical) sense, since selling oneself into slavery was practiced for a variety of reasons in Paul's day (with Barrett, *1 Corinthians*, p. 171). Paul supports this command theologically with the metaphor of salvation as redemption from slavery: 'You have been bought with a price' (7.23). Only an exhortation to use the opportunity for freedom is compatible with this argument against choosing slavery.

72. So apparently Scroggs, 'Eschatological Woman', pp. 294-96. Schüssler Fiorenza (*Memory*, pp. 211-13) thinks, however, that the *pre-pauline* tradition has this sense. It gets a weaker interpretation by Paul, yet his advice to women to remain unmarried is still a 'severe infringement of the right of the *paterfamilias*' (p. 225).

73. Against Pagels, 'Paul and Women', pp. 540-43; R.R. Ruether, 'The Subordination and Liberation of Women in Christian Theology: St Paul and Sarah Grimké', *Soundings* 61 (1978), pp. 168-81 (170-71).

and reflect a realism and a faithfulness to his theological perspective that do not match either of these characterizations.

We can also draw some summary conclusions here about the relationship of creation and eschatology or redemption for Paul and the Corinthians according to their respective interpretations of the declaration, 'There is no "male and female"'. Paul's interpretation shows that he regards the created order neither as completely transcended in Christ, nor as fully determinative for Christians in this age with respect to sex and gender. In the light of the new creation Paul relegates the created order to the past in some respects and in some situations. He does so not out of a belief that creation is evil, but that 'the present form of this world is passing away' (7.31), and what was created 'good' is now being superseded by something better. Thus Paul can say that 'the one who marries...does well', but 'the one who does not marry does better' (7.38a). He is not making a moral judgment, but stating an opinion about the relative advantageousness of marriage and celibacy for Christians living between the cross and the parousia.[74] The charisma of celibacy, an eschatological gift of the Spirit, enables some people to enjoy the advantage of celibacy. Marriage continues to have a place, however, as a context for expression of sexual passion, which Paul accepts as part of the created order without denigrating it. On the other hand, the sexual differentiation of humanity as 'male and female' according to the created order, though it still accurately describes humanity (and rules out androgyny), no longer implies procreation for the purpose of filling the earth. Further, sexual differentiation, which led to subordination on the basis of sex, need not always have such consequences in the new creation.

The Corinthians' understanding of the relationship between creation

---

74. In *this* sense Paul can agree with the Corinthian slogan, 'It is better for a man not to touch a woman' (7.1), i.e., it is advantageous. The unmarried person can escape 'tribulation in the flesh' (7.28; cf. 7.25), be 'happier' (7.40), and pursue 'the things of the Lord' in an 'undivided' way (7.32-35; cf. the implication that abstinence furthers prayer in 7.5). Thus Paul spares no chances to recommend celibacy to those now free from marriage again as well as to those not already committed to marriage (7.7, 8, 15, 26, 27b, 38, 40; cf. 7.11). Cf. R.H. Gundry on 1 Cor. 7.34, where Paul states that the unmarried woman is 'holy in [both] body and spirit': 'the body and the spirit do not diverge but unite in consecration to God, for Paul does not correlate the body with the worldly affairs and the spirit with the affairs of the Lord or pit the body as evil against the spirit as good' (*SŌMA*, p. 141). This comment accurately grasps that at the bottom of Paul's asceticism lies a positive view of the physical body.

and the eschaton differs from Paul's as described above. They want to replace abruptly and aggressively the present created order with their vision of the new creation. This results in simple obliteration of established relationships and roles. Paul's way is perhaps less impressively bold and visionary than theirs.[75] He sees instead a dynamic interrelationship between eschaton and creation that is sensitive to the complexities of life in this world, yet guided by the hope of the new life in Christ already invading the present, and he does not simply acquiesce to the powerful pull of the existing natural and social dynamics. Whatever one might think of Paul's view of the relation of creation and eschaton here, one cannot accuse him of pat solutions.

This essay is affectionately dedicated to Robert Gundry, both mentor and father to me. His guidance and encouragement have graced my whole career, and the excellence of his scholarship has served as an inspiration and a challenge.[76]

75. See Wire's critique of Paul in this sense, *Women Prophets*, p. 126.

76. The research for this article feeds into a project on Gal. 3.28 and the self-understanding of Christian women partly funded through the Pew Evangelical Scholars Program.

THE ESCHATOLOGICAL OUTLOOK IN 2 CORINTHIANS 4.7-15

Jan Lambrecht, SJ

In his *Survey of the New Testament* R.H. Gundry writes, 'The hope of resurrection makes us overlook our present physical dangers in preaching the Gospel'.[1] The author thinks here of passages within 2 Cor. 3.4–7.16. It is a traditional view that vv. 13-14 from ch. 4 refer to the resurrection. This view has recently been challenged. The focus of my 1986 study on 2 Cor. 4.7-15[2] was on Paul's apostolic suffering. In that work, in addition to the position of E. Güttgemanns, the non-eschatological interpretation of vv. 13-14 by N. Baumert was presented and discussed.[3]

Baumert defends the present-life sense of the second ἐγείρω in v. 14: knowing that he who raised Jesus must (or will) 'raise' us also, over and over again, with Jesus. This meaning does not exclude the resurrection after death, but, according to Baumert, Paul here thinks of the new life before death, brought about by God and already mentioned in vv. 7-12. In the same vein, the verb παραστήσει at the end of v. 14 does not point to an eschatological 'causing to stand (before God)', but to a 'presenting (in the public forum)'. Paul says: within the course of ongoing history on earth, God, over and over again, will present us, together with you, Corinthian believers, in the public forum. This presentation corresponds to the manifestation of Jesus' life in vv. 10-11 which is expressed by means of the verb φανερόω.[4]

---

1. R.H. Gundry, *Survey of the New Testament* (Exeter: The Paternoster Press, 3rd edn, 1979), p. 287.

2. J. Lambrecht, 'The Nekrōsis of Jesus: Ministry and Suffering in 2 Cor 4.7-15', in A. Vanhoye (ed.), *L'apôtre Paul: Personnalité, style et conception du ministère* (BETL, 73; Leuven: University Press/Peeters, 1986), pp. 120-43.

3. Lambrecht, 'Nekrōsis', pp. 132-35. N. Baumert explains his position in *Täglich sterben und auferstehen: Der Literalsinn von 2 Kor 4,12–5,10* (SANT, 34; Munich: Kösel-Verlag, 1973) esp. on pp. 72-114.

4. Cf. Lambrecht, 'Nekrōsis', p. 133.

In my evaluation I emphasized that 'both content parallelism and the temporal opposition of ἐγείρας and ἐγερεῖ in v. 14ab make ἐγερεῖ in the sense of a daily (metaphorical) raising...almost impossible'.[5] If this is true of 'raising' it must also be true of 'presenting'. God will place the risen Paul together with the risen Corinthians before him, in the presence of Jesus. I concluded the discussion as follows: 'It would be wrong, we think, to eliminate the eschatological dimension from 2 Cor. 4.7-15',[6] that is, to explain vv. 13-14 *innergeschichtlich*.

In a recent article, 'Faith and Resurrection in 2 Cor. 4.13-14',[7] as well as twice elsewhere,[8] J. Murphy-O'Connor likewise maintains that Paul's 'resurrection' must be understood existentially rather than eschatologically. Murphy-O'Connor distinguishes three meanings of life in Paul's letters: the physical sense of everyday life (e.g. 1 Thess. 4.15; Phil. 1.20), the eschatological sense (e.g. 1 Cor. 15.22; Phil. 4.3) and the 'existential' sense, a true life to God present in those who have been delivered from the death of sin (e.g. Rom. 6.13).[9] According to Murphy-O'Connor, in 2 Cor. 4.13-14 this third meaning of authentic Christian life on earth is intended by Paul.

I must first explain the position of Murphy-O'Connor as objectively as possible. A critical discussion of his argumentation will follow. In a third

5. Lambrecht, 'Nekrōsis', p. 134.

6. Lambrecht, 'Nekrōsis', p. 135. Cf. R. Penna, 'Sofferenze apostoliche, antropologia ed escatologia in 2 Cor 4,7–5,10', in C.C. Marcheselli (ed.), *Parola e Spirito: FS S. Cipriani*, I (Brescia: Paideia, 1982), pp. 401-31, esp. 402.

7. J. Murphy-O'Connor, 'Faith and Resurrection in 2 Cor 4.13-14', *RB* 95 (1988), pp. 543-50. In this article the author refers to the monograph of Baumert several times and manifests his agreement with it, although the repetitive sense of Baumert's interpretation is rejected.

8. J. Murphy-O'Connor, *The Theology of the Second Letter to the Corinthians* (New Testament Theology; Cambridge: University Press, 1991), pp. 48-49; and the discussion after the article of M. Bouttier, 'La souffrance de l'apôtre. 2 Co 4,7-18', in L. De Lorenzi (ed.), *The Diakonia of the Spirit (2 Co 4:7–7:4)* (Benedictina: «Benedictina» Publishing; Rome, I, 10; 1989), pp. 29-49; discussion on pp. 50-74, with the intervention of Murphy-O'Connor on pp. 62-63. Cf. in the same publication G. Strecker, p. 64. 'Ich muss gestehen, von da aus [= von einer Entwicklung innerhalb der paulinischen Eschatologie] ergeben sich auch für mich Gründe, Herrn Murhpy-O'Connor zuzustimmen, diese Verse weniger eschatologisch und mehr innergeschichtlich zu verstehen'.

9. Murphy-O'Connor, 'Faith and Resurrection', pp. 545; *Theology*, pp. 31, 45-47, 49, 57. He finds the notion 'anticipation of eschatological life' for this third sense too vague (cf. 'Faith and Resurrection', p. 545).

section I will integrate my own understanding of vv. 13-14 into the line of thought of 4.7-15.

The Present-Life Interpretation

Before the analysis proper of 2 Cor. 4.13-14 Murphy-O'Connor mentions that generally v. 14 is considered to be a parallel of both 1 Cor. 6.14 and Rom. 8.11.[10] 'Despite the lack of verbal identity' it is often concluded to be a pre-Pauline fixed formula consisting of two assertions: 'God's past action in Christ and his future action in believers'.[11] Yet 2 Cor. 4.13 differs from the other two verses in that in the first passage Paul deals only of his own 'resurrection', not that of the Corinthians, and the noun that indicates the direct object of God's past action is not the 'Lord' as in 1 Cor. 6.14 or 'Christ' as in Rom. 8.11, but 'Jesus'.[12] 'Hence, there are grounds for a re-examination of the meaning of v. 14 and its function in the context'.[13] There are three steps.

1. *'Jesus' in Verses 10-11 and 14*[14]

In his first remark Murphy-O'Connor investigates Paul's use of the proper name Ἰησοῦς in v. 14. If in v. 14 Paul means his resurrection after death, the phrase σὺν Ἰησοῦ is problematic in a twofold way. Why does Paul not write 'with (the risen) Christ'? What is the exact sense of 'with'? Murphy-O'Connor reviews and rejects a number of proposals. For the use of 'Jesus' and 'with' him one should not refer to 1 Thess. 4.14 and 17 since here the risen Jesus first 'descends' from heaven. In 1 Thessalonians there is an evident eschatological scenario, not so in 2 Cor. 4.13-14. Furthermore, it is hardly justified to interpret σύν as 'through' or 'like'. In all these attempts the meaning of the phrase intended by Paul is ignored. 'Such [exegetical] diversity betrays the weakness of the underlying assumption that Paul is speaking about survival after death'.[15]

---

10. For this section see Murphy-O'Connor, 'Faith and Resurrection', pp. 543-44.

11. Murphy-O'Connor, 'Faith and Resurrection', p. 543.

12. In 'Faith and Resurrection', p. 543 n. 3, Murphy-O'Connor supports his choice for the reading without 'Lord' in ὁ ἐγείρας (τὸν κύριον) Ἰησοῦν of 2 Cor. 4.14.

13. Murphy-O'Connor, 'Faith and Resurrection', p. 544.

14. Murphy-O'Connor, 'Faith and Resurrection', pp. 545-45.

15. Murphy-O'Connor, 'Faith and Resurrection', p. 545.

In 2 Cor. 4.7-15 Paul uses the proper name 'Jesus' to point to the earthly Jesus. The same 'existential' life that was in Jesus on earth was also present and manifest in the persecuted, dying Paul (see esp. vv. 10-11). If 'Jesus' in vv. 10-11 and 14a refers to the earthly Jesus, 'it is highly probable that one function of σὺν 'Ιησοῦ is to indicate that the "resurrection" of Paul in v. 14b takes place within the framework of terrestrial existence'.[16]

2. *'Resurrection' and Verse 13*[17]

Murphy-O'Connor then sets out to undermine the two reasons why the verb ἐγείρω is generally understood as referring to the eschatological resurrection. Firstly, he does not accept the validity of the argument which the two parallel verses, 1 Cor. 6.14 and Rom. 8.11, are assumed to provide. As already said, the author maintains that they are not really parallels. Moreover, there is 'the basic principle that the meaning of a phrase is determined by its context'.[18] The discussion above (cf. 1) has established a present-life context.

Secondly, it is generally assumed that the verb λαλέω in the clause ἡμεῖς πιστεύομεν διὸ καὶ λαλοῦμεν of v. 13 is technical insofar as it refers to the proclamation of the gospel. Jesus' past resurrection and the future resurrection of Paul (and all Christians) are the main part of the gospel content which is mentioned in v. 14. Murphy-O'Connor is of the opinion that the context does not require this technical sense. Paul sometimes uses this particular verb λαλέω to point back to what he has just written (see 1 Cor. 9.8; 15.34; 2 Cor. 11.17, 23), and 'it is this sense that is most appropriate in v. 13. In vv. 7-12 Paul gives an interpretation of his suffering that is based on faith. He *believes* that God's power is at work in him and that he manifests "the life of Jesus"; and this is what he has just *said*.'[19]

Moreover, the expression τὸ αὐτὸ πνεῦμα τῆς πίστεως in v. 13 should not be interpreted—as most commentators do—as the spirit of strong, persevering faith, the same as that of the psalmist. No, 'of faith' is a genitive of content: the spirit which is faith. Paul here polemicizes

---

16. Murphy-O'Connor, 'Faith and Resurrection', p. 545.
17. Murphy-O'Connor, 'Faith and Resurrection', pp. 546-48; cf. in L. De Lorenzi (ed.), *Diakonia*, p. 63.
18. Murphy-O'Connor, 'Faith and Resurrection', p. 546.
19. Murphy-O'Connor, 'Faith and Resurrection', p. 547; cf. in De Lorenzi (ed.), *Diakonia*, p. 63.

with the Corinthian *pneumatikoi* and Judaizers. They are despising Paul's lack of strength, his weakness, his poverty of speech. 'In such circumstances it is only natural that the "spirit", which Paul desires the Corinthians to possess, should be defined as faith'.[20] Only faith will enable them to detect the authenticity of Paul's apostleship. Murphy-O'Connor concludes his explanation of v. 13: 'Nothing in v. 13... demands that it be understood generically. On the contrary, there is every indication that it is the continuation of Paul's reflection on his experience as described in vv. 7-12. This in turn suggests that v. 14 should be interpreted in the same way.'[21]

3. *Verse 14 and 2 Corinthians 13.4b*[22]

In what can be called a third step Murphy-O'Connor first returns to the absence of 'the Corinthians' as direct object of the verbs 'will raise'. As becomes evident from a comparison with v. 12, the Corinthians do not need a (metaphorical) resurrection. In v. 12 Paul says that they have life in themselves.[23]

Murphy-O'Connor then compares v. 14bc with 2 Cor. 13.4b: καὶ γὰρ ἡμεῖς ἀσθενοῦμεν ἐν αὐτῷ, ἀλλὰ ζήσομεν σὺν αὐτῷ ἐκ δυνάμεως θεοῦ εἰς ὑμᾶς. The numerous similarities between the two verses 'legitimize the use of 13.4 to unlock the meaning of 4.14'.[24] The future tense in both verses points to Paul's planned visit to Corinth. In 13.4b life is not eschatological life (so in 1 Cor. 15.22), but existential life, that is, forthcoming strong apostolic action towards the disobedient Corinthians. So also in 4.14 'he will raise us' is not an eschatological promise of survival after death but Paul's trust and expectation of

---

20. Murphy-O'Connor, 'Faith and Resurrection', p. 548.
21. Murphy-O'Connor, 'Faith and Resurrection', p. 548. Cf. in De Lorenzi (ed.), *Diakonia*, p. 63: 'Despite his weakness he *believes* that God is at work in and through him, and this is what he has just *said*! Once this is seen, all justification for understanding 4.14 as an allusion to the final resurrection disappears.'
22. Murphy-O'Connor, 'Faith and Resurrection', pp. 548-50.
23. Cf. Murphy-O'Connor in De Lorenzi (ed.), *Diakonia*, p. 62: 'If Paul needs resurrection and the Corinthians do not, it can only be because "death" is at work in us, but life in you (2 Cor 4.12)'.
24. Murphy-O'Connor, 'Faith and Resurrection', p. 549. There are five similarities: '(1) the contrast between "we" and "you"; (2) the use of the present and future tenses; (3) the *syn* theme; (4) the power of God (4.7) displayed in weakness (4.8-9); (5) the use of resurrection language' (Murphy-O'Connor, 'Faith and Resurrection', p. 549).

existential life in the midst of tribulation. 'Given the pressures that were wearing him down, and the mortal dangers that he had to survive (4.12a), it is easy to see why he should depict his arrival at Corinth as a "resurrection"'.[25]

Finally, one must not understand the verb παρίστημι eschatologically as 'to place' nor have we, for that matter, mentally to add the complement 'before him' or 'before the judgment seat'. No, the sense of the verb is 'to manifest, to show'. 'Both this meaning, and the only feasible complement "the world, humanity", are appropriate in v. 14'.[26] The verb is parallel with φανερόω in vv. 10-11. 'It is evident that in vv. 10-11 Paul has in mind the world to which his existential proclamation is addressed, and not merely the community of the converted at Corinth. It seems most natural, then, to postulate the same audience in v. 14'.[27] Moreover, v. 14 with its missionary nuance is beautifully leading up to the solemn closing in v. 15. 'Once Paul has been reunited with the community (σὺν ὑμῖν), with whom he has been reconciled (7.7), they will stand together before the world as those whom the power of God has brought from death to life, and thus exercise in common an existential ministry that is the basis of the thanksgiving in 4.15'.[28]

We cannot but admit that the 'existential' explanation of 2 Cor. 4.13-14 offered by Murphy-O'Connor is consistent. The three steps, especially when taken together, are very impressive, indeed. However, a number of factors preclude our acceptance of this at first sight attractive understanding of Paul's text.

Critical Evaluation

In the critical discussion of the arguments brought forward by Murphy-O'Connor, I will follow the same order as in the three-step exposition.[29]

25. Murphy-O'Connor, 'Faith and Resurrection', p. 549; cf. in De Lorenzi (ed.), *Diakonia*, p. 63: 'Paul is speaking metaphorically of his survival, which is the precondition of his being able to rejoin the Corinthians'.

26. Murphy-O'Connor, 'Faith and Resurrection', p. 550; cf. in De Lorenzi, *Diakonia*, p. 63.

27. Murphy-O'Connor, 'Faith and Resurrection', p. 550.

28. Murphy-O'Connor, in De Lorenzi, *Diakonia*, p. 63; cf. 'Faith and Resurrection', p. 550: 'v. 14 has a missionary resonance that facilitates the transition to v. 15'.

29. In his brief reply, 'Résurrection existentielle ou eschatologique en 2 Co 4,13-14?', *BZ* 34 (1990), pp. 248-52, K. Romaniuk has rightly rejected the thesis of

1. *Jesus*

There can hardly be any doubt that in v. 10a Paul refers to the earthly Jesus in writing the expression ἡ νέκρωσις τοῦ 'Ιησοῦ. Paul points here to the physical dying of Jesus of Nazareth. Although we have no absolute certainty which was the original direct object of the traditional *pistis*-formula ('God raised [Jesus or Christ or Jesus Christ or the Lord?]'), there is, theoretically speaking, no difficulty whatsoever in assuming that in v. 14a Paul, again with 'Jesus', refers to this earthly (dead) Jesus who has been raised from the dead by God. This is, however, no longer the case in the other uses of 'Jesus' within 2 Cor. 4.7-15. In the expressions ἡ ζωὴ τοῦ 'Ιησοῦ (vv. 10b and 11b), διὰ 'Ιησοῦν (v. 11a) and σὺν 'Ιησοῦ (v. 14b) Paul understands and intends the risen Jesus. It definitely is the life of the risen Jesus that is manifested through the suffering and dying Paul. It is for Jesus' sake, that is, because of Jesus who lived and died but is now alive again, raised by God, that Paul is given up to death. God will raise Paul with—whatever this 'with' may mean—Jesus, that is, precisely that Jesus who, according to the preceding statement in v. 14a, is already raised.

Once in 2 Cor. 4.7-15 the use of the proper name 'Jesus' is no longer restricted to Jesus' terrestrial existence, the eschatological passage of 1 Thess. 4.13-18 becomes illustrative. In 1 Thess. 4.14a it is the earthly Jesus who died and rose again, but in 4.14b the expression διὰ τοῦ 'Ιησοῦ, which most probably qualifies the preceding τοὺς κοιμηθέντας, it is not just the earthly Jesus but the total, now risen Jesus who is meant. Then in the following verses, without any difficulty, Paul uses the titles κύριος and Χριστός to refer to the same risen Jesus. The 'Lord', whom, according to v. 17, all Christians, those raised and those still alive, will meet at his parousia, is the risen Jesus of v. 14.[30]

Of course, one need not be a Christian in order to lead an 'existential' life. Many a Jew and Gentile, before and after Christ, have lived such a life. Yet does it make sense for a Christian to separate that existential life so radically from eschatological life as Murphy-O'Connor is doing? Grace is the seed of glory.[31] The life we live in Christ is truly an anticipation of eschatological life; in a certain but real way it is already

---

Murphy-O'Connor. It would seem, however, that much more can be brought forward against the latter's arguments.

30. Cf. also the use of 'Jesus Christ' and 'Jesus' in 2 Cor. 4.5. In 2 Cor. 11.4 and 1 Thess. 1.10, 'Jesus' equally means the risen Jesus.

31. Cf., e.g., 2 Cor. 4.17.

resurrection life. We may refer to Phil. 3.7-11: the power of Jesus' resurrection, which Paul will know fully in attaining the resurrection from the dead, is already at work in the transformation process Paul undergoes in his sufferings and dying.

The preposition σύν in 'with Jesus' of 2 Cor. 4.14b is best taken in its simplest meaning: with, together with. Of course, one can put forward that, in Paul's view, we will be raised through or like Jesus. This is, however, not expressed by σύν in v. 14b.[32] Our problem with the phrase 'with Jesus' is one of time.[33] Jesus' resurrection is past, that of Paul (and all Christians) still lies in the future. To be sure, Paul did not reckon with centuries before the parousia. Paul's deep conviction, however, is that, just as all humans are somehow included in Adam, so also all Christians are one with Christ. What happens to him, happens (or will happen) to us. 'For as all die in Adam, so all will be made alive in Christ' (1 Cor. 15.22). In this last verse the 'in Christ' is for Paul more or less the equivalent of 'by or through Christ'. But this basic conviction precisely makes it possible for him to use the expression 'with (the risen) Jesus', notwithstanding the temporal difference between Jesus' resurrection and his own.[34]

2. Resurrection

Three decisive reasons can be brought forward to reject Murphy-O'Connor's position regarding the metaphorical sense of 'he will raise us' in v. 14b.

a. Within 2 Cor. 4.14a Paul most probably employs a traditional *pistis*-formula, more specifically an *Auferweckungsformel*. Although its original wording must to a certain extent remain uncertain, we may, by way of hypothesis, reconstruct the formula as follows: ὁ θεὸς ἤγειρεν τὸν

---

32. Romaniuk, 'Résurrection existentielle', p. 251, assumes, wrongly, it would seem, an instrumental or even a causal sense in this expression. The variant reading διά in 2 Cor. 4.14 (rather poorly attested instead of σύν) must not be retained.

33. Cf. C.K. Barrett, *A Commentary on the Second Epistle to the Corinthians* (BNTC; London: Black, 2nd edn, 1979), p. 143: '*With Jesus* clearly cannot mean "at the same time"'.

34. Cf. C. Wolff, *Der zweite Brief des Paulus an die Korinther* (THKNT; Berlin: Evangelische Verlagsanstalt, 1989), p. 96: With the expression 'with Jesus' is 'vielmehr ausgesagt, dass die Auferweckung der Christen *sachlich* mit der Auferweckung Jesu verbunden ist, aus ihr folgt...und dass die Auferweckten mit dem "Erstling der Entschlafenen"...vereint sein werden'.

130   To Tell the Mystery

Ἰησοῦν ἐκ νεκρῶν.[35] Paul has rewritten this formula and integrated it
into his flow of thought.

1. Because the main point of his affirmation lies in verse 14b with the
focus on his own future resurrection, Paul modifies the personal verb to
a participle and omits the explicit mention of the word God, as well as
the expression 'from the dead'. What remains, ὁ ἐγείρας τὸν Ἰησοῦν,
functions as a subject clause of the verbs in v. 14bc. Moreover, Paul
introduces the whole of v. 14 by means of εἰδότες ὅτι.

2. For Paul Jesus' past resurrection cannot but imply the future resurrection of Christians. In v. 14b, he applies this certainty to himself (and
his fellow apostles): καὶ ἡμᾶς σὺν Ἰησοῦ ἐγερεῖ, 'he will raise us also
with Jesus'. The particle καί is adverbial and underlines the following
word ('us also'); the verb stands in the future tense; as already stated
above, Jesus is the risen Jesus from v. 14a. Of course, the fact that Paul
speaks of his own resurrection does not deny the resurrection of other
Christians. The use of the same verb, the comparison of a future event
with that of the past, the reinforcing καί before ἡμᾶς and, through the
expression 'with Jesus', the repetition of the one of whom it is just said
that God has raised him—all this makes it utterly impossible that ἐγείρω
in v. 14b can be understood metaphorically, in a sense different from the
eschatological one in v. 14a.

3. Paul adds one more clause: καὶ παραστήσει σὺν ὑμῖν. The
direct object is the same as that of the previous verb, ἡμᾶς. The analysis
in the following paragraph (see pp. 135-36) will show that the phrase
'with you' means 'with you, risen Corinthians'.

b. A second reason why ἐγερεῖ in v. 14b should be understood not in a
metaphorical but in an eschatological sense is the parallelism of this verse
with both 1 Cor. 6.14 and Rom. 8.11.[36] A synoptic presentation of the
texts may be helpful.

35. Cf. W. Kramer, *Christ, Lord, Son of God* (SBT, 50; London: SCM Press,
1966), pp. 20-26; K. Wengst, *Christologische Formeln und Lieder des Urchristentums*
(SNT, 7; Gütersloh: Mohn, 1972), pp. 27-48, esp. 31-35; F.J. Froitzheim,
Christologie und Eschatologie bei Paulus (FB, 35; Würzburg: Echter Verlag, 1979),
pp. 79-80. There is uncertainty not only regarding the direct object (cf. above p. 128)
but also concerning the questions whether the participial construction (ὁ ἐγείρας) is
equally original and whether the expansion which mentions the future resurrection of
Christians is already traditional and thus pre-Pauline.
36. Cf. Romaniuk, 'Résurrection existentielle', pp. 248-25; A. Lindemann,
'Paulus und die korinthische Eschatologie. Zur These von einer "Entwicklung" im

2 Cor. 4.14	1 Cor. 6.14	Rom. 8.11
		εἰ δὲ τὸ πνεῦμα τοῦ ἐγείραντος τὸν Ἰησοῦν ἐκ νεκρῶν οἰκεῖ ἐν ὑμῖν,
ὁ	ὁ θεὸς καὶ τὸν κύριον	ὁ
ἐγείρας τὸν Ἰησοῦν³⁷	ἤγειρεν	ἐγείρας Χριστὸν ἐκ νεκρῶν
καὶ ἡμᾶς σὺν Ἰησοῦ	καὶ ἡμᾶς	
ἐγερεῖ	ἐξεγερεῖ	ζῳοποιήσει τὰ θνητὰ σώματα ὑμῶν
	διὰ δυνάμεως αὐτοῦ	διὰ τοῦ ἐνοικοῦντος αὐτοῦ πνεύματος ἐν ὑμῖν.
καὶ παραστήσει σὺν ὑμῖν.		

In Rom. 8.11 we twice have the *Auferweckungsformel*; twice also the raising power is attributed to the indwelling Spirit; the verb ζῳοποιέω replaces ἐγείρω; Paul speaks of the resurrection of his Roman addressees (second person plural); first Jesus is mentioned, then Christ. In 1 Cor. 6.14 the title is the Lord; the second verb is ἐξεγείρω; and the future resurrection of us, that is, all Christians, will be effected by the power of Jesus Christ. As one can see, Paul rewrites the formula to a certain extent and expands it in different ways according to the specific context. Yet the basic structure of his affirmation is three times the same: the past resurrection of Christ guarantees the future resurrection of Christians. It would seem that the two parallel texts confirm our conclusion, namely, that 2 Cor. 4.14b deals with the future eschatological resurrection.³⁸

paulinischen Denken', *NTS* 37 (1991), pp. 373-99, esp. 392.

37. For the choice of the reading without τὸν κύριον see the note added by Metzger himself in B.M. Metzger, *A Textual Commentary on the Greek New Testament* (London: UBS, 1975), p. 579.

38. Cf. 1 Cor. 15.15: ὅτι (ὁ θεὸς) ἤγειρεν Χριστόν; 15.16: εἰ δὲ νεκροὶ οὐκ ἐγείρονται, οὐδὲ Χριστὸς ἐγήγερται; 15.22: ἐν Χριστῷ πάντες ζῳοποιηθήσονται.

c. The third reason is provided by the analysis of v. 13, part of the long sentence that continues in v. 14. The main clause is formed by two verbs: καὶ ἡμεῖς πιστεύομεν, διὸ καὶ λαλοῦμεν. The preceding participle ἔχοντες possesses a motivating nuance: 'since we have'. The particle δέ is slightly oppositional; it marks the introduction of a new idea. 'The same Spirit of faith', a hapax legomenon in Paul, is probably referring to the Spirit who engenders faith in the psalmist.[39] The genitive 'of faith' is thus not one of content. The introductory formula κατὰ τὸ γεγραμμένον is not elsewhere used by Paul. The quotation from Ps. 115.1 (LXX) is the first explicit Old Testament citation in 2 Corinthians. According to the Septuagintal text the speaker in Psalm 115 remembers his past (cf. the aorist indicative of the two verbs ἐπίστευσα, διὸ ἐλάλησα): he was greatly afflicted, he believed and trusted in God his Savior, he has been rescued, and, therefore (διό), he has spoken in the presence of all the people, by his words he has manifested his salvation.

Paul repeats but, at the same time, rewrites the quotation into καὶ ἡμεῖς πιστεύομεν, διὸ καὶ λαλοῦμεν: (1) first person plural of the verbs; (2) present tense; (3) the pronoun ἡμεῖς is added; (4) a first adverbial καί reinforces ἡμεῖς; (5) the second adverbial καί reinforces the verb λαλοῦμεν. Although Paul stresses the sameness of the Spirit of faith, his faith and his speaking are quite different from that of the psalmist. The content of his faith and the basis of his trust are expressed in v. 14; the participle εἰδότες qualifies this faith as faith certainty. The broader context of v. 14 makes it most probable that the absolute λαλοῦμεν points to the proclaiming of the gospel: see 4.2 (φανέρωσις τῆς ἀληθείας); 4.4 (εὐαγγέλιον); 4.5 (κηρύσσω Ἰησοῦν Χριστόν).[40] Driven by faith (διό), Paul proclaims the gospel.[41] He also proclaims the gospel because he believes and because he possesses that faith certainty about his own resurrection (see the two participles ἔχοντες and

---

39. Otherwise A.T. Hanson, *The Paradox of the Cross in the Thought of St Paul* (JSNTSup, 17; Sheffield: JSOT Press, 1987), pp. 39-54. He strangely finds it far more likely that 'Paul...thinks of the Lord himself as uttering this psalm' (p. 51).

40. Cf. 2 Cor. 2.17. See also, e.g., 1 Thess. 2.2, 4 and 16. G. Dautzenberg, '"Glaube" oder "Hoffnung" in 2 Kor 4,13–5,10', in De Lorenzi (ed.), *Diakonia*, pp. 75-104, prefers a *konfessorische* meaning (see pp. 76-78).

41. For Paul's view on the relationship between faith and preaching, see Rom. 10.14-17.

εἰδότες).[42] The motivation of Paul's faith and proclamation (4.14b) is decidedly eschatological.

3. Anticipated Resurrection Life?

a. In vv. 13-14 Paul explicitly speaks of his own future resurrection. For Murphy-O'Connor it is not accidental that the Corinthians are not mentioned as direct object of the verb in v. 14b. In his opinion 'raising' is metaphorical and points to existential life; according to v. 12, the Corinthians already possess that life. We may, however, ask the question whether this is not, paradoxically, true for Paul also. According to vv. 10-11, the life of Jesus will manifest itself in him, notwithstanding suffering and dying (cf. also vv. 8-9). Yet Murphy-O'Connor maintains that both the future tense in v. 14b (ἐγερεῖ) and the phrase 'with you' at the end of v. 14c point to Paul's forthcoming visit to Corinth. God will 'raise' him for this visit, i.e., renew in him existential life in their presence. Murphy-O'Connor detects a similar idea in 2 Cor. 13.4.[43] Is there a content parallelism between 4.14 and 13.4?

b. Paul's main affirmation in 13.1-4 is found at the end of v. 2: 'I warn them...that if I come again, I will not be lenient'. Verse 3a gives a motivation of this warning: 'since you desire proof that Christ is speaking in me'.[44] In v. 3bc, Christ is further qualified: 'He is not weak in dealing with you, but is powerful in you'. The four clauses of v. 4 follow:

a   καὶ γὰρ ἐσταυρώθη ἐξ ἀσθενείας,
b   ἀλλὰ ζῇ ἐκ δυνάμεως θεοῦ
c   καὶ γὰρ ἡμεῖς ἀσθενοῦμεν ἐν αὐτῷ
d   ἀλλὰ ζήσομεν σὺν αὐτῷ ἐκ δυνάμεως θεοῦ εἰς ὑμᾶς.

We have before us two striking parallel sentences (ab and cd). Yet there also are no small differences.

In c the term σταυρόω is missing (which is hardly surprising). The tenses of the verbs disagree: aorist (a), present (b); present (c); future (d).

42. Cf. Barrett, *2 Corinthians*, p. 142: 'since we have the same Spirit of faith'; p. 143: 'because we know that...'.
43. See Murphy-O'Connor, 'Faith and Resurrection', pp. 548-49 and my summary on pp. 126-27.
44. For this whole section cf. my study, 'Philological and Exegetical Notes on 2 Cor 13,4', *Bijdragen* 46 (1985), pp. 261-69. Cf. also M. Chevallier, 'L'argumentation de Paul dans II Corinthiens 10 à 13', *RHPR* 70 (1990), pp. 3-16, esp. 12-15.

The second sentence (cd), with the emphatic ἡμεῖς and the phrases ἐν αὐτῷ, σὺν αὐτῷ and εἰς ὑμᾶς, is much longer...In verse 4, however, the most surprising feature is that the phrase εἰς ὑμᾶς at the end (d) diverges ζήσομεν from resurrection life strictly speaking (so in Christ and so, one would expect, also in Paul) towards the apostle's future powerful encounter with the Corinthians.[45]

Three philological notes must detain us for a moment. Firstly, although there is a formal parallelism between ab and cd, which suggests a comparison between Christ and Paul, we are, as it were, forced to understand the second sentence in a consecutive way: 'For Christ was crucified in weakness but lives by the power of God, *so that* we, too, are weak in him but shall live with him by the power of God in dealing with you'.[46] Behind the parataxis lies hypotaxis: Paul's implication, inclusion in Christ. Secondly, the first adverbial καί (a) applies to the whole sentence ('for indeed...'), while the second adverbial καί reinforces only the following ἡμεῖς ('for we, too'). Thirdly, in the construction (μὲν) γάρ...ἀλλά the real information is not given in the first clause (a and c are common knowledge) but in the second (b and d), which gives us in paraphrase: 'For indeed, although he was crucified because of weakness, he certainly lives because of God's power, so that, although we, too, are weak in him, in dealing with you we shall certainly live with him because of God's power'.[47]

Due attention must be given to the tenses.

The Corinthians know very well that Christ was crucified (a: narrative aorist), but they should also realize that risen he is now living (b: present continuous). The same Corinthians no doubt experience that Paul is weak (c: present continuous), but they must also believe that he will deal with them in a life-filled, powerful way (d: future). The differences in time indicate the limits of the real inclusion of Paul in Christ. Christ was crucified long ago; the apostle still suffers. Christ is living his resurrection life; in Paul that life is already present but its future manifestation before the Corinthians, forceful as it will be, is but a weak anticipation of the fulness of life after death.[48]

Murphy-O'Connor is right on one point. The ζήσομεν of 2 Cor. 13.4d does not point to Paul's survival after death; it refers to his future

---

45. Lambrecht, 'Notes', pp. 261-62.
46. Lambrecht, 'Notes', p. 263.
47. Lambrecht, 'Notes', p. 267.
48. Lambrecht, 'Notes', pp. 268-69.

'existential life' during the third visit. What about the parallelism with 2 Cor. 4.14ab? A contact between the two texts which Murphy-O'Connor mentions is the use of resurrection language.[49] In 13.4b, however, Paul speaks of Jesus' life (present tense) after his resurrection, whereas in 4.14a Jesus' resurrection itself (aorist tense) is mentioned. In 13.1-4 Paul deals with his attitude of strength which he will manifest during his forthcoming visit. This specific context, as well as the phrase εἰς ὑμᾶς, invites us to look for an understanding of ζάω in 13.4d which is strangely different from that in 13.4b.[50] By ζήσομεν Paul means a forceful confrontation with the Corinthians. That confrontation will be filled with anticipated resurrection life. Such a change of sense, however, is not in the least required in 4.14b, neither by the context nor by the wording within the verse itself.

c. The eschatological interpretation of 4.14b requires that v. 14c must be understood in the same eschatological way. This argument which we take from the most immediate context is by far the strongest. Moreover, clauses b and c are chiastically linked.[51] The pronoun ἡμᾶς is the direct object of both verbs; then we have:

σὺν Ἰησοῦ   ἐγερεῖ καὶ
          παραστήσει   σὺν ὑμῖν.

It is scarcely conceivable that the second verb παραστήσει, which also stands in the future tense, would shift from the eschatological sense of ἐγερεῖ in v. 14b to an existential one in v. 14c. Moreover, after 4.15, which is not so strictly eschatological, the whole subsequent passage of 4.16–5.10 is, again, concerned with the end time.

The problem with v. 14c is the absence of a complement in the dative. In the eschatological setting which we must assume, the complement 'world, humanity' does not make sense.[52] What have we to supply mentally? Although the judgment theme comes to the forefront in 5.10

---

49. Murphy-O'Connor's fifth similarity in my n. 24.

50. Otherwise Romaniuk, 'Résurrection existentielle', pp. 251-52.

51. Cf. A. de Oliveira, *Die Diakonie der Gerechtigkeit und der Versöhnung in der Apologie des 2. Korintherbriefes: Analyse und Auslegung von 2 Kor 2,14–4,6; 5,11–6,10* (NTAbh, 21; Münster: Aschendorff, 1990), p. 313.

52. Murphy-O'Connor, 'Faith and Resurrection', p. 549, claims that παρίστημι in Col. 1.28 (without complement) is not used eschatologically. This is strongly refuted by C.K. Barrett in De Lorenzi (ed.), *Diakonia*, pp. 63-64.

(cf. the expression φανερωθῆναι ἔμπροσθεν τοῦ βήματος τοῦ Χριστοῦ) and in Rom. 14.10 the same verb παρίστημι is used in combination with βῆμα (πάντες γὰρ παραστησόμεθα τῷ βήματι τοῦ θεοῦ), that theme does not seem appropriate in the immediate context.[53] Most probably God 'will cause us to stand'[54] with you "to or before him", that is, into his presence'.

2 Cor. 5.10, however, may be of some interest for our discussion, and this for more than one reason. Just as in 4.14, in 5.10 also the idea of an eschatological gathering of 'all of us' (Paul and the Corinthians) is present. According to Murphy-O'Connor, παρίστημι in 4.14 is parallel to φανεροῦμαι in 4.10-11. Yet the verb φανεροῦμαι, which in 4.10-11 is used for present life manifestation, takes an eschatological connotation in 5.10. It is to this last use that παρίστημι is parallel.

Our conclusion can be brief. Neither the presence in 4.7-15 of the proper name 'Jesus' nor Paul's comment on his quotation from Ps. 115.1 (LXX) nor what Paul says in 13.4 legitimatize the interpretation of 'raising' in 4.14b in the metaphorical sense of 'existential' life. In 4.14b Paul means his personal resurrection after death and in 4.14c his lasting presence together with the risen Corinthians before God.

Resurrection and Line of Thought

A division of 2 Cor. 4.7-15 into three (unequal) parts appears to be justified: vv. 7-12, 13-14, and 15.

1. In vv. 7-12 Paul begins with the statement that as an apostle he has the treasure of his ministry in clay jars (v. 7a).[55] This must be so, because in this way it becomes clear that the extraordinary apostolic power belongs to God and does not come from

---

53. Cf. Barrett, *2 Corinthians*, p. 143: 'the stress does not here lie on judgement'. Otherwise, Romaniuk, 'Résurrection existentielle', p. 250; R.P. Martin, *2 Corinthians* (WBC; Waco, TX: Word Books, 1986), p. 90. 'The future tense... points to a final consummation with the note of judgment struck, a thought Paul will return to in 5:10'.

54. Cf. M. Carrez, *La deuxième épître de saint Paul aux Corinthiens* (CNT; Geneva: Labor & Fides, 1986), p. 119. 'Il faut traduire καὶ παραστήσει par "placer près de" et non pas par "comparaître". Ici le verbe ne fait pas allusion au jugement...mais à l'accès auprès de Dieu du croyant.'

55. For this and the following two paragraphs, cf. Lambrecht, 'Nekrōsis', pp. 126-28.

the apostle himself (v. 7b). Paul formulates the antitheses of vv. 8-9 out of his own experience and thus illustrates what he means by the opening opposition in v. 7 between fragile and powerful. In vv. 10 and 11, by means of subtle variations Paul depicts the same antithesis of dying and remaining alive. He is reflecting here upon the christological dimension of his apostolic existence; both the death and life of the apostle are connected with the death and life of Jesus. Verse 12 starts with ὥστε which marks a conclusion. Yet it strikes the reader that Paul brings about a shift; he now restricts death to the apostle and sees life in the Corinthians: 'So death is at work in us, but life in you'.

2. In v. 13 we have a new beginning which is indicated by the particle δέ. Paul no longer insists that, notwithstanding his dying, there is life, already now here on earth. In the complex sentence construction of vv. 13-14 he explains that his apostolic activity of proclamation is grounded in his faith certainty of a final outcome: his resurrection after death—firmly based on Christ's past resurrection—and what can be called a gathering for ever of all Christians with Jesus in the presence of God.

3. With v. 15a 'Paul both summarizes and motivates the main ideas of the first two parts'.[56] Suffering and preaching occur for the sake of the Corinthians. In v. 15b, however, by means of abundant terms and phrases, the ἵνα-clause points out the ultimate aim of all apostolic activity, the glory of God. 'People are to be persuaded to be thankful. God's free gift of the ministry leads, as it were, in a spontaneous manner to giving thanks to God. Having thus increased the thanksgiving by many people, the gift itself redounds to the glory of God.'[57]

Paul repeatedly stresses that his misery is not all-encompassing.[58] He distinguishes between suffering and liberation. Death is not total; life triumphs. One may perhaps think here of a distinction in time: over and over again there is tribulation, but this does not lead to complete destruction (cf. 4.8-11). Yet Paul also speaks of simultaneous dying and

---

56. Lambrecht, 'Nekrōsis', p. 128.
57. Lambrecht, 'Nekrōsis'.
58. For what follows see Lambrecht, 'Nekrōsis', pp. 141-42.

renewal. Is that process by which the 'inner nature is being renewed day by day' (4.16) invisible? The answer cannot be a simple yes. Paul's apostolic endeavor is not an ordinary life-style. Paul's behavior is provocative. People see it; they like it or hate it. The life of Jesus is manifested in Paul's mortal body (cf. 4.10-11). In the midst of labor and affliction, suffering and dying, in the midst thus of hardships and utter weakness, God's power is paradoxically revealed. Living with this profound insight must have provided Paul with a first deliverance out of what often appeared to be a hopeless situation.

There is a second insight that inspires Paul's dedication and makes the affliction bearable. Paul sees his efforts in an apostolic perspective; he knows that they bear fruit. In 4.12 he concludes the first part of this pericope as follows: 'So death is at work in us, but life in you', and in 4.15 he states with even more clarity that everything in his apostolic existence occurs for the sake of the Corinthians: τὰ γὰρ πάντα δι' ὑμᾶς. What kind of life, then, do the Corinthians possess thanks to Paul's work and suffering? Is it, in opposition to that of Paul, glory without distress? Hardly! At the beginning of his letter Paul explains how apostle and Christians 'endure the same sufferings' (2 Cor. 1.6-7).[59] The 'we' of 4.16-17, like that of 3.18, is broader than the apostolic 'we' elsewhere in the letter. Both the wasting away of the outer nature and the renewal of the inner nature apply to all Christians. There is no reason for considering the already present and increasing glory of the Christians to be different from that of the apostle. For the Christians, too, the ongoing transformation, from one degree of glory to another, is not yet a complete and manifest glorification. Yet through their authentic Christian existence the Corinthians are a letter of Christ, to be known and read by all (3.2-3). For the Christians, too, there is thus that paradoxical combination of death and life, of persecution but not total destruction.

The manifestation of God's power within the apostle's weakness, as well as life in others through the apostle's being given up to death—these two reassuring aspects do not yet procure Paul's complete personal peace of mind. The present glory, that is, the experience of anticipated resurrection life in apostle and Christians alike, awaits a final breakthrough. Suffering is still a daily reality, a wasting away. Yet in his faith Paul knows for certain that God who raised Christ from the dead will raise him with Christ and bring him, together with the risen

59. Lambrecht, 'Nekrōsis', pp. 142-43.

Christians, into God's presence. We should not lose heart. 'For this slight momentary affliction is preparing us for an eternal weight of glory beyond all measure' (4.17). What is temporary will yield to what is eternal (cf. 4.18). Resurrection and eschatological life is the lasting outcome. For Paul this inner, indestructible faith certainty is by far the most important basis for encouragement and strength. That God has raised Jesus and will raise Paul also is 'the ultimate source of [his] apostolic boldness'.[60]

God's power is made clear in the midst of weakness; apostolic suffering brings about life in fellow brothers and sisters; through the resurrection both apostle and Christians will live for ever, with Christ in God's presence. With these three inspiring and fortifying insights, the apostolic existence, as well as every genuine Christian life, does make sense. All anthropological considerations, however, must not obscure the ultimate theological outlook. Grace must extend to more and more people; it increases thanksgiving, to the glory of God (cf. 4.15).

---

60. V.P. Furnish, *II Corinthians: A New Translation with Introduction and Commentary* (AB; Garden City, NY: Doubleday, 1984), p. 286.

ESCHATOLOGICAL STRUCTURES IN GALATIANS

Moisés Silva

In the year 1912, two works appeared that, while very different in important respects, proposed an intriguingly similar and somewhat novel approach to our understanding of Paul's theology. One of them was the English translation of Schweitzer's history of Pauline research.[1] After concluding that 'the study of Paulinism has nothing very brilliant to show for itself in the way of scientific achievement', Schweitzer offered a solution that left out of account the Greek influence and based itself entirely on Jewish primitive Christianity. This approach meant, primarily, that 'the Pauline eschatology must be maintained in its full compass, as required by the utterances of the letters'.[2]

The other work was a substantive article by a scholar at Princeton Theological Seminary named Geerhardus Vos.[3] Published as part of a collection of essays by the Princeton faculty in celebration of the seminary's centennial, this article sought 'to investigate to what extent Paul's doctrine of the Holy Spirit shows interdependence with his eschatology'.[4] While critical of the so-called eschatological school for

---

1.   A. Schweitzer, *Paul and his Interpreters: A Critical History* (New York: Shocken, 1964 [1912]). The original work, *Geschichte der paulinischen Forschung*, had appeared in 1911.

2.   Schweitzer, *Paul*, pp. 237, 240.

3.   Born in the Netherlands in 1862, Vos moved to the United States with his family in 1881. He pursued theological studies at Princeton and in 1888 completed a doctoral program in Arabic studies at Strassburg. In 1893, Vos returned to Princeton to fill a newly created chair of biblical theology, from which he retired in 1932.

4.   G. Vos, 'The Eschatological Aspect of the Pauline Conception of the Spirit', in *Biblical and Theological Studies by the Members of Faculty of Princeton Theological Seminary* (New York: Scribner, 1912), pp. 209-59, reprinted in R.B. Gaffin (ed.), *Redemptive History and Biblical Interpretation* (Phillipsburg, NJ: Presbyterian and Reformed, 1980), pp. 91-125 (quotation from p. 94; note also pp. 526-33 for Vos's cautiously positive review of Schweitzer's *Paul*).

exaggerating the element of time and thus the early church's expectation of an imminent parousia, Vos certainly agreed that the apostles made 'the future the interpreter of the present, eschatology the norm and example of soteriological experience'.[5] With that perspective as a starting-point, Vos produced a singularly penetrating exegesis of the relevant passages, showing that, for Paul, 'the Spirit is both the instrumental cause and the permanent substratum of the resurrection-life'; more broadly, 'the Spirit's proper sphere...is the world to come; from there He projects Himself into the present, and becomes a prophecy of Himself in His eschatological operation'.[6]

It is curious that almost two decades later, precisely in the year 1930, full-length studies of Paul's theology would be published by both men.[7] Although the differences between the two scholars become clearer in these volumes, more provocative are their overlapping emphases. Over against the growing viewpoint that Paul was not to be treated as a systematic thinker,[8] both Schweitzer and Vos insisted that he was.[9]

5.   Vos, 'Eschatological Aspect', p. 92.

6.   Vos, 'Eschatological Aspect', pp. 108, 103.

7.   A. Schweitzer, *Die Mystik des Apostels Paulus* (Tübingen: Mohr, 1930), ET *The Mysticism of Paul the Apostle* (repr. New York: Seabury, 1968); and G. Vos, *The Pauline Eschatology* (repr. Grand Rapids: Eerdmans, 1968).

8.   This viewpoint was exemplified particularly by A. Deissmann, *Paul: A Study in Social and Religious History* (London: Hodder & Stoughton, 1912). Arguing that the 'doctrinaire interest' of 19th-century scholarship had led the study of Paul astray (p. 5), he sought to prove the following thesis: 'St. Paul is essentially a hero of piety first and foremost. That which is theological is secondary with him. The naïve is stronger with him than the premeditated, the mystic stronger than the dogmatic; Christ means for him more than Christology, God more than the doctrine of God. He is far more a man of prayer and witness, a confessor and prophet, than a learned exegetist and brooding dogmatist' (pp. 6-7).

9.   Schweitzer, *Mysticism*, p. 139: Paul 'is a logical thinker and his mysticism is a complete system'. Vos, *Pauline Eschatology*, p. 60: 'Paul's mind had by nature a certain systematic bent'; elsewhere he argues that in 'the Pauline system of truth' the forensic and transforming strands 'do not exist side by side in such form as to yield by mere addition of the one to the other the complete body of Paulinism' (p. 148), for 'it stands to reason that in a mind highly doctrinal and synthetic like Paul's a loose juxtaposition of two tracks of thinking without at least an attempt at logical correlation is inconceivable. In such a matter Paul's mind as a theological thinker was far more exacting than theirs who think that with their facile leaning over to one favored side they have done justice to the genius of the greatest constructive mind ever at work on the data of Christianity' (p. 149). On this general question see M. Silva, 'Systematic

142   *To Tell the Mystery*

Furthermore, over against the Reformational teaching that justification
by faith constituted the center of Pauline thought, both scholars sought
to demonstrate that it was rather eschatology that functioned as the
unifying thread. In Schweitzer's reconstruction, this insight was distorted not only by
an unbalanced emphasis on Paul's supposed mysticism but also by a
brand of 'thoroughgoing [*konsequente*] eschatology' that could hardly
account for the Pauline material as a whole. Vos's approach was distinctively different—indeed, it was genuinely innovative:

> What gives dogmatic coloring to [Paul's] teaching is largely derived from
> its antithetical structure, as exhibited in the comprehensive antitheses of the
> First Adam and the Last Adam, sin and righteousness, the flesh and the
> Spirit, law and faith, and these are precisely *the historic reflections of the
> one great transcendental antithesis between this world and the world-to-
> come. It is no wonder that such energetic eschatological thinking tended
> towards consolidation in an orb of compact theological structure.* For in
> it the world-process is viewed as a unit. The end is placed in the light of
> the beginning, and all intermediate developments are construed with
> reference to the purpose a quo and the terminus ad quem.[10]

The section I have highlighted deserves special attention. In particular,
note (a) that Vos views Paul's thought as a 'compact theological
structure'; (b) that its coherence ('consolidation') arises from 'energetic
eschatological thinking'; and (c) that the kind of eschatological thinking
Vos has in mind is the antithesis between 'this world and the world-to-
come' that we find reflected in history.

Regrettably, Vos's seminal work was all but ignored in mainstream
scholarship. Even within conservative circles, his influence has been
largely limited to the Reformed community.[11] On the other hand, the
'salvation-historical' theme associated especially with the name of Oscar
Cullmann[12] has some significant points of contact with the eschatological
approach of Vos. Most important, another Dutch scholar, Herman

---

Theology and the Apostle to the Gentiles', forthcoming in *Trinity Journal*.

10. Vos, *Pauline Eschatology*, pp. 60-61, my emphasis.

11. A particularly valuable attempt to build on Vos's distinctive approach is
R.B. Gaffin, *The Centrality of the Resurrection: A Study in Paul's Soteriology*
(Grand Rapids: Baker, 1978).

12. O. Cullmann, *Heil als Geschichte: Heilsgeschichtliche Existenz im Neuen
Testament* (Tübingen: Mohr, 1965); ET *Salvation in History* (New York: Harper &
Row, 1967).

Ridderbos, has produced a truly monumental synthesis that takes the Pauline conception of the revelation of God's mystery 'in the fulness of time' as the fundamental structure of the apostle's thought.[13] And in more general terms, of course, the concepts of apocalyptic and eschatology are now widely regarded as playing a crucial function in the New Testament as a whole and in Pauline theology specifically.[14]

Now Paul's language in Gal. 4.4, ὅτε δὲ ἦλθεν τὸ πλήρωμα τοῦ χρόνου, gives particularly clear expression to this point of view, and so the verse is frequently cited as evidence that the apostle thought along redemptive-historical lines.[15] Aside from that clause, however, the epistle to the Galatians has seldom been used to explicate or illustrate Pauline eschatology.[16] One can think of several reasons for this state of affairs. Apart from the initial greeting, for example, this letter contains no explicit references to the resurrection, and such a silence seems incompatible with a strong eschatological note. Perhaps more important, the

---

13. H. Ridderbos, *Paulus: Ontwerp van zijn theologie* (Kampen: Kok, 1966); ET *Paul: An Outline of his Theology* (Grand Rapids: Eerdmans, 1975). Ridderbos interacts repeatedly with Vos when dealing with 'the future of the Lord' (ch. 12), but not when treating the fundamental categories (except for an incidental citation on p. 46 n. 7). Cf. R.B. Gaffin's review article, 'Paul as Theologian', *WTJ* 30 (1967–68), pp. 204-32.

14. Cf. J.C. Beker, *Paul the Apostle: The Triumph of God in Life and Thought* (Philadelphia: Fortress Press, 1980). To be sure, Beker's own emphasis on apocalyptic, shared by a number of scholars, is hardly identical with what Vos and Ridderbos have in mind. Cf. below, n. 37, as well as the concluding paragraphs.

15. Indeed, H.N. Ridderbos chose it for the title of his little book, *When the Time Had Fully Come: Studies in New Testament Theology* (Grand Rapids: Eerdmans, 1957).

16. There are exceptions, of course, the best known being J.L. Martyn, 'Apocalyptic Antinomies in Paul's Letter to the Galatians', *NTS* 31 (1985), pp. 410-24. On the basis of Gal. 6.13-14, Martyn suggests that Paul is building on the ancient idea that the structure of the world lies in pairs of opposites, so that 'the letter is about the death of one world, and the advent of another' (p. 414). He then comments on 3.28 and 5.16-17, summarizes various apocalyptic motifs, and discusses in detail 4.21–5.1 (συστοχεῖ = oppositional columns [!]). 'Interpreted in the light of Paul's frequent recourse to the form of the apocalyptic antinomy, the two cosmic announcements stand at the conclusion of a letter fully as apocalyptic as are the other Paulines' (p. 420). 'Paul writes a letter, therefore, that is designed to function as a witness to the dawn of the New Creation, and, specifically, as a witness to the apocalyptic antinomies by which the battles of that New Creation are both perceived and won' (p. 421).

emphasis of this document on the antithesis between ἔργα νόμου and πίστις appears to reflect a message that focuses on the (individual and 'subjective') application of salvation rather than on the (corporate and 'objective') events of redemptive history.[17]

To be sure, recent dissatisfaction with the so-called Protestant or Lutheran reading of Galatians[18] has led scholars to minimize the epistle's teaching on justification by faith and thus to encourage alternate ways of interpreting the document. Yet the eschatological richness of Galatians has not been sufficiently explored. And while it is not possible in this brief article to do justice to the topic, we can at least identify the areas that deserve further study. Moreover, I hope to show that a full appreciation for the redemptive-historical foundation of the message of Galatians does not entail abandonment of the traditional Protestant understanding.

Perhaps the clearest way to appreciate how pervasive in this epistle are the eschatological undercurrents is by considering the relevant passages in sequence. While this approach precludes a satisfactory exegetical discussion of all the material, it does have certain distinct advantages, as will become clear in the course of the article.

Galatians 1.1

As already mentioned, the lone explicit reference to the resurrection is in the greeting, at 1.1, Παῦλος ἀπόστολος οὐκ ἀπ' ἀνθρώπων οὐδὲ δι' ἀνθρώπου ἀλλὰ διὰ 'Ιησοῦ Χριστοῦ καὶ θεοῦ πατρὸς τοῦ ἐγείραντος αὐτὸν ἐκ νεκρῶν. Scholars who point out that Galatians puts no emphasis on Christ's resurrection fail to note, however, that (aside from Romans) this is the only letter in which Paul at the very beginning calls attention to that event. This peculiarity can hardly be devoid of significance. When Paul alters his standardized greeting, it is

---

17. To use the classic terminology, Galatians, particularly ch. 3, has been understood as dealing with *ordo salutis* rather than with *historia salutis*.

18. Without denying that there are some elements of truth in the view (most freqently associated with E.P. Sanders) that Paul was not attacking Jewish legalism, I do not find this 'new look' on Paul convincing. Cf. my review article, 'Law in the New Testament: Dunn's New Synthesis', *WTJ* 53 (1991), pp. 339-53. Possibly the most effective response to Sanders has been written by the honoree of this volume; see Robert H. Gundry, 'Grace, Works, and Staying Saved in Paul', *Bib* 66 (1985), pp. 1-38.

normally for a reason directly related to the concerns of the letter.[19] At the outset, then, the apostle reminds his readers of the central event in redemptive history.[20] This mighty act of God (note the typical transitive expression, ἐγείραντος αὐτόν), which includes the exaltation of the Messiah at the right hand of the Father as well as the outpouring of the Spirit—who constitutes believers as the Body of Christ—marks the breaking-in of the kingdom, the dividing line between expectation and fulfilment. By highlighting this truth already in the greeting, Paul effectively lays down his most basic assumption, namely, that the passage from slavery to freedom has been made possible through an eschatological event. And having done so, he prepares the way for such passages as 2.19-21 and (possibly) the quotation of Isa. 54.1 in 4.27 (see below).

Galatians 1.4

The relationship between this redemptive work of Christ and the need for freedom is not left to guesswork. The apostle makes it explicit before he is finished with his expanded opening: ὅπως ἐξέληται ἡμᾶς ἐκ τοῦ αἰῶνος τοῦ ἐνεστῶτος πονηροῦ. The use of the verb ἐξαιρέομαι, only here in the Pauline corpus, is noteworthy. For some, it is evidence that Paul is quoting a confessional formula.[21] More likely, the verb may have been chosen because it is better suited than, say, σώζω or even ῥύομαι, to express the idea of 'rescuing someone from a place'.[22] To

19. Cf. L.A. Jervis, *The Purpose of Romans: A Comparative Letter Structure Investigation* (JSNTSup, 55; Sheffield: JSOT Press, 1991), pp. 35-36.
20. For a genuinely biblico-theological exegesis of this theme, see Gaffin, *Centrality*, esp. part 3.
21. Cf. the well-argued article by W. Kirchschläger, 'Zu Herkunft und Aussage von Gal 1,4', in A. Vanhoye (ed.), *L'apôtre Paul: Personalité, style et conception du ministère* (BETL, 73; Leuven: Leuven University Press and Peeters, 1986), pp. 332-39, esp. p. 335.
22. Paul never uses σώζω + ἐκ to indicate that from which one is saved. He does use ῥύομαι with either ἐκ or ἀπό for that purpose, though the object of the preposition consists normally of people (Rom. 15.31; 2 Thess. 3.2; cf. 2 Tim. 4.17) and what we might call 'circumstances' (Rom. 7.24; 2 Cor. 1.10; 1 Thess. 1.10; cf. 2 Tim. 3.11; 4.18). The closest parallel is Col. 1.13, but even here the object is ἐξουσία. On the significance of syntagmatic relations, cf. M. Silva, *Biblical Words and their Meaning: An Introduction to Lexical Semantics* (Grand Rapids: Zondervan, rev. edn, 1994), pp. 110, 119-20, 141-43, 167-68, 195-97.

put it differently, the term possibly occurs here because of its more natural 'syntagmatic' (i.e. combinatory) relation with αἰών. In any case, what matters is that Paul at the outset highlights two important elements in the teaching of the epistle: (a) Christ's work, since it can be described as an act of rescue, leads to freedom; (b) that which Christ frees us from is the present evil world—a phrase that, as is generally recognized, reflects an eschatological mode of thought.[23] And, as Schlier correctly infers, the work of Christ must signify the dawning of the new age.[24]

Galatians 1.12, 16; 2.2

The next passage that calls our attention is 1.11-12, which marks the beginning of the body of the letter,[25] and which sets forth the thesis to be demonstrated. No doubt responding to an accusation (whether real or implied), Paul denies that his gospel has a human origin; quite the contrary, he received it δι' ἀποκαλύψεως 'Ιησοῦ Χριστοῦ. This construction is very likely to be taken as a so-called objective genitive,[26] and the thought is made explicit almost immediately, when Paul goes on to state that God, graciously, was pleased ἀποκαλύψαι τὸν υἱὸν αὐτοῦ ἐν ἐμοί, ἵνα εὐαγγελίζωμαι αὐτὸν ἐν τοῖς ἔθνεσιν

23. 'Il presente non ha senso se non nel suo rapporto col futuro: in questa prospettiva acquista una valenza escatologica' (B. Corsani, *Lettera ai Galati* [Genova: Marietti, 1990], p. 60).

24. H. Schlier, *Der Brief an die Galater* (MeyerK; Göttingen: Vandenhoeck & Ruprecht, 14th edn, 1971), p. 34: 'Indem Jesus Christus sich gab, um unsere Sünden zu tilgen, schuf er auch die Voraussetzung dafür, dass wir—in der Vorausnahme des künftigen Äons!—dem gegenwärtigen Äon entnommen werden. Die Tat Jesu Christi liess in ihrer unsere Sünden tragenden Hingabe den zukünftigen Äon für uns angebrochen sein'. Betz objects that the text does not really say that; since 'the present evil aeon continues', Paul speaks of liberation out of it 'and not of the change of the aeons themselves' (H.D. Betz, *Galatians: A Commentary on Paul's Letter to the Churches in Galatia* [Hermeneia; Philadelphia: Fortress Press, 1979], p. 42). This objection would be valid only if Paul could not think in terms of an overlapping of the ages.

25. Although there are a few dissenting voices regarding this point (some, for example, begin the body at v. 6, others at v. 11 or v. 13), the consensus is strong that vv. 6-10 should be viewed as an introductory paragraph that sets the occasion for the letter.

26. I have discussed this linguistic detail in *God, Language, and Scripture: Reading the Bible in the Light of General Linguistics* (Grand Rapids: Zondervan, 1990), pp. 110-11.

(1.15-16). Casual readers, perhaps, are wont to understand this 'revelation' vocabulary as pointing to the *individual*, visionary quality of Paul's experience. After all, does not the κατὰ ἀποκάλυψιν of 2.2 refer to a very specific context in the life of the early church, so that the revelation Paul received at that time was perhaps little different from those experienced by New Testaments prophets generally? Even commentators, as a rule, overlook the possibility that the apostle uses this language to place his experience within the framework of redemptive history.

Martyn has rightly argued that the vocabulary of 'revelation' in Galatians must be given its full weight.[27] The clearest evidence is the clause in 3.24, εἰς τὴν μέλλουσαν πίστιν ἀποκαλυφθῆναι. As we shall see, this verse is part of a passage that has explicit eschatological overtones, and it would make little sense to understand the revelation mentioned there as *conceptually distinct* from what Paul describes in 1.12 and 16.[28] Indeed, given the strategic significance of 1.11-12, there is every reason to believe that in this formulation of his thesis Paul is anticipating the redemptive-historical point developed in 3.19-29. Moreover, when in 1.16 he specifies that the purpose of the revelation was the evangelizing of the nations, we can be left with no doubt that the apostle is speaking of 'the revelation of the mystery kept silent from eternity but now manifested', namely, the gospel that leads all nations to 'the obedience of faith' (Rom. 15.25-26).[29] Accordingly, even Gal. 2.2, expressing as it does Paul's deep concerns about the future of the Gentile mission, cannot be wrenched away from its redemptive-historical context.

---

27. Martyn, 'Antinomies', p. 417 (see also p. 424 n. 26); it is probably misleading, however, to speak of Paul's 'apocalypse', since this term today carries a large number of associations that are absent from what the apostle is describing.

28. Of course, the specific events are not identical; my point is that these two passages should not be treated as though they belonged to different categories altogether. One could argue that the experience mentioned in ch. 1 is a subset of the more general event described in ch. 3.

29. Even if these verses be regarded as a post-Pauline addition, most commentators would agree that 'the doxology succeeds quite well in summing up the central themes of the letter', as pointed out by J.D.G. Dunn, *Romans 1-8* (2 vols.; WBC, 38; Dallas, TX: Word Books, 1988), II, p. 913.

Galatians 2.16

That this well-known verse should be mentioned as evidence for an eschatological outlook may come as a surprise, since in the traditional reading of Galatians these words are as a matter of course (though not inappropriately) applied to the individual, and thus 'subjective', experience of believers. Moreover, even writers who want to do justice to the concerns raised by E.P. Sanders and others are usually so preoccupied by the exegetical problems found in this verse that they tend to ignore the redemptive-historical bedrock on which it lies. For example, the most recent critical English commentary on Galatians[30] devotes six long pages to the verse, but only a short and innocuous paragraph to the last clause—ὅτι ἐξ ἔργων νόμου οὐ δικαιωθήσεται πᾶσα σάρξ—in which Paul gives the theological grounds for his claim.

The clause, in fact, is a clear allusion to the LXX rendering of Ps. 143.2 (142.2), μὴ εἰσέλθῃς εἰς κρίσιν μετὰ τοῦ δούλου σου, ὅτι οὐ δικαιωθήσεται ἐνώπιόν σου πᾶς ζῶν. In Rom. 3.20 the allusion is even clearer, for there Paul includes the preposition ἐνώπιον. Although the future δικαιωθήσεται could be understood as a generalizing use of the tense,[31] a reference to the future judgment is most likely.[32] For one thing, the phrasing in the psalm itself (both the Hebrew and the Greek) clearly belongs to a type that indicates the finality of the divine judgment. Moreover, if we may appeal to the parallel, the context of Rom. 3.20 undoubtedly has the final judgment in view (v. 19, ἵνα πᾶν στόμα φαγῇ καὶ ὑπόδικος γένηται πᾶς ὁ κόσμος τῷ θεῷ; cf. also Rom. 2.5-16).

To recognize the apocalyptic overtones of this clause is not to undermine the traditional application of the verse, since in this very passage Paul is stressing the significance of faith for his own personal—yes, present—justification and that of his Jewish-Christian contemporaries. The point, however, is that this truth is set within the context of cosmic, eschatological realities. In other words, the 'subjective' experience of

30. R.N. Longenecker, *Galatians* (WBC, 41; Dallas, TX: Word Books, 1990), pp. 83-88.
31. We could view it as gnomic (implying 'in all circumstances') or even assertive ('certainly'). Lagrange calls it a 'futur logique', that is, 'une pareille justification ne se produira jamais' (M.-J. Lagrange, *Saint Paul, Epître aux Galates* [Paris: Gabalda, 2nd edn, 1950 (1925)], p. 48).
32. So Betz, *Galatians*, p. 119.

justification is not divorced from the 'objective' judgment at the end of the age. Quite the contrary, it is grounded in that final judgment, so that our sense of assurance (cf. 4.6-7) is not a psychological strategy that bypasses reality but rather a proleptic manifestation of God's righteous verdict.

Galatians 2.19-20

These verses form the conclusion to a notoriously difficult passage. Not the least of our exegetical obstacles is identifying the logical relationship among the various clauses, and the γάρ that introduces v. 19 can be interpreted in several ways. My own view is that v. 19 gives the explanation for the paradoxical affirmation of v. 18, though the explanation itself consists of a paradox (!): the reason that I would become a transgressor (of the law) if I were to begin rebuilding the law (which I formerly destroyed when I sought justification through faith rather than by the works of the law) is that the law itself led me to die to it. But we need not come to an agreement regarding the precise logical connection involved in order to appreciate the theological point that concerns us.

Paul affirms: νόμῳ ἀπέθανον, ἵνα θεῷ ζήσω. Χριστῷ συν-εσταύρωμαι· ζῶ δὲ οὐκέτι ἐγώ, ζῇ δὲ ἐν ἐμοὶ Χριστός. Although the language of resurrection is not used here, the concept is implicit and inescapable.[33] Paul's claim that he has already died—by crucifixion no less—and yet has been raised to life (how else could he continue to live?) is unabashedly eschatological. Moreover, note that it is the law that provides the contrast with the new mode of existence. One is left breathless by Paul's temerity in formally opposing God and the law: to die to one is to live to the other. Yet his own words make clear that this opposition needs to be nuanced, for he speaks of the law as responsible for his dying to it.[34] To put it differently, the opposition is between the

33. The fact that Paul does not actually say he has already been raised (in contrast to Eph. 2.5-6) may or may not be significant. What matters for our purposes and can hardly be disputed is that in Paul's thought the believer enjoys even now some of the fruits of the resurrection.

34. In the space at my disposal, it is not possible to discuss adequately the question whether what Paul has in mind is that the law sent Christ to his death (cf. 3.13) and believers share in it, or that the law leads people to believe in Christ and thus to separate from the law (anticipating the thought of 3.23-24). In my view, those two explanations are not so distant from each other as is generally thought; an argument can be made that they are two sides of the same coin.

law and the law! There could be no clearer evidence that Paul can consciously speak of the law in more than one sense or aspect, even if those aspects are apparently contradictory.[35] What matters for our purposes, however, is to acknowledge the antithesis between the old existence as represented by the law—presumably the Mosaic economy as a whole—and the new life made possible by Christ's crucifixion. It is curious that among the 'apocalyptic antinomies' discussed by Martyn this one does not show up. One could reasonably argue that, at least with respect to its practical consequences, no antithesis is more significant than that between the *old* existence based on the law and the new life that comes from faith.

Galatians 3.2-5

The antinomy between these two forms of existence is spelled out in very direct terms as we move to the third chapter of the letter. The way that Paul addresses the Galatians here marks a significant movement in the argument. While it would be an overstatement to say that this passage should be the starting-point for a proper interpretation of the document,[36] it would be an even graver mistake to downplay the role played by the battery of questions found in vv. 2-5.

The importance of this passage for our concerns is that Paul, who had already contrasted πίστις with ἔργα νόμου in ch. 2, now sets that contrast more clearly within a redemptive-historical framework by the use of the term πνεῦμα for the first time in this letter. Pauline research during the past few decades has firmly established that, for the apostle, the Holy Spirit is the clearest evidence that the time of fulfilment, the new aeon, has arrived.[37] In Gal. 3.2, therefore, he appeals to the fact that

35. Cf. M. Silva, 'Is the Law against the Promises? The Significance of Galatians 3:21 for Covenant Continuity', in W.S. Barker and W.R. Godfrey (eds.), *Theonomy: A Reformed Critique* (Grand Rapids: Zondervan, 1990), pp. 153-67, esp. pp. 158, 165.

36. C.H. Cosgrove, *The Cross and the Spirit: A Study in the Argument and Theology of Galatians* (Macon, GA: Mercer University Press [Peeters], 1988), p. 38: 'The place *for us* to begin in Galatians is with the *first unit that addresses the Galatian problem with directness and specificity*', and Cosgrove identifies that unit as 3.1-14. Actually, 1.6-7 is, to my mind, specific enough and it is certainly no less direct!

37. The evidence for this interpretation is widely accessible. Cf. Ridderbos, *Paul*, pp. 64-68; E. Schweizer, 'πνεῦμα', *TDNT*, VI, p. 422 (the Spirit 'must be

his readers had received the Spirit and asks them by what means that event took place (ἐξ ἔργων νόμου τὸ πνεῦμα ἐλάβετε ἢ ἐξ ἀκοῆς πίστεως;). Their movement away from the gospel of freedom signifies a return to the old aeon, that is, the present evil age (1.4), the age of the flesh (3.3, ἐναρξάμενοι πνεύματι νῦν σαρκὶ ἐπιτελεῖσθε;). By thus linking the πίστις-ἔργα νόμου contrast with the πνεῦμα–σάρξ antithesis, Paul unmistakably locates the Judaizers' message in a bygone stage of redemptive history. The mode of existence that is based on the works of the law is eschatologically obsolete.[38] Faith, on the other hand, is the way to new life. This perspective, of course, anticipates and thus informs the contrast between Hab. 2.4 and Lev. 18.5 later in this passage.

Galatians 3.8, 14, 16

The next paragraph, which begins with v. 6 (or v. 7), addresses more directly the historical dimensions of the debate between Paul and the Judaizers. At this point, by appealing to the Genesis narrative, the apostle identifies the central element of that debate: how does one become a child of Abraham? If there is a legitimate criticism of the traditional interpretation of Galatians, it can be found here. The typical sixteenth-century Protestant reading of Galatians 3, focusing as it did on the believer's personal ('subjective') appropriation of justification, did not sufficiently recognize that the Jewish–Gentile issue is the overarching motif that brings unity to this passage. To be sure, that hardly

understood as a sign of that which is yet to come'). Although Beker seems to downplay the concept of realized eschatology out of fear that it will neutralize the future-apocalyptic dimension (cf. *Paul the Apostle*, pp. 278, 356 and elsewhere), he forcefully affirms the eschatological significance of the Spirit's present function: 'The Spirit is for Paul determined by the apocalyptic future and does not signify the perfected state of present spirituality. It is the power that *transforms the created order and directs it toward its consummation*. When the Spirit is divorced from apocalyptic categories, it distorts the meaning of the gospel by unduly spiritualizing it' (*Paul the Apostle*, p. 172; my emphasis).

38. Although we normally think of the recipients of the epistle to the Hebrews as quite different from the Galatian Christians, perhaps they had this fundamental error in common—their sense of redemptive history was distorted. If so, could this factor account for the apparent points of contact between the two epistles? Cf. B. Witherington, 'The Influence of Galatians on Hebrews', *NTS* 37 (1991), pp. 146-52.

means, as many seem to think, that the Reformers were *wrong* to focus on the doctrine of personal justification; all it means is that this doctrine can stand some exegetical nuancing. Far from undermining the dogma of justification by faith, however, such nuancing provides a richer biblico-theological context for it.

Two specific points need to be made with regard to this section of Galatians. One is the emphasis on promise and fulfilment: προευηγγελίσατο (v. 8); ἵνα τὴν ἐπαγγελίαν τοῦ πνεύματος λάβωμεν διὰ τῆς πίστεως (v. 14); αἱ ἐπαγγελίαι (v. 16). The reference in v. 14 is particularly significant, for it identifies the reception of the Spirit as the fulfilment of the Abrahamic promise,[39] and thereby the concept of faith is once again associated with a new stage in redemptive history. The second point to be appreciated in these verses is their explicit reference to the Gentiles. Indeed, the term τὰ ἔθνη is used in vv. 8 and 14. Verse 16, which uses τὸ σπέρμα, identifies the seed with Christ, but Paul clearly has his eye on the truth spelled out in v. 29, namely, that those who are in union with Christ also constitute the seed. As already noted in connection with 1.16, the evangelizing of the Gentiles is a distinctively eschatological concept.

Galatians 3.19–4.7

A superficial reading of the text up to this point could have missed the eschatological structures that inform Paul's thought. Beginning with 3.19, however, there is simply no room for equivocation. Although the point is so obvious that it hardly requires demonstration, it may be helpful to bring out the emphasis of the passage, first, on *the law as a redemptive-historical period that has come to an end*: ἄχρις οὗ ἔλθῃ τὸ σπέρμα (3.19); οὐκέτι ὑπὸ παιδαγωγόν ἐσμεν (3.25); ἐφ᾽ ὅσον χρόνον (4.1); ἄχρι τῆς προθεσμίας τοῦ πατρός (4.2). Moreover, the apostle identifies the end of this period with *the coming of faith*:

---

39. However we may understand the genitival construction of τοῦ πνεύματος (genitive of apposition or objective genitive), the resulting thought is the same: 'the promised Spirit'. We might note, incidentally, the potential ambiguity in the Pauline affirmation that the patriarch Abraham, who lived in an early stage in redemptive history, had a relationship to God that was characterized by faith, even though faith is one of the signs of the *new* aeon. This peculiarity is hardly an inconsistency; it is rather a clue to Paul's understanding of the theological issues involved. See below on 3.23-25.

πρὸ τοῦ δὲ ἐλθεῖν τὴν πίστιν ὑπὸ νόμον ἐφρουρούμεθα συγκλειόμενοι εἰς τὴν μέλλουσαν πίστιν ἀποκαλυφθῆναι (3.23); ἐλθούσης δὲ τῆς πίστεως (3.25). Finally, and decisively, the new stage in redemptive history is identified as τὸ πλήρωμα τοῦ χρόνου (4.4), which is described as the time when the promises of God are applied to believers even beyond their expectation. In effect, Gentiles are now regarded not merely as the children of Abraham (3.29), but also as children of God himself (3.26; 4.6-7).

Three issues deserve further comment. 1. Paul's focus on the universal, 'objective' events of redemptive history hardly excludes a concern for the personal, 'subjective' application of those events: ὅσοι γὰρ εἰς Χριστὸν ἐβαπτίσθητε, Χριστὸν ἐνεδύσασθε (3.27); ἵνα τὴν υἱοθεσίαν ἀπολάβωμεν (4.5); εἰς τὰς καρδίας ἡμῶν (4.6); and so on. When scholars, interested in doing justice to the Jewish–Gentile issues in early Christianity, minimize or ignore (sometimes even deny outright) the relevance of Galatians for the doctrine of personal justification, they tend to fall into dichotomies that are totally foreign to Pauline teaching.

2. A related matter of interest—and one that affects how we evaluate E.P. Sanders' thesis—is the ease with which Paul moves back and forth from the Jewish to the Gentile experience, even to the point of identifying the two. One might argue that the first person plural of 3.23-25 (e.g. ὑπὸ νόμου ἐφρουρούμεθα συγκλειόμενοι) can only refer to Jewish individuals, yet he immediately (and using γάρ as his transition!) proceeds to apply the thought to his Gentile readers. Then in ch. 4 the apostle's analogy ('when we were children') again seems applicable only to Jews (τοὺς ὑπὸ νόμον, v. 5), but without batting an eye he shifts to the second plural (ἐστε υἱοί). It is apparent, therefore, that when the Protestant Reformers appropriated the message of Galatians in the context of their own ecclesiastical struggles, they were hardly doing violence to Paul's mode of thinking. After all, Paul himself draws a crucial correspondence between the Galatians' previous ceremonialism in the pagan world and the legal requirements of Judaism (4.8-11). In other words, the experience and sense of spiritual imprisonment that Paul describes was not at all the exclusive property of Israelites who lived under the law.

3. An additional problem has to do with the implications of Paul's statement that there was a temporal point when 'faith came', as though prior to the coming of Christ there had been no faith. I am fully aware

154 To Tell the Mystery

that this issue cannot be adequately treated in anything less than a whole article. The discussion has been further (and I think unnecessarily) complicated by the view, accepted by a growing number of scholars, that πίστις 'Ιησοῦ Χριστοῦ is a subjective genitive referring to the faith (or the faithfulness) of Christ himself. My own view is that the linguistic data make such a claim highly improbable.[40] In the specific case of Galatians 3, I find this interpretation perplexing, for Paul had introduced his argument in this chapter by focusing on the Galatians' *believing* reception of Christ through the preaching of the gospel and by clearly relating their faith to Abraham's *believing* as the pattern to be followed.[41] It would create ambiguity and even confusion for Paul, without any warning, to begin speaking of πίστις from a crucially different perspective.

But if this modern interpretation does not really solve our problem, neither can we be totally satisfied with the traditional understanding, which views πίστις in vv. 23-25 as a metonymy for the object of faith, that is, Christ, and then infers that the faith of the patriarchs had Christ as its object in a proleptic fashion. To be sure, this view that 'the coming of faith' is a figurative way of referring to the coming of Christ can be strongly supported by the context, since earlier in the passage (v. 19) Paul had established a connection between the verb ἔρχομαι and the substantive σπέρμα, identified with Christ in v. 16. A simple identification of 'faith' with 'Christ', however, while correct as far as it goes, does not do justice to the surprising formulation used by Paul. The apostle is in fact telling us that the age of faith began after the period of law had come to an end. Does he really suggest then that there was no faith before the coming of Christ?

Such an inference is of course precluded by the earlier part of the chapter, which explicitly attributes faith to Abraham.[42] But to point that

40. For a brief discussion of this problem, set within the larger question of how nominal cases function in language generally, see Silva, *God, Language, and Scripture*, pp. 107-8.
41. Rather far-fetched is the argument that Gal. 3.6-7 sets forth Abraham not as a model of believing but as a type of Christ in his faithfulness. In view of the initial (and repeated) contrast between ἔργα νόμου and ἀκοὴ πίστεως, which sets the background for vv. 6-14, it must be said that such an interpretation disturbs the context acutely. For an attempt to mediate between this recent perspective and the traditional view, see H.W. Johnson, 'The Pauline Typology of Abraham in Galatians 3' (PhD dissertation, Westminster Theological Seminary, 1993), ch. 3.
42. In Rom. 4, Paul includes David as another Old Testament figure who believed

out is to use a subjective-experiential perspective, whereas vv. 23-25 are clearly informed by a redemptive-historical outlook. The fact that the period of the law has come to an end does not mean that the law ceases to exist or to function experientially (thus Paul in 5.14 can readily quote the law as in some sense functioning within a believing community; see below). Conversely, to acknowledge that the period of faith begins with the coming of Christ is not to deny that faith was experienced prior to the cross. The dawning of the new creation results in an overlapping of the ages and so does not immediately do away with all vestiges of the present evil world, such as the flesh and the law. If there is such a thing as an overlapping of the ages, we should be ready to recognize as well that preliminary signs ('vestiges' in reverse!) of the new creation could be manifested even before the days of fulfilment. Nevertheless, if we wish to do justice to the Pauline conception, an effort must be made to keep the two perspectives distinct from each other. In particular, we must not allow the experiential realities of faith-before-Christ and law-after-Christ to neutralize the significance of this epochal distinction.[43]

Galatians 4.25-27

Paul's eschatological point of view shows up again in his handling of Sarah and Hagar, particularly in his reference to ἡ ἄνω Ἰερουσαλήμ. This phrase, by itself, could be thought to reflect an idealistic outlook, Platonic-style, which views the world above and the world below as two simultaneous modes of existence. Of course, Paul's thought as a whole points in a different direction. More significant, the explicit contrast that the apostle draws with that phrase is not 'the Jerusalem below' but rather ἡ νῦν Ἰερουσαλήμ.[44] Thus the slave woman and the free woman represent two covenants that belong to two ages.

for forgiveness, so we can safely gather that, in the Pauline understanding, people who lived prior to, or during, the period of the law could exercise saving faith.

43. As my colleague Richard Gaffin has suggested (in conversation), there is continuity in *ordo salutis* but discontinuity in *historia salutis*.

44. It is worth noting that, depending on the perspective of a specific context, Paul can use νῦν either with reference to the old age (as he does here, which is an exceptional case) or when speaking of the age to come that has already dawned (as he does more frequently, e.g., 2 Cor. 6.2 and several times in Romans). Of course, the use of the term in a nontheological sense is also very common. This fact should be a warning not to expect Paul's vocabulary to be quite as inflexible as many scholars take it to be.

This perspective is highlighted by the quotation from LXX Isa. 54.1, a strongly eschatological passage that in its use of the term στεῖρα alludes to Sarah (cf. LXX Isa. 51.1-2, which associates Abraham and Sarah with those who pursue δικαιοσύνη). In a recent article that builds on Richard Hays's suggestions, Karen Jobes has explored the rich echoes provided by this quotation. She further proposes that the citation contributes logically to the flow of Paul's argument because, in fact, Sarah has given birth. The key is Jesus' resurrection: Paul 'construed the resurrection of Jesus Christ to be the miraculous birth which would transform Jerusalem the barren one into Jerusalem the faithful mother-city in accordance with Isa. 26.1'.[45] If this interpretation can be sustained—and there is much to be said in its favor—it would provide an important corrective to the usual perception that Galatians shows little interest in the resurrection. More, it would indicate that Jesus' resurrection informs the argumentation of the letter at its very foundations.

It remains to be noted that 4.25-27 is framed by references to the divine promise. In v. 23, the phrase δι' ἐπαγγελίας is contrasted with κατὰ σάρκα (and the κατὰ σάρκα–κατὰ πνεῦμα antithesis of v. 29 makes clear again that the Spirit and the promise are corresponding eschatological terms). Then in v. 28 Paul applies the quotation from Isaiah by reassuring the Galatians that, after the manner of Issac, they are ἐπαγγελίας τέκνα. In short, they live in the age of fulfilment.

Galatians 5.1, 13-14

Although the theme of freedom has surfaced earlier in this letter (especially in 2.4), the beginning of ch. 5 contains the first instance of the verb ἐλευθερόω. It can hardly be claimed that this verb by itself indicates an eschatological perspective. Within the context of the letter, however, such a perspective provides the most natural way of reading the verse, especially since Paul is seeking to prevent the Galatians' returning (μὴ πάλιν...) to an old way of life that is incompatible with the grace they have received (cf. 1.6). Accordingly, the triumphant

---

45. K.H. Jobes, 'Jerusalem, our Mother: Metalepsis and Intertextuality in Galatians 4.21-31', *WTJ* 55 (1993), pp. 299-320, esp. pp. 313-15, building on R.B. Hays, *Echoes of Scripture in the Letters of Paul* (New Haven: Yale University Press, 1989), p. 120.

statement, τῇ ἐλευθερίᾳ ἡμᾶς Χριστὸς ἠλευθέρωσεν, must surely be a reminder that the Galatians have been rescued from the present evil world (1.4). The theme of freedom is thus associated with the new age of faith, and the point is highlighted in 5.13-14 (ἐπ' ἐλευθερίᾳ ἐκλήθητε), where ἐλευθερία is contrasted to σάρξ, anticipating the σάρξ–πνεῦμα antitheses of vv. 16-26. To put it differently, true freedom comes through the blessing of the eschatological Spirit (2 Cor. 3.17, οὗ δὲ τὸ πνεῦμα κυρίου, ἐλευθερία).

Galatians 5.5-6

It may seem strange that we should have to wait until this point in the letter to find an explicit indication of futurist eschatology. Even more unexpected, perhaps, is the context in which it is found. After portraying in harsh terms the status of those who seek to be justified through the law (v. 4; for the idea of being separated from Christ and grace, cf. again 1.6), Paul contrasts them with 'us', using a description that brings together in one short clause three of the most fundamental themes of the letter (Spirit, faith, righteousness) and introduces a new one (hope): ἡμεῖς γὰρ πνεύματι ἐκ πίστεως ἐλπίδα δικαιοσύνης ἀπεκδεχόμεθα. In effect, the apostle distinguishes two groups of people on the basis of their hope.

At this stage in the argument of Galatians, one is certainly not surprised to see the concepts of the Spirit and faith so tightly interwoven (note, however, the exceptionally heavy emphasis given to faith in v. 6—faith is all that matters—a verse that appears to give the grounds [γάρ] for the previous affirmation). The verse does raise several exegetical questions, the most interesting of which is, perhaps, the significance that should be attached to the genitive δικαιοσύνης. Why would Paul speak of righteousness as a future blessing when so much of this epistle—to say nothing of other passages, such as Rom. 5.1—emphasizes its present enjoyment? And would not a future reference weaken his argument?[46] In order to avoid these problems, some commentators have understood the construction as a subjective genitive: 'we are cherishing the hope which it [i.e. the righteousness we now have]

---

46. So John Eadie: the legalists 'think themselves justified—we hope to be justified. To describe a condition opposed to their delusions about justification, something stronger than mere hope might be expected' (*Commentary on the Epistle of Paul to the Galatians* [1894; repr. Grand Rapids: Zondervan, n.d.], p. 386).

excites and sustains'.[47] While it would be difficult to disprove this interpretation, most recent commentators have with good reason understood the phrase as an objective genitive (or perhaps a genitive of apposition), so that the resulting meaning is something like 'the righteousness we hope for'. As pointed out in connection with 2.16, justification is viewed by Paul as an apocalyptic event.

The fact that for believers 'the eschatological verdict of "not guilty" is already realized'[48] does not suspend or even minimize the significance of the future judgment. Quite the contrary. It is precisely because we at the present enjoy God's righteousness that we can with confidence await (ἀπεκδεχόμεθα) the final and definitive verdict.

Finally, notice the parallelism between 5.6 and 6.15. Although it would take a second reading of the letter to appreciate the point, Paul clearly identifies the concept of faith-working-through-love with that of the new creation.[49] How the new creation manifests itself in loving behavior is subsequently expressed with such language as fulfilling (πληρόω) the law by loving one's neighbor, producing love as the fruit of the Spirit (which is described with understatement as conduct that the law does not condemn), and fulfilling (ἀναπληρόω) the law of Christ by bearing one another's burden (5.14, 22-23; 6.2).

47. Eadie, *Galatians*, p. 387. Similarly Lagrange (*Epître aux Galates*, p. 137): 'l'espérance qui est celle de la justice, que la justice fait espérer'. In a very substantive discussion, Corsani (*Lettera ai Galati*, pp. 317-19) appeals to ἐλπίδα σωτηρίας in 1 Thess. 5.8 and rejects this reading of the genitive; uncomfortable with the future reference, however, he suggests that the verb ἀπεκδεχόμεθα 'indica la rinuncia alla fiducia in noi stessi per riporla unicamente in Dio e nella sua azione, dalla quale *aspettiamo* già ora la δικαιοσύνη' (p. 319).

48. Bruce, *Galatians*, p. 232.

49. Note also that the parallelism shows up in 1 Cor. 7.19: ἡ περιτομὴ οὐδέν ἐστιν καὶ ἡ ἀκροβυστία οὐδέν ἐστιν, ἀλλὰ τήρησις ἐντολῶν θεοῦ. This remarkable correspondence among the three passages is routinely ignored by Pauline scholars, no doubt because the usual interpretation of Paul's view of the law cannot account for the possibility that the apostle identifies 'keeping the commandments of God' with the 'new creation'. For an important argument that 1 Cor. 7.19 does cohere with Paul's teaching as a whole, see P.J. Tomson, *Paul and the Jewish Law: Halakha in the Letters of the Apostle to the Gentiles* (CRINT, 3/1; Assen: Van Gorcum; Minneapolis: Fortress Press, 1990), pp. 17, 270-71, 281.

Galatians 5.16-26

The strongly ethical character of this passage has led readers to ignore its eschatological foundation. Earlier commentators often viewed the σάρξ–πνεῦμα contrast as indicating two sides of human nature, and even those scholars who recognize that these terms must be understood in line with Paul's teaching elsewhere do not always attempt to integrate the material.

In reaction to this state of affairs, Walter Russell has recently attempted to provide a 'doggedly consistent reading of the σάρξ–πνεῦμα antithesis within the historical setting of the Galatian conflict'.[50] Arguing that the terms should be viewed in a corporate rather than individualistic sense, he understands σάρξ as 'circumcised bodily existence' and denies that the term has 'the immaterial sense of "a nature"'.[51] Whether it is necessary to exclude this latter sense altogether may be debatable, but Russell is absolutely correct that the antithesis in Galatians 5 must be understood in a way that coheres with the letter as a whole.

The redemptive-historical thrust of the passage is especially evident in vv. 24-25. Echoing 2.20, Paul in effect claims that believers, by virtue of their crucifixion (τὴν σάρκα ἐσταύρωσαν) and resurrection (ζῶμεν πνεύματι), have already been transferred from an old to a new form of existence. It follows, then, that the ethical antitheses of the preceding verses are understood by the apostle as a struggle between two aeons. To use language that has unfortunately almost become a cliche, the imperatives of this passage are grounded in a glorious indicative: believers, through the Spirit, have indeed been rescued from the old age of the flesh and the law (πνεύματι περιπατεῖτε καὶ ἐπιθυμίαν σαρκὸς οὐ μὴ τελέσητε...εἰ... πνεύματι ἄγεσθε, οὐκ ἐστὲ ὑπὸ νόμον, vv. 16, 18).

---

50. W.B. Russell, 'Paul's Use of Σάρξ and Πνεῦμα in Galatians 5–6 in Light of the Argument of Galatians' (PhD dissertation, Westminster Theological Seminary, 1991), p. 260.

51. Russell, 'Σάρξ and Πνεῦμα in Galatians 5–6', pp. 250, 252, 260. On pp. 257-59 Russell describes how his position is similar to, and different from, that of J.M.G. Barclay, *Obeying the Truth: A Study of Paul's Ethics in Galatians* (Studies of the NT and its World; Edinburgh: T. & T. Clark, 1988). For Vos's perceptive comments on σάρξ, cf. his *Pauline Eschatology*, pp. 298-302.

Galatians 6.8

The fundamental continuity between the realized and the futuristic aspects of the σάρξ–πνεῦμα contrast is made unequivocally clear by the presence of this verse in the context of Galatians. In effect, when the apostle affirms that the future judgment[52] grows out of one's mode of existence during the overlapping of the ages (ἐκ τῆς σαρκός–ἐκ τοῦ πνεύματος), he simply makes explicit what may be deduced from the rest of the letter. Notice in particular how naturally Paul had earlier introduced a reference to the future βασιλεία in the midst of his ethical warnings (5.21). The implications of this outlook will be addressed below (see conclusions).

Galatians 6.13-17

One would expect the closing of Galatians to reflect the apostle's more basic concerns in writing the letter. Curiously, such themes as righteousness and faith do not show up explicitly. Instead, as Martyn has pointed out, the passage highlights the apocalyptic antinomy that informs Paul's argument.[53]

In a recent article, moreover, Jeff Weima has demonstrated just how important these verses are for our understanding of the theological structures of the letter.[54] In his view, the closing makes clear how central for Paul's argument is the cross of Christ as 'the decisive event in salvation history that marks an end of the old "world" and ushers in the "new creation"'.

> Paul has constructed this letter closing in such a fashion that it sharpens to a razor-point the theological issue at stake in the letter as a whole. Ultimately the Achilles heel of the 'other gospel' that was being advocated by his Galatian opponents is its incompatibility with the cross of Christ.

---

52. 'Durch die eindeutig eschatologisch gebrauchten Akkusativobjekte φθοράν bzw. ζωὴν αἰώνιον ist in V 8 θερίσει ebenso eindeutig eschatologisches Futur' (F. Mussner, *Der Galaterbrief* [HTKNT, 9; Freiburg: Herder, 1974], p. 405).

53. Martyn, 'Apocalyptic Antinomies', pp. 412-14.

54. J.A.D. Weima, 'Gal. 6:11-18: A Hermeneutical Key to the Galatian Letter', *CTJ* 28 (1993), pp. 90-107. Quotations from pp. 103 and 104. I am very thankful to Professor Weima for reading an earlier draft of this article and offering valuable suggestions.

It could be argued, then, that Paul's fundamental criticism of his opponents was that, by failing to recognize the eschatological significance of the crucifixion, they sought to remain in the old world of circumcision. Those who belong to the καινὴ κτίσις, on the other hand, share in Christ's crucifixion and are therefore no longer alive to the old age (ἐμοὶ κόσμος ἐσταύρωται κἀγὼ κόσμῳ). They live according to a different pattern of existence (τῷ κανόνι τούτῳ στοιχήσουσιν, alluding to Spirit-led conduct, 5.25) and constitute the true, eschatological people of God ('Ισραὴλ τοῦ θεοῦ).[55]

Conclusions

Christiaan Beker, having (perhaps unwittingly) dichotomized the present eschatological from the apocalyptic, and being misled by 'the virtual absence of the resurrection of Christ in Galatians', remarks that 'Galatians threatens to undo what I have posited as the coherent core of Pauline thought, the apocalyptic coordinates of the Christ-event that focus on the imminent, cosmic triumph of God'. He concludes, 'Because the Christocentric focus of Galatians pushes Paul's theocentric apocalyptic theme to the periphery, Galatians cannot serve as the central and normative guide for all Paul's letters and theology'.[56]

Not only does this description fail to do justice to the character of the epistle—I would further argue that Galatians more than any other epistle provides a central guide for Paul's apocalyptic outlook. Precisely because this document grounds the future triumph of God's righteousness in a carefully developed view of realized eschatology, the teaching of Galatians is ideally suited to serve as a norm for understanding the core of Paul's theology. True, since one of Beker's main concerns is to avoid a 'deapocalypticizing' of futurist eschatology,[57] it could be argued that Vos's emphasis on the 'semi-eschatological' character of Paul's

---

55. In spite of many attempts to evade the conclusion that in v. 17 Paul views believers (therefore, the church) as the new Israel, this is the only conclusion that coheres with the argument of the letter, and most recent commentators have accepted it.

56. Beker, *Paul the Apostle*, p. 58. In the preface to the first paperback edition (esp. p. xix, in response to Martyn), Beker does recognize that he had overstated his case, but the problem is more basic than that.

57. *Paul the Apostle*, p. 356.

teaching runs against Beker's thesis. As if anticipating such a concern, Vos commented,

> It has sometimes been asserted that this deflection from the straight prospective line of vision to the upward bent towards the heavenly world represents a toning down of the eschatological interest. Nothing could be farther from the truth. In reality this whole representation of the Christian state as centrally and potentially anchored in heaven is not the abrogation, it is the most intense and the most practical assertion of the other-worldly tenor of the believer's life. Precisely because it is to a large degree *incipient* realization, it bears the signature of eschatology written clear on its face. And because there is in it no *going back upon*, but a *reaffirmation of* the absolute ultimate hope, the other, more simple line of projection into the future continues to exist side by side with it in full validity.[58]

The attempt to describe a whole document by focusing, as I have done, on one single theme runs the risk of distorting the material. It is certainly not my intention to claim that such a description can do full justice to the message of Galatians. Much less, however, can we do justice to the letter if we *exclude* or *even downplay* the eschatological dimension. More to the point, I would want to argue that this redemptive-historical undercurrent, which surfaces in the passages discussed here, provides the foundational framework for everything of importance found in the letter. A genuine appreciation of the eschatological structures that inform the epistle to the Galatians, therefore, not only becomes an essential hermeneutical instrument for understanding this document itself but also furnishes us with the means of identifying the coherence of Paul's theology as a whole.

---

58. Vos, *Pauline Eschatology*, pp. 39-40. Indeed, most of Vos's book is devoted to Paul's futuristic teaching.

THE 'BODY' IN COLOSSIANS

James D.G. Dunn

A study of the Pauline concept of the 'body' would not usually focus on Colossians. Its eight references are outnumbered by Romans (10), 1 Corinthians (46!), 2 Corinthians (10) and even Ephesians (9). In fact, however, there are more variations played on the σῶμα-theme in Colossians than in any of Paul's other letters (1 Corinthians not excepted). It would seem, therefore, to be a highly appropriate subject for an essay in honour of Bob Gundry, who has himself made a specialist study of σῶμα in biblical theology and whose contribution also came at the topic from an unusual angle.[1]

The basic facts are straightforward and it is simplest to proceed by noting the eight texts in Colossians in which the term occurs, plus the single use of the equivalent adverb, σωματικῶς, which occurs only here in the New Testament.

1.18	He is the head of the body, the church
1.22	You... he has now reconciled in the body of his flesh through his death
1.24	I complete what is lacking of the afflictions of (the) Christ in my flesh on behalf of his body, that is, the church
2.9	In him dwells all the fulness of the deity in bodily form (σωματικῶς)
2.11	In him you were circumcised with a circumcision not performed by human hand in the stripping off of the body of flesh
2.17	These are the shadow of things to come, but the reality (σῶμα) is Christ
2.19	...not holding to the head, from which the whole body, supported and held together by joints and ligaments, grows with the growth of God

---

1. R.H. Gundry, *Sōma in Biblical Theology with Emphasis on Pauline Anthropology* (SNTSMS, 29; Cambridge: Cambridge University Press, 1976).

2.23 ...severe treatment of the body, not of value to anyone in
regard to the gratification of the flesh
3.15 the peace of Christ...into which you were called in one body

Several of these seem at first sight to be straightforwardly Pauline,
insofar as 'Pauline' is determined by the usage of the Hauptbriefe.[2] But
on closer examination an increasing number of surprising features come
to light. We will proceed by studying the texts in the most obvious
groupings, starting with the most frequent.

1. *The Body, the Church*

The most distinctive feature of the earlier Pauline σῶμα-theology is
undoubtedly his use of 'the body of Christ' as a way of characterizing
Christian churches as charismatic communities (Rom. 12.4-8; 1 Cor. 12),
where the functions (πράξεις) of the body (Rom. 12.4) are the
individual believers functioning charismatically, and where the body is
the local church in a particular place—as 1 Cor. 12.27 indicates: 'You
[Corinthian believers] are Christ's body [in Corinth], and each of you a
limb or organ of it' (REB).[3] In comparison, in each of the four
ecclesiastical references in Colossians there are notable variations and
developments.

1.1. The most familiar variation is the identification of Christ as the *head*
of the body (1.18; 2.19), rather than with the body itself (cf. Rom. 12.5,
'so we the many are one body in Christ'; 1 Cor. 12.12, 'Just as the
body is one and has many parts, and all the parts of the body, though
many, are one body, so it is with Christ'). As has regularly been pointed
out, whereas in 1 Corinthians 12 the head is simply one part among the
rest (12.21), in Colossians the role of Christ as head *over* the body is a
major feature.

In addition, in 1.18 there is the question whether τῆς ἐκκλησίας has
been added to what was originally a reference to the cosmos understood
as a body and, if so, what effect the addition of τῆς ἐκκλησίας has

---

2. The discussion does not require a decision to be made on the authorship of
Colossians. The differences that will become apparent are there whether penned by
Paul or by a close disciple (Timothy?).

3. See further my *Jesus and the Spirit* (London: SCM; Philadelphia:
Westminster, 1975) pp. 260-65; also *Romans* (WBC, 38; Dallas: Word Books,
1988), pp. 722-26.

had. To keep the analysis orderly I will postpone fuller discussion of this aspect to §3. Here we need simply note that in the 'hymn' as it now stands (1.15-20) the emphasis is on the cosmic primacy and ultimacy of Christ—'image of the invisible God, first-born of all creation', 'all things were created in him...through him and for him', 'he is before all things and all things hold together in him' (1.15-17). The implication is that Christ's headship has the same significance. That is, as 'head' Christ is supreme, authoritative ruler over the body (cf. 2.10),[4] with perhaps the idea of κεφαλή = ἀρχή ('beginning, principle') also in play.[5]

In 2.19, on the other hand, the idea of the headship of the body is more that of the body's complete dependence on the head for its nourishment and growth. Although that idea could follow from the model of the cosmic ruler (1.18), the head as the controlling organ ultimately determining all that happens in the body,[6] the description of how this control operates here assumes a physiological understanding of the body.[7] Through the 'joints and ligaments'[8] the whole body is supported, supplied with what it needs (ἐπιχορηγέω), and held together (συμβιβάζω). In the imagery used the emphasis seems to be more on the interconnectedness of the members of the body than on the joints and ligaments as actually channels of nurture. Such an emphasis on the interconnectedness, and thus interdependence, of the members of the body is characteristically Pauline (particularly 1 Cor. 12.14-26).[9] And

---

4. The observation is regularly made that in the LXX κεφαλή often translates שׁאר in the sense 'ruler' or 'leader', interchangeable with ἀρχή (e.g. Deut. 28.13; Judg. 10.18; 11.11; 2 Sam. 22.44; 1 Kgs 20.12; Isa. 7.8-9) (see H. Schlier, *TDNT*, III, p. 675).

5. S. Bedale, 'The Meaning of κεφαλή in the Pauline Epistles', *JTS* 5 (1954), pp. 211-15.

6. So E. Schweizer, *TDNT*, VII, p. 1076.

7. J.B. Lightfoot, *Colossians and Philemon* (London: Macmillan, 1875), pp. 198-99; J. Gnilka, *Kolosserbrief* (HTKNT, 10.1; Freiburg: Herder, 1980), p. 153. M. Barth, *Ephesians* (AB, 34; New York: Doubleday, 1974) has shown that at this time (Hippocrates fifth/fourth century BCE, and Galen second century CE) there was a physiological understanding of the brain as the coordinator and integrator of the body's sensations (pp. 187-88).

8. See particularly Lightfoot, *Colossians*, pp. 196-98.

9. For the development in thought from the earlier letters see my '"The Body of Christ" in Paul', in M.J. Wilkins and T. Paige (eds.), *Worship, Theology and Ministry in the Early Church: Festschrift R.P. Martin* (JSNTSup, 87; Sheffield: JSOT Press, 1992), pp. 146-62.

though, as already noted, the identification of the head as the most important part of the body is a step beyond the earlier Pauline theology of the church as body, there is no other sense of hierarchy within the body apart from that of the head,[10] and the sense of mutual interdependence remains strong. In short, the use of the physiological model for the 'body' provides a valuable means of integrating the older imagery with the newer emphasis on Christ's headship.

1.2. The third of the ecclesiastical-body references (1.24) does not develop the idea of body as such but instead relates it to 'the afflictions of Christ' in a neat interplay—his afflictions, my flesh, his body. Since this reference follows closely on the preceding interplay of body and flesh (1.22) it would be sensible here too to clarify other aspects of the Colossians' σῶμα-motif (§2) before commenting further.

Col. 3.15 is the final variation on the complex body-theme played in Colossians. And here more than in any of the preceding variations it is the main emphasis of the earlier Paulines (Rom. 12.5-8; 1 Cor. 12) which is to the fore. That emphasis was on the body as a metaphor of unity, but precisely as a unity composed of the complementarity and integrated wholeness of different parts. In this case the primary influencing thought seems to have been the common idea in the ancient world of the city or state as a body (the body politic), which served just the same function, that is, to inculcate a sense of mutual belonging and mutual responsibility among the diverse constituents within the city or state, as in the famous fable of Menenius Agrippa in Livy, *Hist.* 2.32 and Epictetus 2.10.4-5.[11] As in the earlier Paulines, the thought seems to be primarily of the local (Colossian) church as the 'one[12] body' (of Christ in Colossae), that is, with reference to the house church where they would meet for worship (3.16). But the same presumably applies to the church now seen as the universal body of Christ (1.18, 24; 2.19). Nevertheless, it is rather striking that it is only in this almost passing way that the earlier emphasis

10. It is hardly the intention of the metaphor to identify the 'joints and ligaments' as particular ministries or offices; see E. Schweizer, *Colossians* (London: SPCK, 1982), pp. 164-65.

11. E. Schweizer, *TDNT*, VII, pp. 1038-39, 1041, 1069; see also my 'Body in Paul', pp. 153-56.

12. The reason why 𝔓[46] and B omit the 'one' is not at all clear; perhaps as a result of haplography (ἑνί following ἐν). Few commentaors consider the variant worthy of mention, let alone discussion.

(on the body as a model of unity in diversity) is retained, and without the earlier emphasis that the church is only 'one body' as being the body of Christ or one body in Christ (Rom. 12.5; 1 Cor. 12.12).

To sum up, even within the limited scope of 'the body as church' we find a remarkable variation—an adaptation of the cosmic body (1.18), a correlation of the church as Christ's body with his afflictions (1.24), use of a physiological understanding of bodily function to integrate the earlier idea of interdependence with that of Christ's headship (2.19), and a half-casual recalling of the primary emphasis in the earlier Pauline letters on the oneness of the body (3.15).

2. The Fleshly Body

Of particular interest in the second group of 'body' references in Colossians is the interplay between 'body' and 'flesh'.

2.1. We begin with the uniqueness of the phrase 'the body of flesh', τὸ σῶμα τῆς σαρκός (1.22; 2.11). The two words (σάρξ and σῶμα) are, of course, characteristically Pauline (each occurs more than 90 times in the letters attributed to him, more than 60% of the New Testament usage). And they never appear linked together elsewhere in Paul, presumably because their ranges of meaning overlap to such an extent. The basic distinction seems to be that (a) σῶμα denotes the fact of embodiment, that aspect of human (and other) existence which gives it place in its world and makes it possible for embodied entities to interact upon each other (so e.g. 1 Cor. 6.16-18; 7.4), while (b) σάρξ (in its primary sense) is the material substance of which the body is composed in this world.

Here it is important to reassert that in Paul σῶμα does not mean 'physical body' as such.[13] Thus most clearly, the distinction he makes in 1 Cor. 15.44, between the body of this age, σῶμα ψυχικόν ('natural body'), and the resurrection body, σῶμα πνευματικόν ('spiritual body'), shows that different embodiments are necessary for different environments. Since in Hebrew anthropology disembodied existence was scarcely conceivable, transformation of the 'body' was simply the means by which transition from this world to the next takes place (cf. Phil. 3.21). In contrast, 'flesh' remains rootedly of this world,

---

13. This, regrettably, in response to the main thesis of Gundry's *Sōma*, in which he tries to overthrow the prevailing consensus.

inextricably part of it, so that 'flesh and blood' cannot inherit the kingdom (1 Cor. 15.50). Nevertheless, since the embodiment of which Paul speaks most frequently is that within this world, a physical (three-dimensional) world, the individual σῶμα in Paul does in fact usually denote physical body.[14] A fair degree of overlap between 'body' and 'flesh' is therefore inevitable.

From the other side of the overlap between the two words in Paul, σάρξ in its range of meaning quickly gathers to itself a characteristically negative note. The degree to which σάρξ belongs to and is part of this world means that it shares this world's weak, ephemeral character (contrast σῶμα, 2.17), and that its corruptibility leaves it ready prey to the powerful enticements of sin (classically expounded in Rom. 7.7–8.3). The resulting morally negative tone is at its sharpest in Paul's blunt antithesis between 'flesh' and 'Spirit' (Rom. 8.4-8; Gal. 5.16-17).[15] In contrast, σῶμα as such is characteristically neutral and only rarely negative (Rom. 8.13 is exceptional).

In Pauline terms, then, the usage here is highly unusual. Evidently it was chosen, as the immediate context implies, because of its appropriateness in a reference to death. That is to say, it is the body's fleshliness, its subjection to decay and death (or as we today might say, that which makes the physical body subject to the entropic principle), which is in view here. This supposition is strengthened by the use of the same phrase in 1QpHab 9.2 (בנוית בשרו) and in the Greek of *1 En.* 102.5 (τῷ σώματι τῆς σαρκὸς ὑμῶν),[16] where it clearly denotes human vulnerability to disease and decay, and in 4QpNah/1Q169 2.6 (בנוית בשרם), where it refers to corpses.

The result is a fascinating variation on the earlier Pauline balance between the more typically negative σάρξ and the more typically neutral (not essentially physical) σῶμα. For here it is precisely by means of adding τῆς σαρκὸς that the material character of Jesus' body, its subjection to death, is brought out. This in turn highlights a further feature of Colossians—the degree to which σάρξ initially and more

---

14. Failure to appreciate this contingent character of the physical body is, I take it, the cause of Gundry's misplaced emphasis.

15. See further my 'Jesus—Flesh and Spirit: an Exposition of Romans 1.3-4', *JTS* 24 (1973), pp. 40-68; a more popular treatment is to be found in *Paul for Today* (Ethel M. Wood Lecture, 1993; University of London, 1993).

16. Details in E. Lohse, *Colossians and Philemon* (Hermeneia: Philadelphia: Fortress Press, 1971), p. 64 n.20.

consistently in this letter denotes mere physical presence or existence (1.22, 24; 2.1, 5, 11).[17] In the earlier Paul a more strongly moral tone would likely have been prominent. Here, however, the force of the τῆς σάρκος is to distinguish Jesus' physical body in death from the cosmic body implied in 1.15-18 (see §3) and from 'his body, the church' (see §1). 'The body of flesh' was as much, if not more, 'his body' than the others, and (note the fine sense of dramatic irony) it is precisely this body in all its material subjection to decay and death that provides the middle term between these other two.

2.2. In 2.11 precisely the same phrase is used, 'in the stripping off of the body of flesh' (ἐν τῇ ἀπεκδύσει τοῦ σώματος τῆς σαρκός). ἀπέκδυσις is not attested independently of Paul, but is obviously drawn from the verb meaning 'take off, strip off (clothes)' (as in 2.15). The lack of an αὐτοῦ, 'his flesh', would normally indicate that the phrase should be rendered 'the body of the (= your) flesh'. But all the 'flesh' references so far in the letter have denoted physical flesh (1.22, 24; 2.1, 5), and the most obvious way to take the combination 'body of flesh' is once again as a way of emphasising the physicality of the body and its consequent vulnerability to death.[18] 'Stripping off the body of flesh', therefore, can hardly mean anything else than literal death (as in 1.22). If then the phrase was chosen precisely to emphasize the physical nature of the death, it is difficult to see it being referred primarily to something that had already happened to the readers. For there is no suggestion that believers have already stripped off the flesh or the body of flesh (to the contrary, 2.1 and 5).[19]

More likely, as the preceding words suggest ('circumcised with a circumcision not performed by human hand'), the phrase is an adaptation of the description of physical circumcision = a stripping off of the

17. See below nn. 26, 27.

18. This is lost sight of by several translations which seem to want to avoid using 'flesh' at all costs and which produce unjustifiably tendentious translations (NEB 'lower nature'; REB 'old nature'; NJB 'your natural self'; NIV 'sinful nature'; GNB 'sinful self').

19. This conclusion represents a change of mind from my earlier *Baptism in the Holy Spirit* (London: SCM Press, 1970; Philadelphia: Westminster, 1975), p. 153, in which I followed the consensus (e.g. Lightfoot, *Colossians*, p. 182; C. Masson, *Philippiens* [CNT, 10; Neuchâtel: Delachaux & Niestlé, 1950], pp. 126-27; Schweizer, *Colossians*, p. 143) that 'body of flesh' was in effect synonymous with 'body of sin' (Rom. 6.6) and 'body of death' (Rom. 7.24).

flesh (of the foreskin). This is applied to Jesus' death in deliberate echo of 1.22: in this case the flesh that was stripped away was the whole physical/fleshly body.[20] We might even translate, 'in the stripping off of the body, the flesh/as the flesh (= the flesh)'. This likelihood is strengthened when we look ahead to 2.15 (where the equivalent verb is used, 'strip off') and realise that we are caught up in a further play on the body of Christ theme. On the cross there was a double 'stripping off'—his physical body in death, and the rulers and authorities in triumph. It follows that the final phrase, 'in the circumcision of Christ', is best seen simply as a summary expression of the larger imagery of the preceding phrases. That is, not primarily as a circumcision effected by Christ,[21] but as a concise description of the death of Christ under the metaphor of circumcision. It is clearly implied, of course, from the first phrase ('In him you were circumcised with a circumcision not performed by human hand'), that conversion-initiation could consequently be understood as a sharing in that circumcision; but the thought is precisely of a sharing in his circumcision-death, not of an independent act of their own circumcision-death.

2.3. The third interplay between 'body' and 'flesh' comes in 2.23, in a passage notorious for its syntactical difficulty. Without allowing ourselves to be sidetracked by these difficulties we need simply note that important in the text is the contrast between a semi-commendatory reference to 'severity of the body' (ἀφειδίᾳ σώματος) and the implied condemnation of 'gratifying the flesh' (πλησμονὴν τῆς σαρκός). Most commentators explain the contrast by arguing that 'flesh' is being

20. So also C.F.D. Moule, *Colossians* (CGTC; Cambridge: Cambridge University Press, 1957), pp. 95-96; R.P. Martin, *Colossians* (NCB; London: Oliphants, 1974), pp. 82-83; P.T. O'Brien, *Colossians, Philemon* (WBC, 44; Waco: Word Books, 1982), pp. 116-17. Failure to appreciate the allusion to circumcision and the force of 'body' and 'flesh' thus combined, which retains the neutral force of σῶμα as such and makes possible the positive play on σῶμα which is such a feature of the letter, must lie behind G. Bornkamm's otherwise surprising judgment that 'stripping off the body of flesh' is a 'completely un-Jewish expression' and must presuppose a Gnostic context of thought ('The Heresy of Colossians', in F.O. Francis and W.A. Meeks, *Conflict at Colossae* [Missoula, MT: Scholars Press, 1975], p. 128).

21. As NEB/REB; NIV; GNB; and e.g. E.F. Scott, *Colossians* (Moffatt; London: Hodder, 1930), p. 45 and P. Pokorný, *Colossians* (Peabody, MA: Hendrickson, 1991), pp. 124-25. In the earlier Paul the 'circumcision of the heart' is always attributed to the Spirit (Rom. 2.29; 2 Cor. 3.3; Phil. 3.3).

used with the negative, moral force so characteristic of the earlier Paul (cf. Rom. 13.14 and Gal. 5.16-17, the desires of the flesh).[22] The difficulty is that the phrase itself suggests gratification of physical needs in terms of food and drink, as the Fathers clearly understood.[23] But if that sense of the phrase was pressed it would reduce the contrast to something of an absurdity: the practice of severity to the body, including self-mortification and fasting (ταπεινοφροσύνη),[24] does not make any difference to the satisfaction of physical appetites.

It may be, therefore, that we need to look for a third option, which gives more weight to the physical sense of 'flesh', in line with the consistent emphasis of the word in the letter. Such a sense has already been given in 2.13—'the uncircumcision of your flesh'. Self-evidently this is a Jewish description of Gentiles, and one which both values highly 'circumcision' and devalues the state of 'uncircumcision'. It immediately follows that the 'flesh' thus 'uncircumcised' should not be understood as a moral category, as most do (e.g. NEB 'morally uncircumcised'; NIV 'the uncircumcision of your sinful nature'). Rather, in a way similar to 2.11, the phrase echoes the classic description of circumcision as marking God's covenant with Israel (Gen. 17.11-14, 'so shall my covenant be in your flesh an everlasting covenant'), a characteristic echo in Pauline usage (Rom. 2.28; Gal. 6.12-13; Phil. 3.3-5). 'The uncircumcision of your flesh' therefore means simply 'your status as Gentiles', that is, primarily an ethnic distinction.[25] The thought, in fact, is precisely that of Eph. 2.11—'Gentiles in the flesh, those called "uncircumcision" by the so-called "circumcision" made by human hand in the flesh' (note also 3.11).

22. Hence NEB/REB 'in combatting sensuality'. '"Flesh" is man in his own resources (Selbstmächtigkeit) and thereby in his opposition (Widerspruch) against God' (A. Lindemann, *Kolosserbrief* [ZB; Zürich: TVZ, 1983], p. 52).

23. BAGD, *s.v.* πλησμονή; G. Delling, *TDNT*, VI, p. 133.

24. ταπεινοφροσύνη usually means 'humility', but most follow the observation that the LXX uses the repeated phrase 'to humble one's soul' in the sense of 'to mortify oneself' (Lev. 16.29, 31; 23.27, 29, 32) or more specifically 'to fast' (Ps. 35.13; Isa. 58.3, 5; Jdt. 4.9; see also Ps. 69.10 and *Pss. Sol.* 3.8); ταπεινοφροσύνη is clearly used in this latter sense in Hermas, *Vis.* 3.10.6 and *Sim.* 5.3.7.

25. This is recognized by GNB; cf. JB/NJB; T.K. Abbott, *Colossians* (ICC; Edinburgh: T. & T. Clark, 1897), p. 253; Masson, *Colossiens* p. 127 and n. 3; N.T. Wright, *Colossians and Philemon* (TNTC; Leicester: InterVarsity Press; Grand Rapids: Eerdmans, 1986), p. 109; M.J. Harris, *Colossians & Philemon* (Grand Rapids: Eerdmans, 1991), p. 106.

Since there is such a consistent physical emphasis in the use of σάρξ in Colossians,[26] it is likely that in 2.23 σάρξ also refers to physical and ethnic identity (as regularly in the phrase κατὰ σάρκα—Rom. 1.3; 4.1; 9.3, 5, 8; 1 Cor. 10.18; Gal. 4.23, 29). Certainly, similarly negative phrases are used elsewhere by Paul to denote too much value being placed in that flesh, ethnic flesh rather than moral flesh, as we might say—in particular, the 'boasting in the flesh' of Gal. 6.12-13 and the 'confidence in the flesh' of Phil. 3.3-4, which in Pauline terms were as much a distortion of the terms of grace and a pandering to the flesh as any physical greed or overindulgence. 'Gratification of the flesh' may well, therefore, be taken as a reference to satisfaction felt by the Colossian Jews in their ethnic (fleshly, κατὰ σάρκα) identity as Jews, the people chosen by the one God to be his own elect.[27] This would fit well with the various other indications that the most clearly discernible features of the Colossian 'philosophy' are Jewish in character,[28] which in

26. Even 2.18, 'mind of flesh', once again a phrase unique in Paul, should not be taken in a non-physical way. For in a Hellenistic context, as Philo again well illustrates, it was precisely the 'mind' which would have been the medium by means of which the person could enter the higher realms, the logos of human rationality itself part of the medium of the divine Logos that interpenetrated the cosmos (see e.g. J. Behm, *TDNT*, IV, pp. 954-56). In such a scheme 'mind' and 'flesh' were quite antithetical, since it was impossible for the divine substance to mingle with the material. To speak of 'the mind of flesh' therefore was a stinging rebuke, in effect denying that such a Colossian participation in angel-worship could ever have 'lifted off' from earth: even the mind was 'flesh', fast earth bound.

27. The only other σάρξ reference in Colossians is also κατὰ σάρκα, but again slightly unusual in the Paulines as being a description of the relationship between master and slave (otherwise only Eph. 6.5), where it is precisely the 'thingness' of the slave that gives the κατὰ σάρκα its force.

28. Note particularly 2.11, 13, 16, 20 and 3.11; with 2.8 and 20 cf. Gal. 4.3 and 9. On 2.18 see F.O. Francis, 'Humility and Angelic Worship in Col. 2.18, in Francis and Meeks, *Conflict*, pp. 163-95; also N. Kehl, 'Erniedrigung und Erhöhung in Qumran und Kolossä', *ZKT* 91 (1969), pp. 364-94; A.J. Bandstra, 'Did the Colossian Errorists Need a Mediator?', in R.N. Longenecker and M.C. Tenney (eds.), *New Dimensions in New Testament Study* (Grand Rapids: Zondervan, 1974), pp. 329-43; O'Brien, *Colossians*, pp. 141-45; C.A. Evans, 'The Colossian Mystics', *Bib* 63 (1982), pp. 188-205; C. Rowland, 'Apocalyptic Visions and the Exaltation of Christ in the Letter to the Colossians', *JSNT* 19 (1983), pp. 73-83; T.J. Sappington, *Revelation and Redemption at Colossae* (JSNTS, 53; Sheffield: JSOT Press, 1991). See further my forthcoming *Colossians* (NIGTC; Grand Rapids: Eerdmans; Exeter: Paternoster, 1995).

turn strengthens the likelihood that what is being critiqued here was an assumption on the part of (many of) the Colossian Jews that rules for living and worship practices were ways of expressing (maintaining and marking out) their distinctiveness as Jews.

In short, the line of criticism in 2.23 is probably to acknowledge much that appeared admirable in the religious praxis of the Colossian Jews here in view, but with the added final rejoinder that such severity to the body can be just another form of pandering to the flesh (cf. 1 Cor. 13.3). This further variation on Paul's σῶμα–σάρξ theme suggests a subtle interplay in the writer's thought between the fleshly body of the Christ (1.22), the stripping off of the flesh in Christ's death (1.22; 2.11), the circumcision of those (Gentiles) uncircumcised in flesh (2.11, 13), and the failing of those (Jews), albeit circumcised in flesh (whose flesh was stripped off in circumcision), who were nevertheless still gratifying the flesh (2.23).

3. The Cosmic Body

3.1. The third category brings us back to to the first line of 1.18, καὶ αὐτός ἐστιν ἡ κεφαλὴ τοῦ σώματος τῆς ἐκκλησίας. If the last two words are additions to the line (as most believe), then the original meaning would be clear, and entirely consistent with what has gone before. For the likening of the cosmos to a body is very ancient in Greek thought, the cosmos understood as an ensouled and rationally controlled entity. Most often cited are the *Timaeus*, where Plato speaks of God constructing τὸ τοῦ παντὸς σῶμα (31b, 32a) and of τὸ τοῦ κόσμου σῶμα (32c); and the Orphic fragment 168 which describes Zeus as the 'head' (κεφαλή) of the cosmos.[29] As might be expected, this way of envisaging the cosmos also penetrated Hellenistic Judaism, or

29. O. Kern, *Orphicorum Fragmenta* (Berlin: Weidmann, 1922), p. 201. See e.g. E. Lohmeyer, *Philipper, Kolosser und Philemon* (MeyerK; Göttingen: Vandenhoeck & Ruprecht, 1930), p. 62 n.1; J. Dupont, *Gnosis: La connaissance religieuse dans les Epîtres de Saint Paul* (Paris: Gabalda, 1949), pp. 431-44; Lohse, *Colossians*, p. 53; Gnilka, *Kolosserbrief*, p. 68; A.J.M. Wedderburn, in A.T. Lincoln and A.J.M. Wedderburn, *The Theology of the Later Pauline Letters* (Cambridge: Cambridge University Press, 1993), p. 17. E. Schweizer, *TDNT*, VII, pp. 1029-30, 1032, 1035, 1037-38, sums up his careful analysis of the data: 'Undoubtedly, then, in NT days there is identification of the cosmos and God, and undoubtedly too the cosmos is regarded as the body which is directed by the supreme God as world-soul or head' (pp. 1037-38).

at least Philo's philosophical theology, influenced as he was to such an extent by Platonic-Stoic thought in every aspect of his reflections on reality. So, for example, a human being like the world 'consists of body and reasonable soul' (*Rer. Div. Her.* 155); heaven in the cosmos is like a soul in a body (*Abr.* 272). And the Logos (divine reason) is the head of this body, of all things (*Som.* 1.128; *Qu. Ex.* 2.117).[30]

In an original hymn (lacking the last two words), then, the imagery would be a variation on what has already been said, identifying the one praised as being over the body, ruler of the cosmos, without posing that idea as in any degree of tension with the correlated thought of the Logos as pervading the body. And as applied to Christ the significance attached to Christ would be little different from that already discussed in 1.15-17. In other words, here would be a most striking variation in the σῶμα-theme—the body of Christ not merely as the church, not merely as his physical body on the cross, but also (or even) as the cosmos itself. The Christology had already been prepared for in Hellenistic Judaism by the substantial reflection on the figures of Wisdom and Logos.[31] But when set alongside the earlier and more typically Pauline use of 'the body of Christ' motif the further leap in thought is astonishing.

To be sure, some dispute the suggestion that 'the body (of Christ)' here is being (still) identified with the cosmos. For them the addition of τῆς ἐκκλησίας has completely altered the thought; the reference is exclusively to the body, the church.[32] But did the writer (Paul or whoever) intend such an abrupt jump within the hymn, given that the πάντα/τὰ πάντα leitmotif so prominent in 1.15-17 is continued into 1.18b-20? The idea that Christ is 'head of every ruler and authority' (2.10) stands in direct continuity with the idea that Christ is head of the cosmic body (2.18) which includes the 'rulers and authorities' of 2.16. And Eph. 1.22-23, which could justifiably be regarded as the earliest commentary on Col. 1.18a, did not hesitate to push forward with the

---

30. See H. Hegermann, *Die Vorstellung vom Schöpfungsmittler im hellenistischen Judentum und Urchristentum* (TU, 82; Berlin: Akademie, 1961), pp. 58-67. Schweizer, *TDNT*, VII, pp. 1054-55 is more cautious on the latter point (also Schweizer, *Colossians*, p. 58 n. 9) but Lohse, *Colossians*, p. 54 is more confident.

31. See e.g. my *Christology in the Making* (London: SCM Press, 2nd edn, 1989), pp. 163-96, 213-30.

32. So particularly O'Brien, *Colossians*, pp. 49-50; F.F. Bruce, *Colossians, Philemon and Ephesians* (NICNT; Grand Rapids: Eerdmans, 1984), p. 66.

idea of the church as the cosmic body of Christ.[33]

It will not do, therefore, simply to say that the earlier Pauline theology of the 'church' has been thrust into the hymn and has radically modified it without suffering any modification itself. On the contrary, in what may seem a rather forced fashion, the church has been equated with the body of the universe (τὰ πάντα). In which case the way is opened up to the idea of the church as the church universal, and not only so, but identified, moreover, with the cosmic body of which Christ is head (Eph. 1.22-23). This suggests that the church under Christ's headship is being consciously depicted as the microcosm which is to mirror the divinely ordered cosmos, the coherence of Christ's headship over the church and his priority over all things indicating that one ought to reflect the other or provide a model for the other. As the creative power of divine wisdom is now defined in terms of Christ, so the cosmos of divine purpose can/ should) now be defined in terms of the church.

3.2. This is probably the point at which to refer to 2.9 (ἐν αὐτῷ κατοικεῖ πᾶν πλήρωμα τῆς θεότητος σωματικῶς), since it echoes so closely the earlier thought of the hymn as expressed in 1.19 (ἐν αὐτῷ εὐδόκησεν πᾶν τὸ πλήρωμα κατοικῆσαι). Without labouring the point, the thought here, as in 1.15-20, is thoroughly Jewish in character.

It is true that a cosmological reference for πλήρωμα as such is not attested before this time; the word is never taken up in this connection by Philo, usually a sure guide to contemporary philosophic usage in the wider Hellenistic world. However, the idea of God or his Spirit as filling the world is another way of expressing the divine rationality which permeates the world in Stoic thought (Seneca, *Ben.* 4.8.2, 'nihil ab illo vacat, opus suum ipse implet', 'nothing is void of him [God], he himself fills all his work'; Aelius Aristides, *Or.* 45.21, Zeus τὸ πᾶν πεπλήρωκε). And again, as we might expect in the light of 1.15-17, the same language was used in Hellenistic Judaism of divine Wisdom. Thus, in Wis. 1.6-7, 'Wisdom is a kindly spirit...Because the Spirit of the Lord has filled the world (πεπλήρωκεν τὴν οἰκουμένην)'. Philo quite often uses similar phrases: 'God (who) has filled/fills all things' (πάντα πεπλήρωκεν ὁ θεός and πάντα πεπληρωκὼς ὁ θεός) (e.g. *Leg. All.* 3.4; *Gig.* 47; *Conf.* 136; *Mos.* 2.238). At the same time, we should

33. On Eph. 1.22-23 see particularly A.T. Lincoln, *Ephesians* (WBC, 42; Dallas: Word Books, 1990), pp. 66-82.

by no means attribute such conceptuality solely to the influence of wider (Stoic) thought, since it is already present in Jer. 23.24 ('Do I not fill heaven and earth? says the Lord'), not to mention Isa. 6.3 and Ps. 139.7; cf. also *Ep. Arist.* 132 ('God is one and his power is manifest through all things, every place filled with his sovereign power').[34] So too the thought of divine indwelling (κατοικέω) in human beings is also familiar in Jewish thought (Wis. 1.4, wisdom; *T. Zeb.* 8.2 and *T. Ben.* 6.4, God/the Lord; *1 En.* 49.3, the Spirit; so also Eph. 3.17, Christ). The claims made in both passages regarding πᾶν (τὸ) πλήρωμα are very similar. In 2.9 the only modification to the language, apart from the change in tense, is the addition of τῆς θεότητος and σωματικῶς (both *hapax legomena* in biblical Greek). The former was sufficiently familiar in literary Greek to denote the nature or essence of deity, that which constitutes deity.[35] The only difference on this point, then, is that the divine fulness which indwelt and continues to indwell (κατοικεῖ) Christ is expressed in more abstract terms.

The latter addition (σωματικῶς), however, is more interesting for us, since it reinforces the encounterable reality of the indwelling: as the human σῶμα was what enables the person to be in relationship with other persons, so the somatic character of this indwelling meant that God could be encountered directly in and through this particular human being. Here as in 1.19 (and as with the use of the adjective in Lk. 3.22) σωματικῶς underscores the accessibility (come-at-ableness) of the divine epiphany,[36] and can hardly refer to anything other than Jesus' life on earth, though including his death (as the next few verses imply). At the same time the present tense indicates this function of Jesus as ongoing: Christ in his historical embodiment still brings fully to focus the character of deity.[37] In all this a common concern for access to the

---

34. See further Dupont, *Gnosis*, pp. 469-670; G. Delling, *TDNT*, VI, pp. 288-89; N. Kehl, *Der Christushymnus im Kolosserbrief* (SBM, 1; Stuttgart: Katholisches Bibelwerk, 1967), pp. 116-25; J. Ernst, *Pleroma und Pleroma Christi* (Regensburg: Pustet, 1970), pp. 26-36. This background would be sufficient to explain why the term could be introduced here without explanation, despite, e.g., M. Dibelius and H. Greeven, *Kolosser, Epheser, Philemon* (HNT, 12; Tübingen: Mohr, 1953), p. 18.

35. BAGD, *s.v.* θεότης; for the distinction from θειότης see Lightfoot, *Colossians*, p. 179. The later christology of 'divine nature' and 'essence' is clearly prepared for, but is by no means yet present.

36. Cf. the data in Lohse, *Colossians*, p. 100 n. 46.

37. See particularly Lightfoot, *Colossians*, p. 180 and Moule, *Colossians*, pp. 92-94.

ultimate reality is presupposed; to be a Christian is to recognize Christ as the point and means of that access.

Not to be ignored is the further variation on the theme of 'body', probably in deliberate counterpoint with 'the body of flesh' (2.11): in terms that foreshadow the Fourth Evangelist's theology of Christ's glorification, the embodiment of divine fulness is presented as one with the crucified body of flesh. To take the word, in contrast, as a reference to the body = the church[38] is a too simple solution which diminishes the richness of the play on the term.

4. *The Eschatological Body*

The only remaining σῶμα reference to be considered is 2.17, a reference that stands completely on its own in the New Testament: ἅ ἐστιν σκιὰ τῶν μελλόντων, τὸ δὲ σῶμα τοῦ Χριστοῦ. The language is ultimately Platonic, but here, as in so much of the cosmic theology in §3, it is probably drawn from the Hellenistic Judaism which we find most clearly expressed in Philo. Basic to Plato's view of reality was the distinction between the heavenly original and the earthly copy, the former being the true reality, the latter, even in its physical objectivity, only a 'shadow' of the idea(l) or archetype. Philo makes a fair use of the term shadow (σκιά) in a number of variations of this Platonic distinction (e.g. *Leg. All.* 3.100-103; *Plant.* 27; *Abr.* 119-20). Most significant is the fact that he sets σκιά over against σῶμα, as name to that which it represents (πρᾶγμα) (*Decal.* 82), or as copy to archetype (ἀρχετύπος) (*Migr.* 12); or again, 'the letter is to the oracle as the shadow to the substance (σκιάς τινας ὡσανεὶ σωμάτων) and the higher values therein are what really and truly exist' (*Conf.* 190, LCL translation).[39]

The contrast intended here is evidently along similar lines,[40] but with two important modifications. The first is signalled by the τῶν μελλόντων, 'the things to come'.[41] This no doubt is a reflection of Jewish eschatology in which the longed for new age can be described as ὁ αἰὼν μέλλων, 'the age to come' (as in Isa. 9.6 LXX v. 1; Mt. 12.32;

38. Masson, *Colossiens*, p. 124; Lohse, *Colossians*, p. 101; Gnilka, *Kolosserbrief*, p. 129.

39. See also S. Schulz, *TDNT*, VIII, p. 396; Lohse, *Colossians*, p. 116; Gnilka, *Kolosserbrief*, p. 147.

40. Gundry however regards σῶμα here as 'physically substantial' (p. 42).

41. For this use of the participle see BAGD, *s.v.* μέλλω 2.

Eph. 1.21). By the addition of this phrase an essentially static Platonic dualism (between heaven and earth) has been transformed into an expression of Jewish eschatological hope. The strongest parallel is in Hebrews, where precisely the same amalgam of Platonic cosmology and Jewish eschatology has been carried through most effectively. So most noticeably in Heb. 10.1: 'For the law has a shadow of the good things to come instead of the (true) form of these things (σκιὰν τῶν μελλόντων ἀγαθῶν, οὐκ αὐτὴν τὴν εἰκόνα τὼν πραγμάτων)' (see also 2.5; 6.5; 9.11; 13.14).[42]

The second modification is christological: the reality, the substance thus foreshadowed is 'of Christ, belongs to the Christ'. The Christ (the definite article should be given due weight here) is the fulfilment of Jewish eschatological hope. Here the closest parallel is in Paul, Rom. 5.14—Adam as the 'type of the one to come (τύπος τοῦ μέλλοντος)' (Christ). In contrast to Platonic-Philonic thought, it is the Christ in all the concrete bloodiness of the cross who is the true reality. The amalgam thus echoes the Christology of the earlier hymn (1.15-20): Christ embodies the heavenly reality that lies beyond and sustains the perceptible cosmos. But, as in Hebrews, it is also affirmed that Christ is the substance to the shadow of the food laws and feasts by which Jewish social life and time were structured (2.16), he is the reality that casts its shadow backward in time; they are the provisional, inferior copies whose inadequacy is now evident in the light of the real.

In short, in this last fascinating variation on the σῶμα-theme the whole dimension of time is brought in to supplement the different interplays between head and body, body and flesh, and cosmos and church.

5. *The Body of Christ*

The final question has to be whether all these variations actually make up a single theme. Are they quite separate themes whose use of the common term (σῶμα) is coincidental? Or do they make up a coherent

---

42. Schweizer (*Colossians*, pp. 156-57) has no doubt that 'Paul, in speaking of the law, could never use the relatively innocuous image of the shadow of that which is to come'. But the images of the law in Gal. 3.23-24 and 4.1-7 are not so negative as is usually assumed to be the case (see my *Galatians* [BNTC; London: Black, 1993]); in fact they are quite complementary to the image here. See also Lohmeyer, *Kolosser*, pp. 122-23, Scott, *Colossians*, p. 52 and Bruce, *Colossians*, p. 116.

theology of the body of Christ? It would seem likely that a positive answer can be given to this question.

This is suggested by the fact that all four themes overlap and interweave with each other in some degree. We have already noted that the idea of the body as church (§1) is deliberately linked to the idea of the cosmic body (§3). But 2.9 makes a further link with the body of Christ's earthly life (§3), which in turn links up, by means of the repeated talk of Christ's headship over every ruler and authority (2.10), with the very different thought of Christ's 'body of flesh' given to death (2.11) (§2). And the thought of Christ as the substance (σῶμα) to the shadow which is Israel's ancestral traditions (2.16-17), relates to the idea of the cosmic Wisdom-Logos which is the solid reality behind the imperfections of the visible world, as well as to the model of apocalyptic hope fulfilled in Christ (§4).

So too we can speak of what appears to be a sequence of deliberate plays on the σῶμα–σάρξ theme. First between 1.22 (§2) and 1.24 (§1), where the reconciliation accomplished in Christ's body of flesh is complemented by Paul's filling up in his flesh what is lacking of the afflictions of Christ for the sake of Christ's body, the church. Then more faintly between 2.11 and 2.13, where again Christ's putting off his body of flesh, the circumcision of the Jewish Messiah, proves to be an effective circumcision for the uncircumcision of Gentile flesh. Again between 2.17 and 2.18 and 2.19, where the reality (σῶμα) of Christ stands in some contrast to 'the mind of flesh'—the mind being the very medium by which the embodied human should in Greek thought be able to communicate with the realm of substance and reality—and finds its true expression in the church, supported and held together from Christ its head. Finally in 2.23 the criticism of a severity to the body that is intended to promote participation in heavenly worship (2.18), but which only serves to gratify a flesh hungry to maintain its ethnic distinctiveness.

The themes of this 'body-theology' thus become clear. It has several strands.

1. The body of Christ is the key that unlocks the mystery of the cosmos and of God's purpose for all things (1.26-27). If the universe is to be understood as an organism, a body, then the divine rationale (wisdom) that permeates it and makes sense of it is most clearly seen in Christ, that is, in his body (1.15-17). Not the same body, of course, but as different embodiments of the same divine wisdom. Alternatively expressed, when the rationale behind creation and history

To Tell the Mystery

is sought, Christ is the (eschatological) reality that gives body (= substance) to what otherwise are but shadows, the imperfect attempts at human rationalization (2.17).

2. The non-cosmic body of Christ, in the first instance, means his body of flesh, his physical body done to death on the cross. In contrast to a heavenly existence in the form of Wisdom (1.15-17), and in contrast to a σῶμα identified either with the universe as a whole or with the church in particular (1.18a), the σῶμα with which Christ achieved his act of reconciliation was merely that of one single frail human being (the 'of flesh' ensures that this σῶμα could never be confused with the σῶμα of 1.18). That is the profundity of the paradox proclaimed by the first Christians: that the wisdom behind and permeating the universe is to be most clearly seen and its character most clearly perceived in the cross. It is precisely for this reason that his death can be seen as the reconciliation of all things (1.20), precisely for this reason that the cross can be seen as a victory over hostile forces in the cosmos (2.15). The fulness of deity is thus most tangibly (bodily) manifested in this Christ (2.9). In the body of Christ creation and redemption are one.

3. The body of Christ, in the second instance, is the church. Again not the same body, but correlated with the cosmic body as being that corporate organism of human integration and interdependence which should express the divinely intended working of the organisms of creation and society. This will only be possible (1) if Christ is recognized as head over both (1.18), his embodiment of the fulness of deity not only giving him priority over all the forces that may influence human society, but also making a share in that fulness possible for the church (2.9-10), and (2) if the necessary inspiration and enabling are drawn from him (2.19). It is because Christians share in a body that transmutes, as it were, from cosmic body, through body of flesh done to death, to his body the church, that their conversion has cosmic and eschatological implications and even more astonishing corollaries can be drawn out for the church subsequently in Eph. 1.22-23.

4. Nor is the physical body of Christ to be identified simply with his body, the church. Again it is more a matter of two different embodiments of the same reality—the same forgiving, reconciling love embodied both in the cross and in Christian relationships (3.13). At the same time, however, there is an important body–flesh interplay in that the destruction of Christ's flesh, which was the death of his physical body to reconcile all things (1.20, 22), is reflected in the sufferings of

Paul's flesh for the sake Christ's body, the church (1.24)—his body of flesh for us, our flesh for his body. In other words, if the body, the church, is to be the body of Christ there must be the same commitment in killing off that which is of the earth (3.5) as Christ displayed on the cross.

5. For Colossians (as elsewhere in the New Testament) the test case for the reconciliation and integration of creation and humanity achieved in the body of Christ is the reconciliation of Jew and Gentile across the great ethnic and religious divide that separated them. In particular this means that the solution to the 'uncircumcision of the flesh' (Gentile status outside 'the circumcision') (2.13) is not circumcision of the flesh, but the circumcision of Christ, the stripping off not merely of an individual male foreskin but of Christ's whole body of flesh (2.11). To maintain that 'circumcision of the flesh' still counts with God is just another form of pandering to the flesh (2.23), a keeping on rather than a stripping off of the old ways of perceiving creation and redemption (3.9). In contrast, where the purpose of creation is being forwarded and humanity being shaped in God's image, such distinctions as those between Greek and Jew, circumcision and uncircumcision, are no longer of any significance (3.10-11).

EVERYTHING THAT RISES MUST CONVERGE:
PAUL'S WORD FROM THE LORD

J. Ramsey Michaels

1. *1 Thessalonians 4.15*

In what is probably his earliest letter, the Apostle Paul appeals to a 'word of the Lord' as a source of comfort to those grieving over loved ones who had died (1 Thess. 4.15a). Scholars have been unable to agree on whether he is referring to a saying of 'the Lord' Jesus preserved in oral or written gospel tradition (as in 1 Cor. 7.10-11; 9.14; 11.23-26), or to a prophetic utterance given by Paul or someone else in the name of 'the Lord' in a Christian congregation or by Paul for the first time in this letter. Nor have they reached agreement on whether to look for Paul's 'word of the Lord' in vv. 15b, 16-17, or both. In general those who have looked to the gospel tradition have done so not in relation to Paul's statement in v. 15b, 'that we, the living who are left until the coming of the Lord, will not precede those who have fallen asleep', but in relation to his explicit description of Christ's coming and the resurrection of the dead in vv. 16-17:

> For the Lord himself will come down from heaven with a shout, with the voice of the archangel and the trumpet of God, and the dead in Christ will rise first. Then we the living who are left will be caught up together with them in the clouds to meet the Lord in the air. And so we will be with the Lord always.

The common assumption has been that this vivid scenario for the Parousia (vv. 16-17) is what is based on a 'word of the Lord', while the statement that 'we the living...will not precede those who have fallen asleep' (v. 15b) is the conclusion Paul has drawn from it to address the problem at Thessalonica of loved ones who had died.[1] Attention has

---

1. See, for example, D.E. Aune, *Prophecy in Early Christianity and the Ancient Mediterranean World* (Grand Rapids: Eerdmans, 1983), pp. 253-55; also

focused, consequently, on a number of distinctly eschatological passages in the Gospels, for example, those announcing the coming of the Son of Man on the clouds, or with his angels (Mk 8.38; 13.26-27; or 14.62; Mt. 25.31), those emphasizing the suddenness of his coming (Mt. 24.36-44, 45-51; 25.1-13; Lk. 12.35-46; 17.22-37), those in which Jesus promises his disciples that 'I will return' (Jn 14.3, 28; 21.22), and that they will see him (Jn 16.16, 22) or be taken to be with him (Jn 14.3), or that his voice will raise the dead on the last day (Jn 5.25, 28; 6.39, 40, 44, 54). There is nothing close to a consensus as to which of these eschatological passages, if any, Paul had in mind.

Another alternative presents itself when we recognize that, strictly speaking, what Paul claims to be saying 'by the word of the Lord' is v. 15b, and that alone: 'that we, the living who are left until the coming of the Lord, will not precede those who have fallen asleep'. If his 'word of the Lord' is linked specifically to v. 15b, then vv. 16-17 (introduced by ὅτι) become simply an elaboration and further explanation of this brief statement of a principle. This is recognized by a number of scholars, including Robert Gundry, who identifies Paul's 'word of the Lord' with the promise of Jesus to Martha in Jn 11.25-26: 'I am the resurrection and the life. He who believes in me will live, even though he dies; and whoever lives and believes in me will never die.' Gundry reconstructs the original form of the saying as 'The one who has died will rise, and the one who is alive will never die'. He concludes that

> Paul does not formally quote that word in one place, but takes it up in bits
> and pieces throughout 1 Thess. 4.15-17, makes revisions according to his
> textual needs, and adds the fanfare, which details exactly how God will
> bring believers with Jesus and contributes to Paul's portrayal of an impe-
> rial visit in the hellenistic style.[2]

The advantage of Gundry's proposed 'word of the Lord' over most others is that it refers to two distinct groups, and that the groups are

C.A. Wanamaker, *The Epistles to the Thessalonians: A Commentary on the Greek Text* (NIGTC; Grand Rapids: Eerdmans, 1990), p. 171.

2.   'The Hellenization of Dominical Tradition and Christianization of Jewish Tradition in the Eschatology of 1–2 Thessalonians', *NTS* 33 (1987), p. 165. Gundry lists, but rejects, the following other possibilities: Mk 8.35; 9.1; 12.26-27; 13.27, 30; Mt. 10.39; 16.25; 19.28; 20.1-16; 22.32; 23.36; 24.31, 34; 25.6; Lk. 9.24, 27; 11.50-51; 17.33; 20.37-38; Jn 5.25; 6.39-40 (p. 164). An earlier advocate of Jn 11.25-26 as Paul's 'word of the Lord' was P. Nepper-Christensen, 'Das verborgene Herrenwort. Eine Untersuchung über 1. Thess. 4,13-18', *ST* 19 (1965), pp. 136-54.

precisely those who have died and those who are still alive. Probably its greatest barrier to wide acceptance is its assumption that a distinctly Johannine saying of Jesus is in fact primitive, possibly authentic, yet was nowhere picked up in the synoptic tradition. Gundry describes his proposal as the 'best (and, ironically, least regarded)' of the many proposed identifications of Paul's 'word of the Lord'.[3]

More to the point than scholarly fashion is the fact that the latter part of Gundry's reconstruction ('the one who is alive will never die') is precisely the kind of saying that could have created the problem at Thessalonica over dead loved ones in the first place. Those who took such a saying literally, whether as found in Jn 11.26, or 8.51, or any number of other Johannine passages, would be ill prepared to cope with deaths in their Christian communities. Is it possible that Paul is rubbing salt in the wounds by alluding to the troublesome text itself—while balancing it with its companion saying and natural antidote, 'the one who has died will rise' (11.25b)? This would be a bold move indeed, but would require a more explicit treatment of his text than Paul in fact provides. Certainly the rhetoric of the couplet, 'The one who has died will rise, and the one who is alive will never die', places more emphasis on the second clause than on the first, and such emphasis would only tend to heighten the Thessalonians' anxiety. Or was Paul even expecting his readers to grasp a connection between what he says here and a saying of Jesus which both they and he remembered? Is it possible that his reference to a 'word of the Lord' is merely a private reminder to himself of the tradition on which he is relying? Gundry's proposal has merits that other proposals do not, yet it is not quite conclusive and (rightly or wrongly) is unlikely to persuade most interpreters. What it does help establish as a firm point of departure is the recognition that

> Paul's main point, in fact, the *only* point which he identifies as coming from the word of the Lord and which he mentions immediately after referring to the word of the Lord [is v. 15b], 'that we who are alive, who remain till the coming of the Lord, will not precede the ones who have fallen asleep'.[4]

Another important recent article limiting Paul's word from the Lord to v. 15b is that of Helmut Merklein.[5] In contrast to Gundry, Merklein

---

3. 'The Hellenization of Dominical Tradition', p. 164.
4. 'The Hellenization of Dominical Tradition', p. 165.
5. 'Der Theologe als Prophet: Zur Funktion prophetischen Redens im

gives up any search for a link to the gospel tradition.[6] He concludes that Paul has in mind a prophetic word, not someone else's but his own. Thus the expression, 'For this we tell you by a word of the Lord' in 1 Thess. 4.15a is equivalent to 'Look, I tell you a mystery' in 1 Cor. 15.51a, introducing a similar kind of pronouncement ('We will not all fall asleep, but we will all be transformed', 1 Cor. 15.51b). Merklein argues for this view in the context of a whole series of suggested parallels between 1 Thess. 4.13-18 and 1 Cor. 15.51-58.[7]

There is much to be said for Merklein's contention that Paul himself functions as a prophet in these passages, but it does not follow that his prophetic insight must be entirely independent of the gospel tradition. Moreover, if Paul's 'word of the Lord' is confined to v. 15, there is no reason why he had to have had a distinctly *eschatological* saying of Jesus in mind. The core of v. 15b is not the nature of 'the coming of the Lord' but the simple assertion that the living 'will not precede' (οὐ μὴ φθάσωμεν) those who have died. Paul is asserting a kind of parity or equality between the two groups. In determining his 'word of the Lord', therefore, it may be helpful to look for a pronouncement of Jesus emphasizing equality among those who will enter the Kingdom of God.

This is where the title of the present essay comes in. I lifted the title directly from Flannery O'Connor's second collection of short stories, *Everything That Rises Must Converge*. I do not feel guilty about this because O'Connor, one of my favorite writers, herself took the title from one of her favorite writers, the Roman Catholic paleontologist and philosopher Pierre Teilhard de Chardin.[8] I am not of course claiming O'Connor in support of my proposed interpretation of 1 Thess. 4.15. What I am suggesting is that people like Robert Gundry and myself,

theologischen Diskurs des Paulus', *NTS* 38 (1992), pp. 402-29.

6. Merklein ('Theologe als Prophet', p. 413 n. 37) lists a number of suggested identifications of Paul's 'word of the Lord' (including Mt. 10.39; 16.25, 28; 24.31, 34; 25.6; 26.64; Lk. 13.30; Jn 5.25; 6.39-40; 11.25-26), but dismisses them all with the comment that 'Die Vielzahl der Stellen, die vorgeschlagen wurden, unterstreicht nur die Fragwürdigkeit des Postulats'.

7. Merklein, 'Theologe als Prophet', pp. 414-18.

8. For the quotation from Teilhard from which the title was taken, see R. Wood, 'The Heterodoxy of Flannery O'Connor's Book Reviews', *The Flannery O'Connor Bulletin* 5 (1976), p. 26. 'Remain true to yourselves, but move ever upward toward greater consciousness and greater love! At the summit you will find yourselves united with all those who, from every direction, have made the same ascent. For everything that rises must converge.' Here we are very far from both the New Testament and

who work as professionals in biblical studies, can learn a great deal from fiction writers like O'Connor who in their own way are interpreters of the Bible—even when they are dealing (as they usually are) with no specific text but with many texts at once—all in the context of their first priority of telling a good story. In Flannery O'Connor's case, I have found in a number of instances that her sensitivity to the Christian gospel in general has opened the door for me to new readings both of Paul and of Jesus. Her fiction affords me a springboard from which to engage my friend Bob Gundry on a classic Pauline text of great interest to us both.

The theme of several of O'Connor's stories in *Everything That Rises Must Converge* is social reversal, especially in the context of distinctions of race and class in the American South. This is evident in the story for which the collection is named, in another well-known story called 'Revelation', and in the very title of one of her lesser efforts, 'The Lame Shall Enter First'. In the face of disconcerting social change, Mrs Chestny in 'Everything That Rises Must Converge' laments that 'the bottom rail is on top'. Of the black people in her city she says, 'They should rise, yes, but on their own side of the fence'.[9] Mrs Turpin, the protagonist in 'Revelation', shouts at her God in defiance, 'Put that bottom rail on top. There'll still be a top and bottom.'[10] The echoes of Jesus' ministry, where the status of rich and poor, sick and well, clean and unclean, righteous and sinner, were reversed by Jesus' words and actions, are unmistakable. The question raised by such stories is whether any meeting, or reconciliation, ever takes place between the poor who are lifted up and the rich who are pulled down from their places of privilege, or whether the two groups are like ships passing in the night. Surely the title, *Everything That Rises Must Converge*, suggests O'Connor's hopes for healing and reconciliation.

2. *Matthew 20.16*

One pronouncement in particular in the gospel tradition speaks both to Flannery O'Connor's questions and to the search for Paul's 'word of

Flannery O'Connor, and Wood suggests (quite plausibly) that O'Connor's title 'looks very much like a parody of the cosmic optimism' of this philosopher rather than a serious use of his language.

9.   F. O'Connor, *The Complete Stories* (New York: Farrar, Straus & Geroux, 1972), pp. 407-408.

10.   O'Connor, *Complete Stories*, p. 507.

the Lord'. This is the statement of Jesus at the end of the parable of the vineyard workers in Matthew, 'So the last will be first, and the first last' (Mt. 20.16). The saying occurs in slightly differing forms in all three synoptic Gospels. Mk 10.31 has it, 'But many first will be last, and [the] last first'. Mt. 19.30 follows Mark almost verbatim, 'But many first will be last, and last first'. Lk. 13.30 reads, 'And see, there are last who will be first, and first who will be last'.[11] There is a subtle difference between the wording of Mt. 20.16 and that of the three other occurrences of the saying (including Matthew's own alternate version of it in 19.30). Aside from Mt. 20.16, the Gospel writers have taken the pronouncement as having to do with the *reversal* of expectations in the kingdom of God. The outsiders will be on the inside and the insiders will be left out. The kingdom will belong not to the righteous but the sinners (for the idea, see Mt. 21.31b; Lk. 7.29-30), not to the rich but the poor (see Lk. 6.20-26), not to the Jews but the Gentiles (see Mt. 8.11-12 and Lk. 13.28-29, the latter followed immediately by Luke's version of the saying in question).

When the saying is understood in this way, it always includes a qualifying word such as 'many' (Mk 10.31; Mt. 19.30), or else finds expression in a qualified manner (as in Lk. 13.30, 'there are [those who are] last who will be first, and [those who are] first who will be last'). The qualification is necessary because when taken literally, the reversal cannot be total or absolute. Jesus cannot be made to say that *all* the righteous will be lost while *all* the sinners are saved, or that *all* Jews will be lost and *all* Gentiles saved, or that *all* the rich are lost and *all* the poor are saved, or that *only* tax collectors and prostitutes will enter the Kingdom. This is the difficulty with Gundry's remark in his commentary on Matthew that '"Many" does not distinguish people inside each category, but describes the people in each category as numerous. Thus "many" is almost synonymous with "all"'.[12] I am suggesting rather that the saying as found in Mark, Luke and Mt. 19.30 is more aptly taken as meaning not total reversal, but simply that there will be a great many surprises when the kingdom of God comes.

Mt. 20.16 is different. There is no qualifying 'many'. If there is reversal here, the reversal is absolute. But the parable to which the

---

11. Notice that Mt. 20.1-16 occurs on Gundry's list of rejected possibilities (see above, n. 2), pp. while Lk. 13.30 is found on Merklein's list (n. 6).

12. *Matthew: A Commentary on his Literary and Theological Art* (Grand Rapids: Eerdmans, 1982), p. 395.

saying is attached suggests that reversal is *not* the point. The story of the vineyard workers does *not* end with some of the workers being fired or receiving no wages while others are given a partnership in the vineyard. Instead, all the workers received *the same* wages. When wages were paid at the end of the day, the owner began with the 'last' ones hired, and then went on to reward those who had come 'first' (20.8). The complaint of those hired first was that 'these last worked one hour, and you have made them *equal to us* (ἴσους ἡμῖν) who have borne the burden and heat of the day' (20.12). The point of the story, therefore, and consequently the point of the saying that follows it in Matthew, is not reversal but equality. In a purely formal sense the owner had paid the wages of 'the last' first, and 'the first' last (v. 8), but the outcome was that they all were given the same amount. To Matthew, the import of the concluding pronouncement that 'the last will be first, and the first last' (v. 16) is that all the old distinctions between 'first' and 'last' will be abolished in the kingdom of heaven. There will be no 'first' or 'last' any more, none who are intrinsically advantaged or disadvantaged. Everyone—rich or poor, sick or well, righteous or sinner, Jew or Gentile—is on the same plane before God, and all will be judged equitably on the basis of what they have done. Equality, not reversal, is the point of this saying in Matthew—at least in the context of the parable of the vineyard workers.

In the canonical Gospels, Mt. 20.16 seems to stand alone in interpreting the saying about the first and the last in this way, but his interpretation surfaces again in the *Gospel of Thomas*. This is the more surprising in view of the fact that the form of the pronouncement in the *Gospel of Thomas* includes the qualifying 'many' found in Mark and Luke. According to *Gospel of Thomas* 4,[13]

> Jesus said, 'The man old in days will not hesitate to ask a small child seven days old about the place of life, and he will live. For many who are first will become last, *and they will become one and the same* [italics mine].

Equality has become in the *Gospel of Thomas* virtual identity. Bertil Gaertner, one of the earlier commentators on *Gospel of Thomas*, remarked in 1961 that

---

13. *The Nag Hammadi Library in English* (San Francisco: Harper & Row, 1988), p. 126. The corresponding pronouncement in POxy 654 adds the clause, 'and the last first', as in the canonical Gospels. See E. Hennecke and W. Schneemelcher, *New Testament Apocrypha*, I (Philadelphia: Westminster, 1963), p. 102.

What is...strange is that the meaning of the words in *Logion* 4 is the opposite of that of the New Testament text. In the New Testament, the despised and the least of all shall be the first on 'that day', whilst the first and greatest in the world shall be the last. In *Logion* 4 it is vice versa: the first shall be the last, and as this is the same as the creation of a unity, these are the ones who will be saved, 'and they shall be a single one'.[14]

As we have seen, the gap between the perspective of *Gospel of Thomas* and that of the canonical Gospels is not so wide as Gaertner thinks. His view takes account of the accent on reversal in most forms of Jesus' saying, but does not do justice to the accent on equality in Mt. 20.16.

Another saying in *Gospel of Thomas* celebrates the abolishment of a whole range of this world's distinctions or dualities when the Kingdom of God comes:[15]

> Jesus saw infants being suckled. He said to his disciples, 'These infants being suckled are like those who enter the kingdom'. They said to him, 'Shall we then, as children, enter the kingdom?'

> Jesus said, 'When you make the two one, and when you make the inside like the outside, and the outside like the inside, and the above like the below, and when you make the male and the female one and the same, so that the male not be male nor the female female; and when you fashion eyes in place of an eye, and a hand in place of a hand, and a foot in place of a foot, and a likeness in place of a likeness; then you will enter [the kingdom]' (*Gos. Thom.* 22).

In light of *Logion* 4, and the reference to infants in both sayings, the compiler of the collection might easily have added in *Logion* 22, 'When you make the first as the last', without changing the meaning.

---

14. *The Theology of the Gospel according to Thomas* (New York: Harper, 1961), p. 227. Because of his interpretation of *Gos. Thom.* 4 as a promise of salvation, Gaertner proposed that the saying's real New Testament parallel was Mk 9.35: 'If any one would be first, he must be last of all and servant of all'. He commented, 'This saying fits in better, for Logion 4 would then mean that "the first"—the old and wise, and those who have some position in the world—must become "the last", the smallest and least important in the world, "the suckling babes". But if they become "little", i.e., "Gnostics", they then reach salvation and unity can be created' (p. 227). But Gaertner's suggestion overlooks the longer form of the pronouncement in the Greek parallel in POxy 654 (see above, n. 13). Moreover, Mk 9.35 deals not with those who are 'first', but with those who *want* to be first.

15. *Nag Hammadi Library*, p. 129. For an early 'orthodox' interpretation of this saying, see 2 *Clem.* 6.2-6.

3. *The 'First and the Last' in a Pauline Context*

Paul too envisioned an end to the distinctions and dualities of the present world. According to Gal. 3.28, 'There is neither Jew nor Greek, there is neither slave nor free, there is no male and female; for you are all one in Christ Jesus'. According to Col. 3.11, 'There is no Greek and Jew, circumcision and uncircumcision, barbarian, Scythian, slave, free, but Christ is all, and in all'. Paul, like Jesus in the *Gospel of Thomas*, wants to break down barriers between various pairs of advantaged/ disadvantaged groups. Sometimes in doing so he echoes the familiar distinction between 'first' and 'last'. The gospel, he says, is 'the power of God to salvation, to the Jew *first*, and to the Greek' (Rom. 1.16). 'Trouble and distress', he claims, 'are on every human soul who does what is evil, the Jew *first*, and the Greek. Glory and honor and peace are on everyone who does what is good, the Jew *first*, and the Greek' (Rom. 2.9-10). The terminology of 'first'—and, implicitly, 'last'—is retained, possibly from the gospel tradition, but in the setting of a powerful emphasis on equity or equality.

Despite the terminology, Jew and Gentile are no longer related as 'first' and 'last' in any determinative sense, least of all chronologically. The point is not the same as in the book of Acts, where Paul's missionary strategy depended on going 'first' to the Jews and to the synagogue in every city he visited (see, for example, Acts 13.46, and compare the similar terminology used by Peter in Acts 3.26). Rather, Paul's overriding emphasis in Romans is that the gospel is 'the power of God to salvation' *both* to Jew and Gentile, and that judgment and blessing rest on Jew and Gentile alike, without distinction or favoritism. His conclusion to the matter is on the one hand, 'There is no distinction, for all have sinned and fall short of God's glory' (Rom. 3.22b-23), and on the other, 'There is no distinction of Jew and Greek, for the same Lord is over all' (Rom 10.12a). In Ephesians, Paul (or one of his followers) reflects on all this and concludes,

> For he is our peace, who made both one and broke the dividing wall, the hostility, in his flesh, and abolished the law's commands and decrees, so that he might create the two in himself into one new man by making peace, and reconcile both in one body to God through the cross, and by it put to death the hostility (Eph 2.14-16).

In 1 Thessalonians, because of certain anxieties in the congregation,

Paul turns his attention to a very different pair of advantaged–disadvantaged groups, the living and the dead. There is no disputing that the dead are the ultimately disadvantaged group—more disadvantaged than the poor, or sinners, or slaves, or women, or the Gentiles. One of Flannery O'Connor's lesser known stories has as its title, 'You Can't be any Poorer than Dead'.[16] But Paul, in light of the principle that 'the last will be first, and the first last', argues that neither group—the living or the dead—has an advantage over the other. The two stand on an equal footing before God.

The problem of the relationship of the many generations of the dead to the generation surviving to the end of the age was a familiar one in certain early Jewish apocalyptic writings, notably *4 Ezra* 5.42, where the Lord says in reply to Ezra's persistent questions,

> I shall liken my judgment to a circle; just as for those who are last there is no slowness, so for those who are first there is no haste (RSV).

So appropriate did this text seem to the situation addressed in 1 Thessalonians 4 that a German scholar over a century ago proposed it as the 'word of the Lord' to which Paul was referring in 4.15. His motive was to prove that 1 Thessalonians was written later than *4 Ezra* and was, consequently, inauthentic.[17] Clearly, the saying of Jesus, 'the last will be first, and the first last', lies much closer at hand. The text in *4 Ezra* suggests, however, that similar pronouncements were known in early Judaism, and interpreted in relation to the respective destinies of the living and the dead. Another example is *2 Bar.* 51.13:[18]

> For the first will receive the last, those whom they expected; and the last, those of whom they had heard that they had gone away.

In contrast to *4 Ezra* and *2 Baruch*, where the dead are 'the first' because they were the first to die, Paul assumes that the dead are 'the last' because they are the disadvantaged group. Paul, after all, is dealing not with dead generations of the past, but with the dead of his own time and of the Thessalonians' own community. His intent is not to quote verbatim Jesus' saying about the first and the last. Not a word of it, in fact, is visible in 1 Thess. 4.15. Paul's intent is rather to bring the

---

16. O'Connor, *Complete Stories*, pp. 292-310.
17. R. Steck, 'Das Herrenwort 1. Thess. 4,15', *Jahrbuch für protestantische Theologie* 13 (1883), pp. 509-23.
18. See J.H. Charlesworth (ed.), *The Old Testament Pseudepigrapha* (Garden City, NY: Doubleday, 1983), I, pp. 638.

pronouncement to bear on the specific problem at Thessalonica. As we have seen, the core of his application of the saying is the οὐ μὴ φθάσωμεν, 'will not precede', of v. 15b. The living will have no advantage over the dead at the Parousia.[19] Only when he adds his own further explanation in vv. 16-17 does Paul introduce (as an adverb) the word 'first' (πρῶτον) from the saying of Jesus: 'the dead in Christ will rise first'.[20]

Just as in the parable of the vineyard in Matthew, where wages were paid starting with the last and ending with the first, 'the last' have become 'the first' in a purely formal sense. But it does not matter to Paul's argument whether the living or the dead are literally to rise first at the Parousia. What matters above all is that the dead, just as surely as the living, will be there. Paul's real point is that the living and the dead are equal before God, and that the Parousia will prove it. The core of his further explanation of his 'word of the Lord' in vv. 16-17 is the phrase, 'together with them' (ἅμα σὺν αὐτοῖς, v. 17a). His encouragement of the Thessalonian believers depends on the notion that in the resurrection the living and the dead, 'the first and the last', will come together as one, even as both groups are united to Jesus Christ (cf. ἅμα σὺν αὐτῷ, 'together with him', in 5.10).

If Paul's 'word of the Lord' is indeed 'the last will be first, and the first last', then his interpretation of the saying corresponds to that of Mt. 20.16 and the *Gospel of Thomas*, and contrasts with that of Mark, Luke and Mt. 19.30. Yet the fact that even Matthew (in 19.30) and *Gospel of Thomas* testify to a qualified form of the saying ('*Many* who are first will be last, and the last first') suggests that this form of the pronouncement may be the more original. If so, then Jesus' own emphasis was

19. The notion of 'preceding', or having an advantage when the Kingdom of God comes, recalls again the *Gospel of Thomas*, this time Saying 3. 'Jesus said, "If those who lead you say to you, 'See, the kingdom is in the sky', then the birds of the sky will precede you. If they say to you, 'It is in the sea', then the fish will precede you. Rather, the kingdom is inside of you, and it is outside of you. When you come to know yourselves, then you will become known, and you will realize that it is you who are the sons of the living father. But if you will not know yourselves, you dwell in poverty and it is you who are that poverty."' Although this text has no direct bearing on the relation between the living and the dead, it is followed immediately by the pronouncement in *Gos. Thom.* 4 about the equality and unity of the first and the last.

20. Some Western manuscripts in v. 16 (the first hand of D, as well as F, G, the entire Latin tradition and Tertullian) read the substantive πρῶτοι, as in the Gospel tradition, instead of the adverb πρῶτον.

probably more on radical social reversal rather than on the ideal of equality or unity. That question, however, lies outside the scope of this paper.

In terms Flannery O'Connor would have understood, the point at issue is whether Mrs Turpin in the story, 'Revelation', was right when she shouted to God, 'Put that bottom rail on top. There'll still be a bottom and a top'. Quite clearly, O'Connor's own view was that Mrs Turpin was wrong, for in her final revelatory vision that gives the story its name, there was no bottom or top, no first or last:

> A visionary light settled in her eyes. She saw the streak as a vast swinging bridge extending upward from the earth through a field of living fire. Upon it a vast horde of souls were rumbling toward heaven...And bringing up the end of the procession was a tribe of people whom she recognized at once as those who, like herself and Claud, had always had a little of everything and the God-given wit to use it right. She leaned forward to observe them closer. They were marching behind the others with great dignity, accountable as they had always been for good order and common sense and respectable behavior. They alone were on key. Yet she could see by their shocked and altered faces that even their virtues were being burned away.

Radical reversal has taken place in Mrs Turpin's vision, but not as an end in itself. Its sole purpose is to bring about equality, in the sense of Mrs Turpin's realization of the common humanity and need of salvation she shared with blacks, with those she considered white trash, and with the 'battalions of freaks and lunatics' ahead of her in the procession, 'shouting and clapping and leaping like frogs'.[21] When the first becomes last, and the last first, the terms no longer have any meaning. This, Mrs Turpin learned, is how it will be in the kingdom of God.

Long before Mrs Turpin or Mrs Chestny, long before Flannery O'Connor or Pierre Teilhard de Chardin, the Apostle Paul knew that 'everything that rises must converge'. But unlike Teilhard de Chardin and the *Gospel of Thomas* (centuries apart and in very different ways), Paul did *not* make the principle into a new eschatology replacing the old.[22] Instead, he made it his way of articulating a very traditional Jewish

---

21. *Complete Stories*, p. 508.
22. On O'Connor's appropriation of the title from Teilhard de Chardin, Robert Fitzgerald comments significantly, 'It is a title taken in full respect and with profound and necessary irony. For Teilhard's vision of the "omega point" virtually at the end of time...has appealed to people to whom it may seem to offer one more path past the

and Jewish Christian eschatology to the Gentile believers at Thessalonica—specifically, of introducing them to the ancient but (to them) alien Jewish notion of the resurrection of the dead.

Again Robert Gundry's comment is illuminating: 'If Paul has hellenized the dominical eschatological and apocalyptic tradition in 1 Thess. 2.19-20; 3.13; 4.15-17, he Christianizes Jewish eschatological and apocalyptic tradition in the rest of 1–2 Thessalonians'.[23] I am suggesting here that Paul 'Christianizes Jewish eschatological and apocalyptic tradition' in 1 Thess. 4.15-17 as well—specifically that he Christianizes the traditional Jewish resurrection hope by linking it to Jesus and to one of Jesus' sayings. He links it to Jesus in 4.14a, 'for if we believe that Jesus died and rose, so too, through Jesus, will God bring with him those who have fallen asleep'. The dead will rise because Jesus rose from the dead. Paul then links the traditional Jewish resurrection hope to a saying of Jesus ('The last will be first, and the first last') in v. 15. Instead of trying to impose an alien Jewish notion on these Gentile Christians by his personal authority, Paul appeals to two things: first, to the precedent of Jesus, which they had accepted as part and parcel of their initial acceptance of Paul's gospel (cf. 1.9-10); secondly, he appeals to simple fairness as articulated in one of Jesus' well-remembered sayings. To Paul, 'the last will be first, and the first last' was a promise of equity or equality between the advantaged and the disadvantaged, in this case equity at the time of the Parousia between the dead and the living. If— as the Thessalonians already believed—the living were to meet their Lord at the Parousia, would a just God exclude other believers simply because they had died? Of course not, and Jesus had said as much in his pronouncement about the first and the last. This was something Gentile Christians could understand without being initiated into all the particulars of the traditional 'hope of the resurrection of the dead' as articulated and debated within the various sects of Judaism.[24]

Crucifixion. That could be corrected by no sense of life better than by O'Connor's. Quite as austere in its way as his, her vision will hold us down to earth where the clashes of blind wills and the low dodges of the heart permit any rising or convergence only at the cost of agony. At that cost, yes, a little' ('Introduction' to *Everything That Rises Must Converge* [New York: Farrar, Straus & Giroux, 1965], pp. 26-27. Compare Ralph Wood's remarks in n. 8, above.

23. Gundry, 'Hellenization', p. 169.

24. See Acts 23.6, and contrast the way in which the Lukan Paul introduces the theme of resurrection in Acts with the way in which Paul introduces it in

That the future resurrection of the dead was a difficult notion for Gentile Christians to grasp and accept is nowhere better demonstrated than at Corinth, where Paul's preoccupation with the subject finds its deepest expression, and where he begins to move beyond the parameters of standard Jewish teaching. 1 Corinthians lies beyond the scope of this study, but here too Paul appeals to the precedent of Jesus and his resurrection (15.1-11, 20-23). He also appeals to the principle of equity between 'first' and 'last' at the future resurrection. In 1 Cor. 15.45-49, he sharply contrasts 'the first man, Adam', who was 'from the earth, and of dust', and 'the last Adam' or 'the second man', who was 'from heaven' (vv. 45, 47). Yet he brings the two into a kind of eschatological unity: 'Just as we have borne the image of the man of dust, we will also bear the image of the heavenly one' (v. 49), and 'We will not all fall asleep, but we will all be transformed' (v. 51; cf. v. 52b). 'This corruptible thing', he concludes, 'must put on incorruption, and this mortal thing must put on immortality' (v. 53). Here again 'first' and 'last' become one, although in this chapter they no longer represent the living and the dead, but humanity in Adam and humanity in Christ. The 'first' does not simply disappear, to be replaced by the 'last', but is 'transformed' so that the two become one. By now Paul has moved far enough beyond the original saying of Jesus that he prefers to call his vision of rising and convergence not a 'word of the Lord', but 'a mystery' revealed to him alone (v. 51). That, however, is another essay altogether.

---

1 Thessalonians and 1 Corinthians (see, for example, Acts 24.15; 26.6-8; 28.20). When speaking to non-Christian Jews, Paul moves from the known (the general resurrection of the dead) to the unknown (the resurrection of Jesus). When speaking to Christian Gentiles he also moves from the known (the resurrection of Jesus and a saying of Jesus) to the unknown (the general resurrection of the dead).

PNEUMA AND ESCHATOLOGY IN 2 THESSALONIANS 2.1-2:
A PROPOSAL ABOUT 'TESTING THE PROPHETS' AND THE PURPOSE
OF 2 THESSALONIANS[1]

Gordon D. Fee

For whatever reason, Spirit movements are frequently characterized by an unusually heightened eschatological awareness or fervor.[2] Recently Robert Jewett has suggested such a *Sitz im Leben* as the most likely historical context for the Thessalonian letters.[3] While I am less persuaded than Jewett as to the presence of a pervasive millenarianism in this church, it seems highly likely that the existence of such an element, and its relationship to the activity of the Spirit in their midst, may best explain one of the more intriguing texts in the Pauline corpus, namely 2 Thess. 2.2, with its collocation of 'through Spirit' and a distressing pronouncement of 'realized eschatology' (probably as a 'Spirit' utterance). The purpose of this present paper[4] is twofold: (1) to look more

1. The following commentaries are referred to in this paper by author's name only: E. Best (HNTC, 1972); F.F. Bruce (WBC, 1982); E. von Dobschütz (7th edn, 1909); C.J. Ellicott (1861); G.G. Findlay (CGTC, 1925); J.E. Frame (ICC, 1912); W. Hendriksen (1955); D.E. Hiebert (1971); J.B. Lightfoot (1895 = *Notes on the Epistles of St Paul*); I.H. Marshall (NCB, 1983); G. Milligan (1908); J. Moffatt (*EGT*, 1910); A.L. Moore (NCB, 1969); L. Morris (NICNT, 1959); A. Plummer (1918); B. Rigaux (EBib, 1956); C.A. Wanamaker (NIGTC, 1990); D.E.H. Whiteley (NClarB, 1969). Three other significant works are referred to by short titles: Giblin, *Threat* (= C.H. Giblin, *The Threat to Faith: An Exegetical and Theological Re-Examination of 2 Thessalonians 2* [AnB, 31; Rome: Pontifical Biblical Institute, 1967]); Hughes, *Rhetoric* (= F.W. Hughes, *Early Christian Rhetoric and 2 Thessalonians* [JSNTSup, 30; Sheffield: JSOT Press, 1989]); Jewett, *Correspondence* (= R. Jewett, *The Thessalonian Correspondence: Pauline Rhetoric and Millenarian Piety* [Philadelphia: Fortress, 1986]).
2. Perhaps part of the reason for this is the close connection between the prophetic Spirit and prophecy (understood as having to do with future events).
3. See *Correspondence*, especially pp. 161-92.
4. The substance of much of this paper appears in quite different form in *God's*

closely at 2 Thess. 2.2, and especially at the difficult phrase, ὡς δι᾽ ἡμῶν, since I am convinced that many of our difficulties both with 2 Thessalonians as a whole and with this passage in particular are the result of a misreading of this phrase; and (2) to suggest that what Paul says later in 2.15 offers us both a key for unlocking 2.2 and the earliest clue regarding his own perspective on the 'testing' of prophetic utterances, as he had encouraged in 1 Thess. 5.21, and insists on later in 1 Cor. 14.29-32.

I am happy to offer this modest proposal in honor of Robert Gundry, with appreciation both for his own work in New Testament studies and for his and Lois's hospitality on more than one occasion.

I

At the beginning of the body[5] of his second[6] letter to the Thessalonians, Paul[7] says:

Empowering Presence: The Holy Spirit in the Letters of Paul (Peabody, MA: Hendrickson Publishers, 1994). Thanks are due my colleague, Sven Soderlund, whose careful reading of an earlier draft saved me from several infelicities and errors and whose disagreement on the phrase 'as though through us' prodded me to think through the argument more carefully at several points.

5.   This is the more traditional way of referring to the argument of the letter, which I am convinced is still the better way. For the view that this is the 'petitio' of ancient rhetoric, see Hughes, *Rhetoric*, pp. 19-74; for a helpful overview of this whole question and one that takes a position similar to Hughes, see Jewett, *Correspondence*, pp. 61-87, 222-25.

6.   I remain convinced that one can make best sense of this letter as the second of the two. For the opposite view see, most recently, Wanamaker, pp. 37-45. For a helpful overview of the issues, which concludes in favor of the traditional sequence, see Jewett, *Correspondence*, pp. 19-30.

7.   One of the incongruities of New Testament scholarship is the rejection of this epistle as genuinely Pauline. The rejection in this case is based, not as elsewhere on the differences between this letter and the other Paulines, but rather on its high level of similarity to 1 Thessalonians. Paul here is too much like himself to be genuine(!)— although not very far below the surface in every case of rejection is some dissatisfaction with its content, especially the themes of judgment frequently expressed in a more apocalyptic mode of language. But the reasons for inclusion far outweigh any considerations against it. The similarities are precisely what one might expect of a letter written very shortly after the first one, and dealing for the most part with several of the same issues. Moreover, it is nearly impossible to find a reason for pseudepigraphy in this case, especially since so little seems to be gained by it.

1   Now, brothers and sisters, we beg you concerning the coming of our[8]
Lord Jesus Christ and our gathering unto him
2   that you not be too easily[9] shaken in mind or disturbed, whether through
Spirit or through word or through letter, as though through us, to the effect
that the Day of the Lord[10] has come (2 Thess. 1.1-2, my translation).

These opening words are at once the most crucial and most problematic
in this letter. They are the most crucial because Paul now articulates for
his and their sakes his understanding of what has been recently reported
to him about the situation in Thessalonica; thus they serve to communicate the primary occasion of the letter. Indeed, as will be noted
momentarily, the other concerns—their unjust suffering (ch. 1) and the
continuing difficulty with the 'unruly idle'[11] (ch. 3)—are best understood as related to this one.[12]

Furthermore, the exegesis of 2.1-2 and 15 offered here presents a simple and historically viable reason for the letter within the framework of the context of Paul and
Thessalonica that emerges in the first letter. On this whole question, again see Jewett,
Correspondence, pp. 3-18.
     8.   B, Ψ and a few others (including sy[h] and some MSS of the Vulgate) omit the
ἡμῶν. Were this more widely attested, most textual critics, including this one, would
think that the other witnesses had added the pronoun, since this is Paul's more usual
form. But more likely here we have omission for stylistic reasons, in light of the
ἡμῶν that follows a few words later and/or in conformity to the immediately preceding clause (1.12).
     9.   For this sense of ταχέως, see BAGD, who also offer Gal. 1.6 and 1 Tim.
5.22 as further examples. The emphasis is only partly on 'haste'. Rather it lies more
on 'quickly' in the sense of 'too easily' taken in by new things.
     10.   Against all earlier evidence in all forms (Greek, versions, fathers), the Majority
text has substituted χριστοῦ for κυρίου. This seems to be a later attempt to make
sure that 'Lord' equals 'Christ' in this passage, which in fact it undoubtedly does.
     11.   This translation of ἄτακτοι indicates agreement with the lexical evidence
suggested by C. Spicq ('Les Thesaloniciens "inquiets" etaient ils des paresseux?',
ST 10 [1956], pp. 1-13) that the word implies active behavior, not mere passivity (as
in 'laziness'), on their part. This is confirmed especially by the word play in 3.11
between ἐργαζομένους and περιεργαζομένους, the latter meaning something close
to 'busybodies'.
     12.   One of the weaknesses in Jewett's radical (= Spirit 'enthusiasm') millenarian
reconstruction of the historical situation is that he sees such a realized eschatological
point of view as already present when 1 Thessalonians was written, so that he can
speak of this passage in terms of their 'readiness to accept the message reported in
2 Thess 2:2'. But that seems to downplay too much of what is said in this passage,
particularly that they have been 'shaken and disturbed in their minds' about this
matter, and that the responsibility of the declaration has been laid at the feet of Paul,

At the same time, however, this passage is also the most problematic, because, being as crucial as it is for the interpretation of the letter, what it finally means is far from certain. The difficulty is twofold: (1) What has been communicated among them? That is, what does it mean to say, 'the Day of the Lord has come'? (2) How has this 'deceit' (v. 3) been communicated to them (Spirit, word, letter, or some combination of the three?), and how is that question related to Paul (i.e. how has this error been palmed off on them as Pauline)? So problematic is this passage that it is probably fair to suggest that the questions of authenticity and the sequence of the two letters[13] stem in part from its exegetical difficulties, and both of these in regard to how the problems in 2 Thessalonians relate to what Paul has written in 1 Thess. 4.13-18 and 5.1-11.

Much of the problem in interpreting this text lies with the little phrase ὡς δι' ἡμῶν ('as though through us'), mostly because it follows hard on the heels of the preceding triplet of διά clauses, 'whether through Spirit, whether through word, whether through letter'. Despite the fact that it so poorly represents Pauline usage, the common interpretation understands ὡς δι' ἡμῶν as qualifying one or more of these preceding phrases, suggesting that Paul's uncertainty expressed by this phrase refers to the *means* by which the miscommunication took place. That is, he does not know whether someone has prophesied in his name/behalf, communicated orally as though from him, or forged a letter in his name. In terms of Pauline usage and the literary context, however, this phrase is better understood as anticipating what follows, referring to the *content* of the miscommunication, rather than to its form. Paul is thus offering an unqualified denial that what they are presently believing about the Day of the Lord can be attributed to him at all, even though he is not quite sure, but had a pretty good idea, from my point of view, how such a thing happened. This slight shift of perspective regarding the intent of this phrase, it will be argued, not only resolves many of the difficulties in interpreting v. 2, but also clears the way for a better understanding of the letter as a whole.

---

despite what he knows has been clearly communicated to them. The implication is strong that this is a 'new twist' and that they are quite distressed by it.

13. See nn. 6 and 7 above. Evidence for such a judgment may be found in Jewett's historical sketch of the question of authenticity (*Correspondence*, pp. 3-18), where, without his trying to make this point, the discussion about authorship invariably involves a prior understanding of our passage.

II

The first matter—as to *what* had been communicated to them—will not detain us, since to discover what they had come to believe is not essential to our immediate concern. Nonetheless, since it is crucial to the whole letter and in part to how the first part of v. 2 is to be understood, a summary of conclusions is in order.

First, it seems most highly probable that the error referred to in v. 2 is related to some kind of misunderstanding or, more likely, misrepresentation of 1 Thess. 5.1-11, with its repeated mention of 'the Day of the Lord' (vv. 2, 4) and subsequent play on the themes of 'day' and 'night'. After all, it is not as though a letter addressing this subject had *not* come from him; one had indeed. What is at issue in our letter is that some are promoting a *different* view from what Paul had communicated earlier.

Secondly, very likely the content of the misrepresentation has to do with someone's teaching that the Day of the Lord is already present, or, perhaps more likely in light of the emphases in ch. 1, that it had at least already begun in some way. This alone seems to make sense of the argument that follows, in which Paul insists that, just as *he had in fact previously taught them*, both orally (vv. 5, 15) and by letter (v. 15), certain observable events must transpire *before* that Day comes. The Day not only will be preceded by certain events (vv. 3-7), but also the events surrounding the Day will simply be too visible for any of them to miss it when it does come (vv. 8-10a). Hence, he argues, it is quite impossible to derive from anything he himself ever said (whether through word or through letter) that the Day of the Lord has already made its appearance in the present age.

Thirdly, such erroneous teaching about the 'present-ness' of the Day of the Lord also helps to explain the emphases in chs. 1 and 3. In light of what Paul had said in the earlier letter, the increase—and unjust nature—of their sufferings gives them considerable reason for anxiety, if the Day has already made its appearance. This is the reason for Paul's assurance in ch. 1 both of their own (future) vindication and of the just judgment of their adversaries. The same error could also buttress the reasoning of the 'unruly idle'. Since the Day of the Lord has arrived, and since they probably already took a dim view of work quite apart from the eschatological ferment,[14] why should

14. On this matter see esp. R. Russell, 'The Idle in 2 Thess 3.6-12: An

they return to their former occupations?

It is precisely the deleterious effects of such teaching that causes Paul to insist so strongly, first, that he is in no way responsible for it (the present passage), and, secondly, that what he had previously communicated to them by oral instruction (2.5, 15) and letter (2.15) is the singular truth about the Day of the Lord to which they should hold fast.

III

The question for us, then, is *How* has this thoroughly misguided understanding arisen among them? and How is it related to anything Paul may have said or written? The problem is both *linguistic* (What does 'Spirit' mean here, especially as the first member of an apparently equivalent triad that includes 'word' and 'letter'?) and *grammatical* (How is the phrase 'as though through [διά] us' related to the preceding triad of διά phrases?). At issue is what Paul is *denying* by the little phrase ὡς δι' ἡμῶν: (a) that he had written a letter in which this had been stated; (b) that he was responsible for any one of three unknown possible sources for the error; or (c) that he is not responsible for the false pronouncement itself, however it may have been communicated to them. I will argue here that the last of these is the most likely.

1. Let us begin by noting three matters from 2 Thessalonians, two of which are explicit, and the third suggested by Paul's use of language.

a. Paul really does not know the means through which this eschatological falsehood has been communicated to them. In its barest form, Paul's sentence can be displayed thus:

I urge you
        concerning the Parousia
        not to be shaken in mind
            that the day of the Lord has come

His *uncertainty* has to do with the form by which this content has been communicated, as the repeated μήτε διά makes clear. Furthermore,

Eschatological or a Social Problem?', *NTS* 34 (1988), pp. 105-19; and D.C. Aune, 'Trouble in Thessalonica: An Exegetical Study of I Thess 4.9-12, 5.12-14 and II Thess 3.6-15 in Light of First-Century Social Conditions' (unpublished ThM thesis, Regent College, 1989).

although these three phrases (μήτε διὰ πνεύματος, μήτε διὰ λόγον, μήτε δι' ἐπιστολῆς) together modify the compound infinitives in the purpose clause, the thrice repeated διά is probably best understood as carrying its ordinary sense of secondary agency. Thus Paul's grammar indicates that his interest is not in the *source* and *form* of the misinformation—that it came *from* the Spirit, for example, or *from* a letter—but in the *content*, by whatever *means* it may have been communicated. This may be displayed thus:

> I urge you
>> concerning the Parousia
>> not to be shaken in mind
>>> whether through the Spirit
>>> whether through a spoken word
>>> whether through a letter
>>>> that the day of the Lord has come

Putting ὡς δι' ἡμῶν aside for the moment, one can therefore make perfectly good sense of all this. That someone has communicated to them the content of the final clause is certain; that Paul does not know *how* this has been communicated is equally certain, but his best guess is that it came by means of either a prophecy, another form of spoken word, or a letter.

b. What Paul takes issue with in the argument that follows is likewise not the form of the communication, but its content. Indeed, the form of communication is quite irrelevant after v. 2. One of our exegetical questions, therefore, is why this triad of phrases exists at all. At first blush, it appears to have very little bearing on what follows.

What Paul does remind them in what follows is that he himself has spoken clearly to the issue at hand, on two occasions, and that he has said quite the opposite of what is now being promulgated among them. In v. 5 he appeals, 'Don't you remember that when I was with you I used to tell you these things?' (NIV). In v. 15 he again refers to his former teaching when with them, this time by picking up the expression εἴτε διὰ λόγου from v. 2;[15] at the same time he also refers to his former letter, our 1 Thessalonians, and speaks of these two earlier communications as 'the *traditions* which you were *taught*'. Thus, from Paul's point of view, two things matter: he has formerly taught them the

---

15. In this instance διὰ λόγου cannot mean 'report', as the NIV translates it in v. 2, but refers to his (and his companions') own oral instruction when they were present during the founding visit. Thus the NIV here translates 'word of mouth'.

precise opposite of what they are now being told; as far as he is concerned he was also quite clear in what he had taught, and they should hold fast to these 'traditions'.

Thus, in sum, we are faced with a situation in which Paul (1) knows that his own teaching has been either ignored, misunderstood or misrepresented (probably the latter), and (2) that even though he is not quite sure how this came about, he himself is being promoted as responsible for *what* is currently being taught.

c. Now to the more suggestive observation. It is striking that the two realities to which Paul refers in v. 15 as 'the traditions you were taught'[16] are expressed in precisely the same language as the final two members of the triad of διά phrases in v. 2. To be sure, in v. 2 he wrote μήτε διὰ λόγου, μήτε δι᾽ ἐπιστολῆς, while in v. 15 he writes εἴτε διὰ λόγου εἴτε δι᾽ ἐπιστολῆς; but these differences merely reflect the grammar of the two sentences. This repetition may, of course, be quite accidental, with the former referring to *later* possible communications which have recently been spoken or written among them. But there are good reasons to think otherwise, that in both cases the phrases refer to the *same* realities, namely his own previous eschatological communications with them. And this is where the demurrer, 'as though through us', most likely fits in.

2. In light of these various observations about what Paul actually says, the question then is, what is Paul primarily *denying* by the qualifying phrase, ὡς δι᾽ ἡμῶν?[17] To be sure, both the repetition of the διά and the fact that the phrase immediately follows 'whether through letter', makes it appear as though Paul is denying that he has written (yet another) letter to them in which he had taken a position quite the opposite of that taken in his first letter. The qualifier is thus sometimes understood as referring only to the final διά phrase, so that the two should be read together thus: 'whether through an epistle as though it

---

16. Meaning, of course, 'formerly taught personally by me and my companions'.

17. On this whole question, see the helpful discussion in Jewett, *Correspondence*, pp. 18-86, who categorizes three approaches to this phrase: (1) to view the phrase as the work of a forger (which Jewett rightly sees breaks down in trying to interpret 2.15); (2) to deny that the phrase has any implications of forgery; (3) to view 1 Thessalonians as the letter, but to understand it as being misrepresented in some way (the view argued for in this study).

came from us'.[18] This understanding is seen to be supported further by the signature in 3.17; Paul 'signs' off our present letter in his own hand, we are told, so that they will not mistake it for some forgery. But there are several matters that make this view highly suspect, despite its surface appearance of naturalness.

a. This reading of the sentence puts the emphasis in Paul's denial at the wrong place. As noted above, Paul's concern throughout is to deny that he can be held responsible for eschatological teaching that so thoroughly contradicts what he has clearly taught them previously, so much so that he spends the next several sentences reiterating that teaching by way of reminder. This view, on the other hand, puts the emphasis on Paul's denying that he has written a further letter to them (hence if there is such a letter, it is a forgery).

b. While it is possible, of course, that Paul could be denying both things at the same time, namely, that he could be held accountable for the false teaching since he is not responsible for any such letter, this view nonetheless has considerable difficulty with the role of the first two διά phrases. By limiting the denial to the letter only (as the NIV: 'or letter supposed to have come from us'), the first two items are cast adrift as possible sources for attributing this 'new teaching' to Paul. What Paul is thus uncertain about is whether the error springs from a prophecy or an oral communication neither of which is attributed to Paul or a letter which did purport to come from him (thus a forgery). But if so, that makes the reference to λόγος especially puzzling. Why mention it at all, one wonders, if this also is not attributable to Paul? And 'prophecy' also stands quite on its own, as something that sprang from within the community, but not in relation to Paul's own teaching.

The net result is that by understanding ὡς δι' ἡμῶν as denying only a forgery, the attribution to Paul of the present eschatological teaching is no longer an issue unless, of course, its source was the alleged forgery. But such a view makes very little sense either of the mention of the first two members of the triplet or of the argument that follows, where Paul sets about to overturn the attribution of this nonsense to himself.

c. These difficulties have led most scholars, therefore, to view the demurring phrase as qualifying all three of the phrases in the preceding

18. See, e.g., the commentaries by Moffatt, Moore and Bruce; this view is also assumed by those who argue for inauthenticity, as the discussion in Jewett (*Correspondence*, pp. 3-18) makes clear. Indeed, for the latter it is usually a crucial plank in their argument.

triad.[19] Although this 'solution' has more going for it grammatically, it too founders on point (a) above, but even more so on the problem of understanding how 'the Spirit' might have been understood as mediated 'through us', since Paul has not recently been on the scene.[20] Indeed, that Paul should ever have landed on an *alleged prophecy* as having *come from him* in some way as a possible source of this present error seems most remarkable! Someone could easily have misrepresented his earlier—or later—teaching, to be sure, not to mention the ability to forge a letter in his name. But how could a prophecy have been alleged to have come from Paul, which is what this view must necessarily require?

d. All of which leads finally to the primary objection to both of these views, the grammatical one. It seems nearly impossible that Paul could have intended this phrase to mean, 'as though it [the letter] *came from* us'. If reference to a forgery were Paul's present intent, then one would expect ὡς ἀπ' ἡμῶν or παρ' ἡμῶν ('as though *from* us'), not δι' ἡμῶν, which rarely if ever denotes the 'originating source' of anything in Pauline usage. Overlooking or ignoring this point of grammar, as so often happens in the commentaries and translations,[21] will not do, since Paul elsewhere shows considerable precision in the use of these prepositions. When he refers to the originating source of something he uses παρά or ἀπό;[22] when he refers to a secondary agent, that through which something has been mediated, he uses διά.[23] In this regard one

---

19. This is by far the more common option in the English commentaries; cf. the discussion in Rigaux, pp. 650-51.

20. That this is obviously the difficulty for those who take this position can be seen by the way they struggle to make sense of it. See, e.g., Best (pp. 278-79), who waffles at best (cf. Wanamaker and others who follow Best). On the basis of 2.15, he wants the phrase to refer only to the latter two items; but he recognizes how difficult that is to maintain grammatically, so he reluctantly includes all three. Of the first he is then left to comment, 'Paul was probably known to exercise ecstatic gifts...any oral prophecy or statement made elsewhere by Paul or one of his associates could have been wrongly reported in Thessalonica'.

21. Exceptions are Dobschütz, p. 266, and Giblin, *Threat*, p. 149 n. 3.

22. See e.g. 1 Thess. 3.6: 'now that Timothy has come to us from you'.

23. It should be noted in this regard that on four other occasions Paul uses διά with ἐπιστολή (2 Thess. 3.14[!]; 1 Cor. 16.3; 2 Cor. 10.9, 11) and in each case he clearly refers in some fashion to the *content* of the letter(s), not to its origins. One should note further that the δι' ἐπιστολῆς in 2.15 does *not* refer to Paul as the source

need look no further than the well-known demurrer in Gal. 1.1, that his apostleship is neither ἀπ' ἀνθρώπων nor δι' ἀνθρώπου (it neither has its source in humans nor has it been mediated through any human). We must accept it simply as wrong to translate this phrase, 'either *by* spirit or *by* word or *by* letter, as though *from* us' (NRSV; cf. NIV).

3. That leads us, then, to an alternative way of understanding ὡς δι' ἡμῶν, one that takes the grammar more seriously while at the same time fitting better with the various observations made at the beginning of this section.

As noted above, the use of διά in the preceding three phrases does not emphasize the originating source of the error; rather, by means of the διά Paul is already pointing ahead to the content of the error described in the final clause of the sentence. Thus he is not suggesting that either a prophecy or an oral report or a letter may have *originated* with him, but that by any one of these unknown means the *content of the false teaching* has been *attributed* to him. For example, had Paul not gone on to mention λόγος and ἐπιστολή, we would all (correctly) understand him to be urging that the Thessalonian believers not be easily shaken 'through some prophetic utterance' to the effect that 'the Day of the Lord has come'. The same is true with 'through oral instruction' and 'through letter'. In each case the διά refers to a possible source by which this content has been mediated, not that the source itself came *from Paul*.

That further suggests, therefore, that when Paul inserts the qualifying phrase, ὡς δι' ἡμῶν, he is not so much concerned with the form in which the error came to them, but with the fact that the content of the error itself has been attributed to him in some way.[24] In this sense, our phrase does indeed *grammatically* go with the three preceding phrases, but it is not suggesting any of the three items as being *from Paul*; rather,

---

of the letter as such, but to the letter as the means whereby the 'traditions' have been given to them.

24. This view has been suggested, *inter alios*, by Frame, p. 247 ['he disclaims simply all responsibility for the statement: "the day of the Lord is present"']; cf. Dobschütz, pp. 266-67; Dibelius, p. 44; Findlay, p. 165 ['"*supposing that* it is through us", viz. that the announcement of the arrival of "the day" comes from the Lord through His Apostles and has their authority']. For a different solution, see Giblin, *Threat*, pp. 149-50, 243, who sees the issue not to be one of the content of the utterance itself so much as an issue over Paul's authority.

it refers to them as the possible means whereby he has been accredited with the content of the false teaching about the Day of the Lord. Thus Paul almost certainly does not mean, '*through* a letter, as though *from* us'; he means, 'whether through [any of these means], as though through us the present teaching came to you'.

4. If such is the case, and both grammar and the rest of the argument in context seem to point this way, then several matters combine to suggest (1) that the second and third phrases in the διά triad do not refer to a recent report or letter purported to come from him, but rather to his own teaching when first with them and in his previous letter to them, which are now being misrepresented in some way so that they support the new 'teaching'; and (2) that the first member of the triad, which does not fit easily with the second and third under any circumstances, and is noticeably missing in 2.15, may be the key to much.[25] Let us begin with the latter.

a. Much of our difficulty with v. 2 has always lain with the first of the three διά phrases. On the one hand, it is *grammatically* coordinate with the next two, but unlikely so otherwise. That is, even though the three phrases are joined grammatically in Paul's sentence, it is unlikely that they can be coordinate either as to the nature of the communication or in terms of who is doing the communicating. It is generally agreed that διὰ πνεύματος refers to a prophetic utterance of some kind.[26] Although we may be rightly puzzled as to why he may have used πνεῦμα rather than προφητεία, it is not unlike Paul to express himself in this way. This is surely the way we are to understand the use of the plural πνεύματα in 1 Cor. 14.32 (where 'spirits' of the prophets are subject to the prophets; cf. 12.10 and 14.12). The reason for the plural in the 1 Corinthians passage is not that Paul believed in a plurality of 'spirits', but that he understood the one Holy Spirit to be speaking

---

25. Cf. J.T. Ubbink, 'ὡς δι' ἡμῶν (2 Thess 2,2) een exegetish-isagogische puzzle', *NedTTs* 7 (1952–53), pp. 269-95, who, however, still takes the phrase as referring to what precedes, not to what follows.

26. So most commentaries (Best, Bruce, Dobschütz, Ellicott, Frame ['clearly'], Hendriksen, Hiebert, Marshall, Milligan ['ecstatic utterance'], Moore, Morris, Plummer [who allows tongues as well], Rigaux, Wanamaker); cf. the NIV, which actually translates, 'by some prophecy'. Whiteley (p. 97) suggests simply 'ecstatic experience'.

through the several human spirits.[27]
It seems altogether likely, therefore, especially in light of 1 Thess. 5.19-22, that this meaning should prevail in our sentence. If so, then it also seems likely that this alleged means through which the error might have found expression took place *within the believing community at worship*. Furthermore, given that Paul includes such an option at all, one should probably take seriously both that this is a very real possibility from his point of view and that the final clause actually gives the basic content of the oracle itself.[28]

b. Such a possibility would further explain (1) why Paul repeats the final two διά phrases in v. 15, but with the 'Spirit' phrase noticeably missing, and (2) how it is that he knows his own teaching is now being contradicted—even though he is not quite sure how this came about—while at the same time he is being promoted as responsible for what is currently being taught. The reasons for both phenomena lie with a recent prophetic utterance within the community, which has given expression to the present teaching, whose content at the same time has been attributed to Paul.

c. On this view, one can then also make sense of the repetition—and omission—in 2.15, by viewing the twin phrases in vv. 2 and 15 as *referring to the same reality*, namely what he had communicated both when he was himself present with them and in his former letter—our 1 Thessalonians. A prophetic utterance that either contradicts that former teaching, or reinterprets it, could at the same time also attribute to Paul what is being prophesied—if one but have the Spirit's help in 'properly interpreting' what Paul had previously taught! This would explain both the inclusion of prophecy in the triad in v. 2 and also such a clear contradiction to his former teaching could have been laid at his feet. This also how means that 'through letter' has nothing at all to do with yet another letter, as though someone forged such a letter in his name.[29]

---

27. I have suggested the cumbersome 'S/spirit' as a way of translating this idea, which is also the best explanation for the (for us) awkward-sounding, 'my S/spirit prays' or 'sings' in 1 Cor. 14.14-15. On these various matters see the discussion of these texts in G.D. Fee, *The First Epistle to the Corinthians* (NICNT; Grand Rapids: Eerdmans, 1987).

28. As many have suggested; see, e.g., Jewett, *Correspondence*, p. 178; Giblin, *Threat*, p. 243.

29. This also suggests that the whole issue of forgery, which has caught the imagination of so many scholars, is something of a red herring. These two passages

Rather, Paul's (now awkward) sentence gives expression to his own frustration that his own teaching is no longer adhered to while he himself is being given credit for a clear contradiction to it. His solution is found in v. 15, where διὰ πνεύματος is noticeably missing[30] as he now urges them to 'hold fast to the traditions you were taught, whether by direct speech or by letter'.[31] He knows that his former teaching was not ambiguous; they must therefore hold fast to what has been 'handed down' to them directly from him.

5. Putting all of this together, the 'logic' of the sentence thus goes something like this. Given Paul's twofold difficulty—that he is aware that the *misinformation* has ultimately been attributed to him, while he is not quite sure *how* it was communicated—he therefore begins with the latter item, the uncertain form of miscommunication, the first member of which is most likely the key to the whole. By means of the 'Spirit' someone could easily have represented himself/herself as speaking in Paul's behalf (e.g., 'the same Spirit who spoke to us previously through Paul now speaks again in Paul's behalf, saying that...'). But for Paul it would be equally possible—more likely, perhaps, in light of the next two phrases—that such a 'prophecy' had been given in the form of an authoritative interpretation of what he had previously taught or written (e.g. 'the Spirit says that what Paul really meant was...'!). In either case,

---

together (2.2 and 15) do not suggest as much; and the reason for 3.17 is precisely the same as in Gal. 6.11, as a way of emphasizing that, whatever else, he is indeed responsible for the (apostolic) content of what has been written in *this* letter.

30.   Cf. Giblin, *Threat*, p. 45, who also sees 2.15 as 'factoring out' a 'heavy reliance on charismatic utterances', but as a 'modification', rather than a 'follow up', of 1 Thess. 5.19-22 (as I will argue below).

31.   It is the clear statement of 2.15, that Paul has in fact written to them *before* the writing of our 2 Thessalonians, which makes the reversal of the order of these two letters so problematic. Wanamaker's 'solution' of this difficulty is highly questionable. He suggests that the 'letter' mentioned in 2.15 is hypothetical on Paul's part. But that will not work at all, not only because Paul also mentions 'through word', which harks back to v. 5 and therefore cannot be hypothetical, but also because 'through letter' is modified by ἡμῶν, which can scarcely mean 'as though from us'. Paul is clearly referring to a previous letter, '*our* letter', which picks up the plurals from 1 Thessalonians which are carried through this letter as well. That 'our letter' refers to 1 Thessalonians is made the more certain because the content of that letter, as Paul well knows and is now reminding them, stands in utter contradiction to what they are now believing.

having mentioned the uncertain *form* of mediation of this error by the repeated 'whether through...', he begins to move toward the misrepresented *content*.[32] Using the same suppositional language, 'as though through us', he now with this demurral anticipates the final clause in the sentence. Thus, 'Do not be too easily shaken or disturbed', he urges them, 'whether it comes through the Spirit, or through what I have previously taught or written, as though the teaching came through us to the effect that the Day of the Lord has already come'.

Finally, this also helps to make sense of the ὡς ὅτι that introduces the final clause. What Paul intends is clear enough; here finally is the content of what has been said in their midst that is currently troubling them. But the sentence has gotten away from him a bit. The ὅτι ('that') grammatically follows the various possible sources by which this content has been mediated, and thus by direct discourse introduces the content of the oracle itself; the ὡς picks up the same sense of misrepresentation as in the preceding phrase, and thus ties the two together. He does not doubt that the version of the content he is about to offer is basically correct; but he may not have it precisely correct, so he qualifies, 'to the effect that'. The point being made is that under no circumstances may teaching of this sort, or a prophetic oracle with this content, be laid at his feet, as though it had come to them with his imprimatur.

IV

The view suggested here, it should finally be noted, makes good sense of several matters in these letters, and beyond.

1. Let us begin by reiterating the conclusions from above: The answer to the question, How in light of 1 Thess. 5.1-11 (δι' ἐπιστολῆς) and 2 Thess. 2.3-12 (διὰ λόγου) could anyone have attributed to Paul the realized eschatology expressed in 2.2, probably lies with the pneumatism that was apparently alive and active in this congregation. Someone speaking 'by the Spirit' has declared that 'the Day of the Lord has already come'. By 'the Spirit' this eschatological declaration has also

---

32. Thus at issue is not simply a misunderstanding of Paul, as Jewett (*Correspondence*, pp. 185-91) would have it. 'Misrepresented' or 'misconstrued' makes far more sense of the twin facts that Paul knows he has been quite clear on this matter, yet that he is now being put forward as responsible for the current contradiction.

been laid at Paul's feet. But he will have none of it. He will neither disown the Spirit nor despise prophesyings (cf. 1 Thess. 5.19-20); but neither will he allow such prophetic words to go 'untested'. What they are to hold onto, he declares in 2 Thess. 2.15, are 'the *traditions* you were taught previously, whether orally or by our letter'. This does not 'factor out' the Spirit; but it does offer a guideline whereby such Spirit utterances were to be tested.

2. That leads us, in turn, back to the Spirit material in the earlier letter (1 Thess. 5.19-22), to ask how that might be related to what is said here. One of the problems with the 1 Thessalonians passage is its relationship to the larger context of the letter and in particular to the paraenesis that begins in 5.12.[33] The problem is, how do these imperatives relate to the *formal* (structural) aspects of the letter, and how much do they *reflect the known situation* in Thessalonica (as reported to him by Timothy)?

Most likely the answer to both parts of the problem lies in a *via media*. On the one hand, they are part of a 'formal' series of 'staccato' imperatives such as one can find in many of the Pauline letters; on the other hand, and especially since imperatives like those in vv. 19-23 are noticeably missing in all other Pauline letters, this set probably reflects the 'tailoring' of the concluding imperatives to fit the local situation in Thessalonica.

If so, then the question is, what situation? First, some structural observations: As with vv. 16-18 which immediately precede, the five imperatives in vv. 19-22 are intended to be read together. They are given in two sets (vv. 19-20; 21-22); the first is a form of parallelism in which the second member specifies the first (they are not to quench the Spirit by despising prophesying); the second set, which is in contrast to the first, specifies what they are to do instead, this time in a set of three,

---

33. On the one hand, hortatory remarks such as these appear regularly as a part of the concluding materials in the Pauline letters (e.g. 1 Cor. 16.13-18; 2 Cor. 13.11; Rom. 16.17-19; cf. Fee, *1 Corinthians*, pp. 825-26), most often, as here, in the form of 'staccato imperatives'. Sometimes these imperatives pick up specific matters in the congregations; at other times they are simply general exhortations. On the other hand, in some of Paul's letters a section of paraenesis follows the so-called doctrinal section, as a conclusion of the larger argument of the epistle, as, e.g., in Rom. 12–15, Gal. 6.1-10, Col. 3–4. In each case these can be shown to be integral to the argument of the letter, not simply 'ethical instruction' following 'right thinking on the Christian gospel'.

the first giving the general rule, which the final two spell out more specifically. Thus:

> The Spirit do not quench;
> Prophecies do not despise; *but*[34]
>   Test all things:
>   Hold fast to the good;
>   Avoid every evil form.

The basic exegetical issue is to ascertain *where the emphasis lies*: is it on the first two imperatives (are some within the community less than delighted with such phenomena in the assembly?), or on the final three (do the first two set up the final three so that in correcting abuses they will not over-correct?)?[35]

It is common to argue that the problem in Thessalonica results from some disenchantment with, or conflict over, these phenomena,[36] in the form either of too much 'ecstasy' (usually glossolalia, as in Corinth) or of misguided 'ecstasy' (either by the 'unruly idle', who are using prophecy to justify their behavior or by some whose mistaken predictions about the Day of the Lord have brought prophecy into

---

34. The omission of this δέ in the TR (supported by ℵ* A 33 81 104 614 629 630 945 pm), along with the fact that each of these imperatives was assigned a verse number, has tended to destroy altogether the meaning of this series of imperatives—and to cause untold harm in separatist churches. The δέ in this case was in all likelihood omitted by scribes (in conformity to the whole series, all of which lack conjunctions), rather than added early and often by such a wide range of early witnesses (incl. B D G K P J 181 326 436 1241 1739 pm it vg cop goth eth). B.M. Metzger (*A Textual Commentary on the Greek New Testament* [London: United Bible Societies, 1971], p. 633, following Lightfoot, p. 84) suggests that the omission may have resulted from its being 'absorbed by the following syllable', but it is hard to see how that could have happened in this case (since it is followed by the δοκ-, not the -τε, of δοκιμάζετε).

35. It is altogether possible, of course, that Paul is simply trying to offer some guidelines for perfectly valid—and normal—Spirit activity within their own gatherings for worship, since many of his Gentile converts would already have been well acquainted with 'ecstasy' from their pagan past. Wanamaker (p. 201) suggests that 'Paul wished to encourage pneumatic activity as a sign of the eschatological times in which the Thessalonians found themselves'. This passage, however, and others like it, implies that the phenomena are more integral to early Christian initiation and experience than Wanamaker allows. Paul hardly needs to 'encourage' what would have been *presuppositional* in the Pauline churches.

36. See esp. Jewett, *Correspondence*, pp. 100-102, whose discussion notes others who share this perspective (e.g. W. Schmithals, Marshall, D.E. Aune).

disrepute). This is arguably supported by the grammar of the prohibitions themselves.[37]

But it is just as possible, more likely in my view, that Paul is offering something preventative, perhaps related to their former experience with 'ecstasy' of a more uncontrolled sort. In light of the evidence from 2 Thess. 2.1-2, it may well be that Timothy had already informed Paul of some tendencies in worship that needed 'adjustment'—but not elimination. Thus, some months later (2 Thess. 2.2), even though Paul does not know the precise source of the misrepresentation of his teaching, he does know that a prophetic utterance is one of the possibilities. Thus, the evidence from 2 Thess. 2.2 and 15 leads one to think that Paul in 1 Thess. 5.19-22 already had reason to caution this community to be a bit more perceptive about 'Spirit' utterances.[38]

The difficulty with this passage, of course, is that in urging that they 'test all things', and in so doing to 'hold fast to the good and be done with every evil expression', he gives no criteria for such testing. How does one distinguish the good from the evil, in terms of prophetic utterances? Here again is where the combined evidence of 2 Thess. 2.2, 5 and 15 may help. On the one hand, the abuse of 'prophetic utterances' is not in itself directly condemned in the second letter, probably in this case because Paul is not in fact certain that this is the actual cause. On the other hand, if our understanding of 2.2 moves in the right direction, then in 2.15 he is also offering a clear criterion for 'testing the spirits': 'the *traditions* you were taught, whether orally or by our letter'.

3. It is of some interest, in light of these suggestions, to note that in the better known passage in 1 Corinthians 12–14 Paul also calls for 'testing all things' when it comes to prophetic utterances. First, in 1 Cor. 12.8-

---

37. μή with the present imperative often has the force of 'stop doing something', implying the forbidden action as already taking place. This is argued, e.g., by Hiebert, p. 243, and Moore, p. 83; but see Bruce, p. 125, who correctly notes that 'like the positive imperatives in vv 16-18 and 21-22, [these negative imperatives] indicate what they must habitually do (or refrain from doing)'.

38. For a different view on the relationship between 1 Thess. 5.19-22 and 2 Thess. 2.2; 2.15, see Hughes, *Rhetoric*, pp. 56-57, who interprets the author of 2 Thessalonians as denying the validity of 'spirit', which is contrary to the genuine Paul in 1 Thess. 5.19-20 ('a particularly jarring contrast' to the exhortation not to quench the Spirit, as though Paul had not written vv. 21-22 as well!).

10, in his list of primarily extraordinary Spirit manifestations within the gathered community, he lists 'the discerning of "spirits"' immediately following 'prophecy'. That this most likely refers to 'discerning prophecies' is substantiated by the use of this same language in 14.29-32, where he insists that after two or three utterances, the others 'discern' what is said, and that they can take their turn in prophesying because the 'spirits' of the prophets are subject to the prophets.[39] But, again, as in 1 Thess. 5.19-22 Paul neither indicates the process nor gives criteria as to how one goes about the 'discerning'. Earlier, however, in 14.3 he specifically says that the one who prophesies speaks edification, encouragement (or exhortation), and comfort. Even if not intended as criteria for 'discerning', such a direct statement as to the goal of prophecy within the community has the effect of establishing a kind of criterion—the encouragement and building up of the community. This, of course, is precisely *not* what has resulted from a 'Spirit' utterance in Thessalonica about the Day of the Lord, which has led instead to many of them being 'shaken in mind and disturbed'.

V

If all of this approximates both the situation being addressed in 2 Thessalonians and the meaning of these various texts, then a few brief conclusions may be drawn about the purpose of 2 Thessalonians, as well as about 'testing the prophets' in the Pauline corpus.

Whether or not the Thessalonians' present distress was *actually* the direct result of a prophetic utterance that had also laid claim to Paul's authority, Paul himself at least *believed* that such could well have been the case. If so, then the purpose of 2 Thessalonians and the need to 'test all things' with regard to prophecy may well coalesce in 2 Thess. 2.15.

At stake are two issues: the need expressed earlier in 1 Thess. 5.19-22 to 'test' prophetic utterances, and the need to calm this community's distress over false eschatological 'prophecies'. The key to both of these matters is for Paul to remind them of 'the *traditions* you were taught, whether orally or by previous letter'. Since this latest eschatological unrest has apparently caused further distress in their suffering, as well as having furthered the cause of the 'unruly idle', he reminds them of his former teaching on these matters as well. This accounts for all the data in this letter.

---

39. For full arguments in this regard see Fee, *1 Corinthians*, pp. 596-97, 693-96.

What this also means is that here, along with 1 Cor. 14.3, we have a primary criterion for the testing of prophetic utterances. In 2 Thess. 2.15 the basis of the 'test' is *theological or doctrinal content* (= 'the traditions you were taught'); in 1 Cor. 14.3 Paul offers the test of *effect*, as well as content, having to do with its helpfulness to the believing community.[40] Both of these 'criteria' were being abused in Thessalonica, and that is what called for our letter.

A final, contemporary word is perhaps in order, especially in the light of the renewal of Spirit phenomena in so many sectors of the church in our day. First, it should be noted that the earliest mention of prophecy in the New Testament (1 Thess. 5.19-22) includes the imperative that all such prophecies (and by implication all other such 'Spirit utterances' in the community) are to be tested. The awe with which many contemporary charismatics hold prophecy and 'prophets', which in effect causes them almost never to be 'tested', stands in basic contradiction to this Pauline injunction; rather it reflects the Thessalonian attitude toward prophetic utterances, one that needed correcting and harnessing.

Secondly, it is arguable that in 2 Thess. 2.15 and 1 Cor. 14.3 Paul has set the pattern for the church at a later time. On the one hand, all Spirit utterances should be tested in light of the 'traditions', which for us, of course, are now in the form of inspired sacred Scripture. On the other hand, since even 'truth' can be used in an abusive way, all such Spirit utterances should also lead to the encouragement and edification of the local community of believers.

---

40. Among the 'criteria' passages, one might add 1 Cor 12.3, but as I have noted in my commentary (*1 Corinthians*, p. 581), 'Paul's point in context is not to establish a means of "testing the spirits", but to remind them that "inspired utterance" as such is not evidence of being "led of the Spirit"'. Some might want to add Rom. 12.6 ('according to the analogy of the faith'). While this view has several things to commend it, more likely this phrase refers to the actual gifting of the prophet, that he or she is to prophesy in keeping with the faith to do so, which in turn is in keeping with the differing 'portion of faith' that each has received (v. 3). For a full examination of this matter, see Fee, *Presence*, *ad loc.*

THE THREE WITNESSES AND THE ESCHATOLOGY OF 1 JOHN

D.A. Carson

1. *The Challenge of Eschatology in 1 John*

The relationship between the eschatology of the Fourth Gospel and the eschatology of 1 John is hotly disputed. The difficulties in building any sort of consensus view are grounded in the first instance on the fact that there is considerable diversity of opinion on the nature and balance of eschatological perspectives in the two documents taken separately; inevitably, the permutations increase when the two documents are compared.

Virtually everyone acknowledges that the Fourth Gospel is characterized by realized eschatology. Discussion on this theme in the Gospel becomes complex when the passages that are avowedly futurist in their orientation (primarily Jn 5.24-29; 6.43, 54; 11.23-27; 14.2-3; 17.24; 21.22) are dismissed as exceptions, assigned to later redactors,[1] or interpreted in such a way that their futurist orientation is neutralized.[2] But virtually no one would deny that the Fourth Gospel, as we have it, though it includes a few passages with a futurist orientation, lays primary emphasis on realized eschatology.

On the face of it, 1 John lays a little more emphasis on futurist

---

1.   Even most of those who do not accept the detailed source criticism of Bultmann are usually content to assign Jn 21, with its critical reference to Jesus' return (v. 22), to a later hand.

2.   E.g., R.H. Gundry, '"In my Father's House are Many Μοναί" (John 14.2)', *ZNW* 58 (1967), pp. 68-72, argues that 14.2-3 refer to the fellowship the disciples of Jesus will enjoy with Jesus through the Spirit. More dramatic is the work of A. Stimpfle, *Blinde Sehen: Die Eschatologie im traditionsgeschichtliche Prozess des Johannesevangeliums* (Berlin: de Gruyter, 1990), who argues that the apparently futurist passages are nothing of the kind: they are the evangelist's sleight-of-hand, carefully crafted 'misunderstandings' to lead astray the unenlightened. The elect will see them for what they are.

eschatology. Not only do we find apocalyptic expressions (ἐσχάτη ὥρα, παρουσία, ἀντίχριστος) absent from the Fourth Gospel, but there is open anticipation of the future judgment when we shall see Christ (or God—the text could be rendered either way) and be like him (1 Jn 2.28; 3.2). Although believers have already passed over from death to life (3.14), and for them eternal life is a present possession (5.12, 13)—certainly Johannine themes—what does the small change in emphasis signify?

For Dodd, it signals a return to a more primitive eschatology.[3] For Lieu, 'It is wrong to find in 1 John (a return to) a "primitive" future eschatology, although it may be that the author is picking up the language of this type'.[4] She argues that the futurist themes 'are used to say something about the present' (but isn't that true even of all apocalyptic?), and 'they do not change the perspective of the picture'.[5] Bultmann is as happy to assign apocalyptic elements in 1 John to an ecclesiastical redactor as he is to adopt such a course in the Fourth Gospel,[6] though on the face of it the futurist elements are so interwoven into the text that they cannot be so easily dislodged.[7]

Klein argues that in the Fourth Gospel the light that has come into the world is focused in the ministry of Jesus, whereas in 1 John the darkness is gradually passing away and the light is triumphing in the period after Jesus' resurrection.[8] He therefore concludes that there is a greater 'historicizing' of eschatology in 1 John:[9] the Antichrist is not future but present, the last hour has already arrived, and so forth, even while certain futurist elements receive more emphasis than in the Fourth Gospel. But how much of these and related changes owe everything, or

3. C.H. Dodd, *The Johannine Epistles* (London: Hodder & Stoughton, 1946), pp. xxxiv-xxxvi, liii-liv.

4. J. Lieu, *The Theology of the Johannine Epistles* (Cambridge: Cambridge University Press, 1991), p. 90.

5. Lieu, *Theology of the Johannine Epistles*, p. 90.

6. R. Bultmann, *The Johannine Epistles* (Philadelphia: Fortress Press, 1973), *passim*.

7. Cf. G. Strecker, *Die Johannesbriefe* (Göttingen: Vandenhoeck & Ruprecht, 1989), pp. 54-55.

8. G. Klein, '"Das wahre Licht scheint schon." Beobachtungen zur Zeit- und Geschichtserfahrung einer urchristlicher Schule', *ZTK* 68 (1971), pp. 261-326.

9. The expression is much used by R.E. Brown, *The Epistles of John* (Garden City: Doubleday, 1982), who argues that 1 John 'revived an earlier stratum of Johannine thought' (p. 99) in order to combat perceived secessionist distortion.

at least a substantial amount, to the author's (authors'?) decision in the first instance to write a *gospel*, and in the second to write, if not exactly an epistle, some sort of tractate that does not purport to set out the life and ministry and death of the Messiah, however much it insists on the importance of those events? Certainly some of the distinctions discovered by scholars should be assigned to the difference in genre.

Nevertheless, many studies of the eschatology of John and of 1 John use the shape of this theme in the two documents (and often in the sources perceived to underlie these documents) to assist in the re-creation of the history of the Johannine community.[10] Collaterally, some scholars deploy perceived differences in the eschatology of John and of 1 John to argue against common authorship,[11] or at very least to argue for a certain chronological sequence in the writing of the Johannine corpus (something already implicit in persistent scholarly references to 1 John 'returning' to a 'more primitive' form of eschatology).

Clearly one's assessments in this area are tied to a nexus of other complex judgments, for example, whether 1 John is written against the background of some kind of rising proto-gnosticism (still the majority view), and if so what kind, or, alternatively, one of the more imaginative positions—for example, the view of Grayston, that 1 John was written before the Fourth Gospel,[12] or the view of Brown, that the secessionist opponents behind 1 John are arguing their case on the basis of their own reading of the Fourth Gospel, and that this case cannot rightly be said to embrace gnosticism.[13] They are also tied to one's reconstruction of first-century Christianity. Did Christian eschatology develop in a straight line, so that one can reliably plot the date and origins of a document by simply analyzing the eschatology it embraces? Or was there some tension between realized and futurist eschatology from the first, leaving plenty of scope for varied emphases dictated not only by personal preference but also by any author's perception of the most urgent need?

---

10. E.g. M.-E. Boismard, 'L'évolution du thème eschatologique dans les traditions johanniques', *RB* 68 (1961), pp. 507-24; G. Richter, 'Präsentische und futurische Eschatologie im 4. Evangelium', in P. Fiedler and D. Zeller (eds.), *Gegenwart und kommendes Reich* (Stuttgart: Katholisches Bibelwerk, 1975), pp. 117-52.

11. Not least Klein, 'Licht'.

12. K. Grayston, *The Johannine Epistles* (London: Marshall, Morgan & Scott, 1984).

13. Brown, *Epistles*.

In this short paper, it is neither possible nor desirable to introduce the numerous points that are at issue. Instead, I shall probe one passage, the passage on the three witnesses, and draw attention to two or three points that are usually overlooked. This passage is one of several that simultaneously invite reflection on the position of John's opponents, and say something about the Spirit, who is clearly to be reckoned with in any accounting of Johannine eschatology. Then, assuming the exegesis, I shall consider its bearing on the evaluation of the eschatology of 1 John.

2. *The Three Witnesses Reconsidered*

Bonnard has rightly articulated the contribution of 1 Jn 5.6-7:

> On abandonne maintenant la victoire de la foi [see v. 5] pour rappeler inlassablement qu'elle n'est possible que comme la foi à un certain Jésus. L'épître n'a pas été écrite pour susciter la foi, mais pour la sauvegarder, non dans ses propres qualités, mais dans son objet. L'authenticité de la foi lui vient, non de sa radicalité, mais de son objet historique, Jésus 'en chair'.[14]

The three witnesses, then, are meant to add substance and evidence to the repeated christological confession of 1 John: 'the Christ' or 'the Son of God' is Jesus.[15] Any exegesis of these verses must account for at least the following points: (1) the force of διά; (2) the reason why διά governs both 'water' and 'blood'; (3) the reason for the shift to the preposition ἐν in the next line; (4) the reason why the preposition ἐν is repeated before both 'water' and 'blood'; (5) the reason 'water' and 'blood' now become articular; (6) the force of the οὐ μόνον... ἀλλά construction. In addition, it would obviously be helpful if some plausible background could be linked with the proposed exegesis.

The principal interpretations that are regularly advanced are three. In addition, three more or less idiosyncratic proposals have been advanced in recent years.

---

14. P. Bonnard, *Les épîtres johanniques* (Geneva: Labor & Fides, 1983), pp. 106-107.

15. I have argued elsewhere that 'Jesus' is the complement, not the subject, though that will make little difference to my argument here; see D.A. Carson, 'The Purpose of the Fourth Gospel: John 20.31 Reconsidered', *JBL* 108 (1987), pp. 639-51.

1. The water refers to baptism and the blood refers to the eucharist. In this sacramental reading, the Spirit could refer either to a third sacrament that some find in the anointing passages (2.20, 27) or to the Holy Spirit as the agent who in some way renders the other two effective. Although this interpretation was popular in the fourth and fifth centuries (Ambrose, Augustine, Chrysostom, Cyril of Alexandria), and found its supporters in the nineteenth century, it is now relatively rare. It has been espoused by Cullmann,[16] and has more recently been defended by Brooks[17] and Grech.[18] Despite their best efforts to argue that for John the eucharist constitutes a pointer or 'witness' to Jesus' humanity, they are entirely unconvincing. 'Blood' is an unprecedented way of referring to the eucharist; more importantly, there is simply no evidence that John is responding to secessionist doubts about the value of the Lord's Table. Throughout 1 John, the author focuses on the reality of the historical manifestation of the Son of God, not the disputes over the modes by which Jesus makes himself known in the church. And if someone argues, as Brooks does, that the eucharistic presence of Christ might well serve as a pointer to the historical reality that undergirds it, then the argument is surely backward. Quite apart from debates about just what the eucharist actually meant to Christians in the Johannine tradition, the idea of an appeal to the eucharist to defend the incarnation strikes me as a remarkable case of appealing to the weak to defend the strong, or, better, of appealing to the derivative to defend the source. True, two or three decades later Ignatius criticizes an anti-eucharistic group (*Smyrn.* 6–7), but that group may well have been made up of Jewish Christians, and it is far from clear that they are the same people as the docetists who are also occasionally framed from time to time in Ignatius's sights. Moreover, the sacramental interpretation makes little of the exegetical details—why, for instance, that pesky διά? And exactly what does one make of the third witness, the Spirit? What *textual* appeal does one make to fit the Spirit into this interpretation (as opposed to theological arguments in the sacramental tradition)?

16. O. Cullmann, *Early Christian Worship* (London: SCM Press, 1953), p. 110 n. 1.

17. O.S. Brooks, 'The Johannine Eucharist: Another Interpretation', *JBL* 82 (1963), pp. 293-300.

18. P. Grech, 'Fede e sacramenti in Giov 19,34 e 1 Giov 5,6-12', in Puis-Ramon Tragan (ed.), *Fede e sacramenti negli Scritti giovannei* (Rome: Abbazia S Paulo, 1985), pp. 149-63.

But if the sacramental reading of 1 Jn 5.6 is no longer widely accepted as the primary meaning of the passage, several scholars detect either a secondary allusion to the sacraments, or a shift in meaning within the passage itself. Affirmations of *secondary* allusions are notoriously difficult to deny; they are usually highly dependent on antecedent theological commitments. More intriguing is the suggestion that δι' ὕδατος καὶ αἵματος refers to the historical Jesus, while ἐν τῷ ὕδατι καὶ ἐν τῷ αἵματι refers to the sacraments.[19] But most of the same problems apply to this variation of sacramental interpretation. Its one significant variation, the distinction between the διά phrase and the ἐν phrases, is unconvincing, for the οὐ μόνον...ἀλλά construction surely rules it out. If John had written οὐ δι' ὕδατος καὶ αἵματος ἀλλ' ἐν τῷ ὕδατι κτλ, presumably one could have made a case for it. But because the οὐ μόνον part of the construction has already shifted to the preposition ἐν *but covers only the first of the two nouns*, viz. 'water', then the entire construction, if it follows on from the preceding line at all, really must have the same referents for 'water' and 'blood' as in that preceding line. The reason why the preposition changes must then lie elsewhere. In short, from a syntactical point of view this is an exceedingly unlikely rendering.

Yet another variation of the sacramental interpretation distinguishes between the meaning of v. 6 and the meaning of vv. 7-10 or vv. 8-10. In this view, 'water and blood' have some other meaning (still to be explored) in v. 6, but take on sacramental meaning in vv. 7-10. I think this unlikely, but it does not greatly affect my argument. I shall briefly discuss it a little farther on.

2. In recent years a view that has gained substantial support is that the epistolary author is making explicit reference to Jn 19.34-35.[20] The

---

19. See B.F. Westcott, *The Epistles of St John: The Greek Text with Notes* (Grand Rapids: Eerdmans, 4th edn, 1966 [1892]), p. 182. Cf. similarly J. Bonsirven, *Epîtres de Saint Jean* (Paris: Beauchesne, 2nd edn, 1954), *in loc.*; H. Windisch, *Die katholischen Briefe* (Tübingen: J.C.B. Mohr, 3rd edn, 1951), *in loc.* Cf. also E. Malatesta, *Interiority and Covenant* (Rome: Biblical Institute Press, 1978), p. 312.

20. So Brown, *Epistles*, p. 578; R. Kysar, *I, II, III John* (Minneapolis: Augsburg, 1986), pp. 107-108; M.M. Thompson, *1–3 John* (Downers Grove, IL: InterVarsity Press, 1992), pp. 132-33; with some variations, cf. also H. Balz, 'Johanneische Theologie und Ethik im Licht der "letzten Stunde"', in W. Schrage (ed.), *Studien zum Text und zur Ethik des Neuen Testaments* (Berlin: de Gruyter, 1986), pp. 35-56.

strength of this view is that Jn 19.34-35 is the only other Johannine passage where water and blood are joined. The flowing of the blood and water from Jesus' side is understood to anticipate, among other things, the gift of the Spirit (note the apparent connection between water and Spirit in 7.37-39). The secessionists, in this view, are happy to stress Jesus' baptism, but do not take on board the significance of his death for their Christology. They may have believed in some true incarnation, but thought of that incarnation as taking place at Jesus' baptism, with nothing of great Christological significance taking place after that point: 'nothing further was salvifically necessary'.[21] So John is denying that the 'coming' (clearly an important word in 5.6) at Jesus' baptism was sufficient; he is insisting that 'Jesus Christ, the Son of God, fully came as Savior of the world (1 Jn 4.14) *only* [emphasis mine] through his death when he served as an atonement for the whole world (2.2)'.[22]

The apparent weakness of this view—namely, that the οὐ μόνον... ἀλλά construction demands two referents, 'water' referring to one and 'blood' referring to the other, not one 'blood and water' incident—is rebutted by its proponents. The Presbyter, they argue, is denying the secessionist claim that Jesus came by water, by insisting that he came by 'water and blood', that is, he substitutes a different reference point drawn from Jesus' earthly mission.[23] But this will not do. That is precisely what μόνον will not allow: John does not say 'not this, but that'; he says 'not *only* this, but that'. Moreover, on this reading 'water' has to change its referent in midstream (at the risk of a bad pun): the 'not (only)' element has to refer to Jesus' baptism, yet the 'but' element has to be linked with 'blood' so that the two nouns together refer to the incident of Jn 19.34-35. Moreover, as Smalley has pointed out,[24] this interpretation depends to no small degree on a disputed interpretation of Jn 19.34-35. If that passage does not symbolize the giving of the Spirit, or, at some primary level, the provision of the sacraments (a denial many commentators are happy to make),[25] the proposed interpretation of 1 Jn 5.6 seems even more remote.

There are still more reasons for rejecting this second interpretation.

21. Brown, *Epistles*, p. 578.
22. Brown, *Epistles*, p. 578.
23. Brown, *Epistles*, p. 574; Thompson, *Epistles*, p. 133 n.
24. S.S. Smalley, *1, 2, 3 John* (Waco, TX: Word Books, 1984), pp. 277-78.
25. E.g. C.K. Barrett, *The Gospel according to St John* (Philadelphia: Westminster Press, 2nd edn, 1978), pp. 556-57.

(a) In Jn 19.34-35, the order is 'blood and water'; here it is 'water and blood'. If the author of 1 John were trying to make an allusion to Jn 19.34-35, it is strange that he did not cite the crucial words in the same order. The arguments advanced to explain the reversed order might have some minor weight if it were already clearly established on other grounds that direct dependence between the two texts exists; failing such evidence, these arguments sound circular at best, weak special pleading at worst. (b) This view necessarily makes nothing of the change from διά to ἐν. This objection is scarcely fatal to the interpretation, of course; while at least half a dozen explanations of the change have been proposed, nowadays the majority of scholars think there is no difference in meaning, and that the change is purely 'stylistic'. Often they quote Heb. 9.12, 25, where first one preposition and then the other governs 'blood' as that *with* or *by which* one enters (εἰσέρχομαι) the most holy place. Most of these scholars take διά to be governing 'the genitive of accompanying circumstances',[26] and the ἐν rather similarly.[27] But although John is notorious for his slight changes in vocabulary without much (or any detectable) semantic shift, in this case one must notice that, as far as I know, there is no clear evidence that διά plus the genitive ever has anything but local force when it is construed with a simple verb of coming or going.[28] This still leaves some difficulties to face (see below), but if this syntactical judgment is right it tells against this second interpretation of the passage. (c) Brown suggests that this interpretation may be related to the later Mandaean literature (citing *Ginza Right* 2.64.10-14).[29] Of course, this is put forward as nothing more than a mild suggestion. But it is vaguely disquieting to find a willingness to tie a passage in 1 John to sources from a half millennium later, combined with a spirited denial that Cerinthus has anything to do with the background (see further below). (d) Finally, this interpretation, though it rightly sees the importance of Jesus' death in 1 John as the climactic saving point in the mission of the historical Jesus (see especially 2.2, and the quotation from Brown,

---

26. So, for instance, Grayston, *Epistles*, p. 136.

27. In the latter case, scholars often refer to BDF §§198(4), 219(4).

28. 'Denkbar ist freilich auch, dass die Partikel διά in Verbindung mit ἔρχεσθαι, eine lokale Bedeutung impliziert'; so Strecker, *Johannesbriefe*, p. 273 n. 10 and references there.

29. *Epistles*, p. 578. My access to the Mandaean literature is through the Lidzbarski translation.

above), it is curiously reticent about the more obvious Johannine connection, namely, the major christological credal statements on which so much turns (2.22-23; 4.2, 15; 5.1, 5; cf. 2 Jn 7).

In short, this second interpretation does not seem very convincing.

3. By far the most common interpretation (though it has many variations) is the one that sees in 'water' and 'blood' symbols for Jesus' baptism and death respectively. Certainly it has been repeatedly shown that 'water' can easily stand for baptism, and 'blood' for death or sacrificial death. Objections have usually been of two sorts: (a) Why does the one preposition διά govern both 'water' and 'blood'? Brown thinks this syntactical datum tells against this view, and favours his (i.e. the second view, above): coming by (διά) water and blood should be understood as a composite action.[30] I am inclined to agree; but as we shall see, one form of this interpretation not only meets Brown's objection, but is strengthened by it. (b) Increasingly it is argued that the background usually proposed to support this interpretation, namely, the heresy of Cerinthus, cannot be reliably tied to 1 John, and therefore should not enter into the discussion. I shall challenge that point shortly.

How the third witness, the Spirit, is understood on this interpretation of 1 Jn 5.6 varies a great deal. Before offering support for a particular version of this interpretation, I should briefly mention some of the more idiosyncratic views.[31]

4. Grayston offers a significant variation on the second interpretation.[32]

> Since water is associated with life, illumination and truth, and blood is a
> biblical symbol for violence, suffering and sacrifice, the Johannine image
> may mean that the violence endured by Jesus is accompanied by life and
> light to those who have seen and borne witness; or even that the benefits
> symbolised by water cannot be had apart from the sufferings symbolised
> by blood.[33]

As for Spirit, the third witness, Grayston's view depends on his reconstruction of the position of the secessionists: they have adopted the

---

30. *Epistles*, p. 577.

31. By 'idiosyncratic' I mean no opprobrium; I mean only to say that, so far as I know, each of the views (or specific versions of those views) I now mention is held by only one person.

32. *Epistles*, pp. 136-38.

33. *Epistles*, p. 137.

stance that with the reception of the Spirit nothing more is needed; John replies by a reference to Spirit used as in 4.1: spirit prompted prophetic utterance must be controlled by the Johannine tradition.

Grayston's interpretation seems to depend on thematic associations he finds for water, blood and Spirit in biblical and extra-biblical literature, with too little attention paid to the flow of the argument in 1 John 5. It is unclear to me how water and blood, in his view, witness to who Jesus is, which is surely required by both the immediate and the epistolary contexts. It is beyond the scope of this essay to criticize his understanding of the stance of the opponents, on which his grasp of this passage substantially depends, except to say that it is *sui generis*.

5. Richter has argued at some length that both water and blood refer to Jesus' physical birth, that is, to his incarnation. The docetists (understood to be the opponents) denied that the Christ had a genuine human birth; John affirmed it.[34] Richter has been challenged by Wengst[35] and Brown.[36] It is unclear that John specifies exactly when the incarnation took place: why specify the birth, as opposed to the conception (certainly Luke's witness)? Richter assumes that John's opponents were docetists, and argues that they held that Jesus had only an apparent body, made of water. John replies in terms of the physiology of the day (Wis. 7.2): the human embryo is made up of a woman's menstrual blood, and of male semen. His response, in other words, is that Jesus' body is real, of water and blood, not just water. But the connection of 'unreal' bodies with water alone is late. Enosh-Uthra, the Mandaean Saviour, was thought to be garbed in water (*Ginza Right* 1.29.5),[37] but the source is exceedingly late. When much earlier Ignatius emphasizes blood against his adversaries (*Smyrn.* 1.1; 12.2), he is referring to the cross, not the incarnation. And in any case Richter's view does not adequately handle the reference to the Spirit, the third witness.

---

34. G. Richter, 'Blut und Wasser aus der durchbohrten Seite Jesu (Joh. 19,34b)', *MTZ* 21 (1970), pp. 1-21.
35. K. Wengst, *Häresie und Orthodoxie im Spiegel des ersten Johannesbriefes* (Gütersloh: Mohn, 1976), pp. 19-20.
36. *Epistles*, p. 576.
37. Even here, however, as Brown points out, there is no contrast with blood.

6. Witherington ties this passage to one of the possible interpretations of Jn 3.5.[38] He holds that 'born' or 'begotten of water and spirit', read in the light of Jn 3.6 and the background he sketches in, refers to natural birth and spiritual birth. Applying that use of 'water' to 1 Jn 5.6, he argues that the three witness are the incarnation (water, a reference to Jesus' physical birth), the passion (blood), and the Spirit. Elsewhere I have argued against his interpretation of Jn 3.5;[39] here I would only add that, even if he were right on Jn 3.5, it would not follow that he is right here. Water has a variety of symbolic values in the New Testament, and none of the associations it enjoys in Jn 3.5 is carried over here.

The interpretation of 1 Jn 5.6 I wish to defend is a variation on the third: Jesus came through water (his baptism) and blood (his death). Without attempting a detailed exegesis, it may be helpful to organize the discussion around the following points:

1. On this view the διά is significant: Jesus came *through* water and blood—the obvious local meaning of this preposition with the genitive, when bound with a verb of coming or going. It is often objected that whereas this makes good sense with respect to the water (Jesus came *through* the water at his baptism), 'no good sense' can be attached to the notion of coming 'through blood'.[40] But this, surely, confuses the symbol with the thing symbolized. Doubtless Jesus came through water at his baptism, but that is scarcely the point: he came through *baptism*; he came through *death*. The point is especially telling if John is responding (as I shall argue) to a Cerinthian-type heresy. It appears that Cerinthus taught that the Son/Spirit/Christ fell on Jesus at his baptism, and left him while he was still hanging on the cross, that is, *at* his death. John argues that this one person, Jesus Christ, came *through* both the baptism and the death: he was, in other words, one person, Jesus Christ, before the baptism and after the death, and he came *through* both epochal events.

38. B. Witherington, 'The Waters of Birth: John 3.5 and 1 John 5.6-8', *NTS* 35 (1989), pp. 155-60.

39. D.A. Carson, *The Gospel according to John* (Grand Rapids: Eerdmans, 1991), pp. 191-96.

40. So, *inter alios*, I.H. Marshall, *The Epistles of John* (Grand Rapids: Eerdmans, 1978), p. 232 n.6; Smalley, *Epistles*, p. 280; C. Haas, M. de Jonge and J.L. Swellengrebel, *A Translator's Handbook on the Letters of John* (London: UBS, 1972), p. 118.

2. Similarly, it is significant that the one preposition governs both 'water' and 'blood', that the nouns are anarthrous, and that they are in that order (instead of the order found in Jn 19.34-35). Coming *through* both the baptism and the death is one significant composite action. The focus of attention, from this perspective, is not on the baptism itself, or on the passion itself, but on the coming that brought Jesus Christ through both of them, and in that order.

3. The shift to the preposition ἐν, the distribution of the preposition over both nouns, the use of the article with those nouns, and the οὐ μόνον...ἀλλά construction, all serve the same purpose. From one perspective, it was important for John to stress that the one person, Jesus Christ, came *through* both the baptism and the passion; from another perspective, it was important to stress Christ's death over against the baptism; at least the opponents (whether followers of Cerinthus or other gnostic heretics akin to those described by Ignatius and later fathers) had some place for Jesus' baptism. The passion, by contrast, could be dismissed, from their perspective, as quickly as possible. That element of the problem was best addressed by distinguishing the two events: Jesus Christ came *not only* in the one, *but also* in the other. The preposition ἐν, then, does not here govern a dative of accompanying circumstances, namely, water and blood. As in the previous line, that is to confuse the symbol and the symbolized. Christ came in the 'water-event' and in the 'blood-event', that is, not only in his baptism but also in his passion. This is simply a metaphorical use of the simple locative ἐν, a common function of the preposition. The articles, then, are either anaphoric, or help to draw attention to two definite, distinguishable events.

4. A very large number of reasons have been put forward as to why the Spirit is now identified as the third witness. There is little point in canvassing them here; the larger commentaries do a masterful job of surveying most of the options. But if the line of interpretation being advanced here is correct, then it is tempting to think that the 'third witness' theme is directly dependent on Jn 1.32-34, in connection with Jesus' baptism. There John the Baptist testifies,

> I saw the Spirit come down from heaven as a dove and remain on him. I would not have known him, except that the one who sent me to baptize with water told me, 'The man on whom you see the Spirit come down and remain is he who will baptize with the Holy Spirit'. I have seen and I testify that this is the Son of God.

If this is the passage to which the epistolary author refers, then his point is that even in their interpretation of Jesus' baptism they are wrong, and none less than the Holy Spirit contradicts them.

It will not do to protest that the evangelist does not actually describe Jesus' baptism. For that matter, he does not actually describe the institution of the memorial supper, either. Virtually no one doubts that the events themselves are presupposed. But this passage (Jn 1.32-34) has several instructive features that would make it an attractive reference point for the author of 1 John.[41] First, the one to whom the Baptist bears witness is 'the Son of God', twice used in the epistolary christological confessions (1 Jn 4.15; 5.5; cf. 2.23). Secondly, the Baptist's witness is cast in such a way that the text makes clear that the descent of the Spirit does not *constitute* Jesus as the Son of God, but *identifies* him as the Son of God. That is entirely in line with the point derived from the force of διά with a form of ἔρχομαι: against Cerinthus, Jesus the Son of God, one person, existed before the baptism, came *through* the baptism, and was (according to the Baptist) identified to others by the experience of the Spirit's descent. Thirdly, quite clearly it was the Spirit's function, descending as a dove, to bear witness to Jesus the Son of God in this regard. That is precisely why the Spirit is here introduced into the discussion. Thus the heretic who ignores what John says not only misunderstands the true nature of Jesus' baptism and passion, but refuses to listen to the Spirit's witness, clearly given.[42] Fourthly, at the same time this particular announcement to John the Baptist of the role of the Spirit in identifying the Son of God was given by the One who sent him to baptize, that is, by God himself. This paves the way, I suspect, for John's insistence, in 1 Jn 5.9, on the importance of heeding God's testimony—it is God himself who stands behind the three witnesses.

5. If this is correct, there is no need to follow the many commentators who argue that, whatever the interpretation of 5.6, these later verses (5.7-10 or 5.8-10) clearly stress the sacramental. The many nuanced arguments need not detain us here; they have been briefly but

---

41. Although in my view the author of the Fourth Gospel and the author of 1 John are one and the same, my argument in this essay nowhere requires that identification.

42. It follows, of course, that this passage offers no support for some 'internal witness of the Spirit' theme (compare Rom. 8.15-17), *pace* T. Preiss, *Le témoignage intérieur du Saint-Esprit* (Neuchâtel: Delachaux & Niestlé, 1946), pp. 36-39.

competently critiqued by Venetz.[43] If it is God himself who stands behind the three witnesses, then 'human testimony' in v. 9 is what takes place in common experience, while 'God's testimony' has been given in the three witnesses: the argument is *a fortiori*, and reinforces the line of thought already established.

6. Even if we knew nothing of what the fathers say about Cerinthus, the exegesis just advanced makes reasonable sense in its own right. Nevertheless, because at this point the heresy of Cerinthus meshes so closely with this line of interpretation, considerable controversy has broken out as to whether one can responsibly posit such a background. From Irenaeus we learn that Cerinthus taught that the Christ came upon Jesus at his baptism and abandoned him on the cross (*Adv. Haer.* 1.26.1); from some other fathers there is confirming evidence.[44] But doubts have been raised, principally on three fronts: (a) Some minimize the evidence of Irenaeus, once errors have been found in his work; (b) it is sometimes noted that some of the teachings of Cerinthus are not found in 1 John, such as the gnostic distinction between the supreme God and the inferior god who created the universe; (c) so far as our information goes, some themes important to 1 John, such as the rebuke of claims to sinlessness (1.6–2.2), would have no purpose among Cerinthian heretics.

I shall try to exonerate Irenaeus a little in my forthcoming commentary on the Johannine epistles.[45] Suffice it now to say that just because someone is wrong some of the time does not mean he or she is wrong all of the time! There is a sufficiently broad support for certain claims about Cerinthus, even if we rightly discount much of the later source material that becomes more and more speculative as time elapses, that it is premature to write off the evidence too quickly. As for the other two objections, it is surely right to recall that gnosticism was never a coherent and well-defined system. It was, as C.H. Dodd used to say, a 'theosophical hotch-potch'. To cite a contemporary parallel, it is not at

---

43. H.-J. Venetz, '"Durch Wasser und Blut gekommen": Exegetische Überlegungen zu I Joh 5,6', in U. Luz and H. Weder (eds.), *Die Mitte des Neuen Testaments: Einheit und Vielfalt neutestamentlicher Theologie, Festschrift für Eduard Schweizer* (Göttingen: Vandenhoeck & Ruprecht, 1983), pp. 345-61, esp. p. 355.

44. For admirable surveys of the evidence, see G. Bardy, 'Cérinthe', *RB* 30 (1921), pp. 344-73; Wengst, *Häresie*, pp. 24-34; Brown, *Epistles*, pp. 766-71.

45. NIGTC.

all difficult to find 'Christians' who have bought into some form or other of 'new age' spirituality totally inimical to their putative faith. In our (and the first century's!) eclectic age, it is disturbingly common to find people adopting religious convictions in a smorgasbord fashion, with no feel for what belongs together, let alone what is intellectually coherent. Cerinthus should be set forward, then, not as the sole source of John's ecclesiastical problems, but as a telling example of the kind of pressures that nascent gnosticism was beginning to exert on the church. To insist on utter alignment between 1 John and our flimsy sources for Cerinthus before one is permitted to discern any connections is totally unrealistic, not only because of the brevity of the sources (and their secondary nature in the case of Cerinthus), but also because of the intrinisic nature of virtually all branches of gnosticism.

In short, the three witnesses are Jesus' baptism, Jesus' death, and the Spirit-given witness to Jesus' Sonship—all played out to combat a Cerinthian-like gnosticism.

3. *Conclusion: The Bearing of the Three Witnesses*
on the Eschatology of 1 John

Of course, one cannot legitimately infer the entire background of an epistle by a cursory exegesis of one passage, a difficult and disputed passage at that. Nevertheless, if this interpretation of the three witnesses were sustained, along with an acknowledged background in the 'theosophical hotch-potch' that was gnosticism—in this case gnosticism with a Cerinthian flavour—then certain things might be usefully inferred about the eschatological emphases of this document.

1. The more concrete and novel the opponents, the less suitable it is to construct a 'systematic theology' of eschatology from 1 John and place it on some nicely erected trajectory of eschatological development. If both the Fourth Gospel and 1 John were presented as cool, reasoned attempts to set out, in dispassionate form, the convictions of their author(s)—something akin, say, to an ordination statement—then it would be worthwhile investigating the changes *as changes to a system of thought*. But the more obvious it is that one or the other is written in the heat of theological controversy, the less plausible it is to treat the author's eschatological pronouncements, insofar as they bear on the controversy, as reflections of dispassionate and systematic thought.

2. If the background to 1 John is one branch or another of gnosticism,

resulting in fundamental christological aberrations and outright secessionism, then it is entirely understandable why 1 John should reflect a little more emphasis on futurist eschatology than does the Fourth Gospel. All branches of gnosticism were notorious for their emphasis on the present, on what they had already received. John finds himself in the awkward position of having to articulate the true joys of Christian experience *now*, while insisting that the best is still to come. Christianity that loses its eschatological orientation by the simple expedient of focusing all its attention on present blessings is crying out to be corrected by futurist emphases.

3. Talk about returning to a 'more primitive' eschatology is trifling. It assumes a straight line of development in relation to which there are apparent aberrations. The opposing thesis is far more likely: the tension between futurist and realized eschatology was present from the beginning, and in many instances the element that receives emphasis is determined by the need to rebut a particular opponent.

4. It follows that the eschatology of 1 John cannot be deployed as a reliable indicator of the date of the document, or of when it was written relative to the other documents of the Johannine corpus.

5. On the other hand, if the background to 1 John lightly sketched here is judged largely right, then it is plausible to argue, if not on the basis of the eschatological themes themselves, but on the basis of the known rise of gnosticism, that 1 John was written after the Fourth Gospel. Neo-platonic dualism troubled some branches of the church almost from its inception, but the rise of full-fledged gnosticism awaited the end of the first century and beyond. If the kind of docetic gnosticism confronted by 1 John had been a major concern when the Fourth Gospel was written, it is hard not to conclude that it would have been written slightly differently. This is not to agree with Käsemann, who argues that the Christology of the Fourth Gospel is docetic through and through.[46] It is simply to say that it is hard to imagine how the author could have resisted taking far more shots at the docetic errorists, had that been called for, granted some of the themes already present (cf. Jn 1.14!). It appears, then, that the Fourth Gospel was written before the gnostic controversy was really underway, at least in the horizons of the evangelist. By the time 1 John is written, that is no longer the case.

---

46. E. Käsemann, *Testament of Jesus: A Study of the Gospel of John in the Light of Chapter 17* (London: SCM Press, 1968).

6. Finally, the role of the Spirit in the three witnesses passage calls for further comment. It appears that 1 John appeals not to the Spirit's role as set forth in the Paraclete passages, but to the Spirit's role in connection with the baptism of Jesus. The former would have better suited an emphasis on realized eschatology; the latter largely ignores such niceties of the eschatological debate, and focuses on who Jesus Christ is. Granted the author's concern to combat a heresy in the christological arena, that is not surprising. But that is simply another way of saying that eschatological concerns are not at the top of the agenda in 1 John, but are deployed in a variety of ways to serve christological, ecclesiastical and pastoral interests.

'AND THE SEA WAS NO MORE':
WATER AS PEOPLE, NOT PLACE

Thomas E. Schmidt

In his 1987 article, 'The New Jerusalem: People as Place, Not Place for
People', Robert Gundry persuasively articulates the view that Revelation
21–22 depicts redeemed humanity.[1] This article purposes to extend
Gundry's thesis backward to Revelation 17–18 and the depiction
of Babylon, which is generally regarded as antonymous to the New
Jerusalem. More specifically, I will maintain that Babylon and cosmological imagery pertaining to the sea are linked as representations of
unredeemed humanity, and I will explore briefly the implications of this
conclusion for New Testament eschatology in general.

The New Jerusalem and Babylon

Gundry maintains that the language of Revelation concerning the New
Jerusalem is consistently non-spatial in reference. The antonymous characterization of Babylon is not consistent in this regard, but consistency is
not necessary. With respect to Babylon, all things are not yet made new,
and referents may be at once spatial and non-spatial. In other words, the
depiction of the present world involves a reality that transcends space
without denying it.[2] Thus although in the new Jerusalem we observe the
'reciprocal indwelling of God, the Lamb, and the saints in the *futuristic*
eschatology',[3] in 'old' Babylon—the eschatological *present*—a whore
metaphorically denotes a mythical Mesopotamian city which denotes a

1. *NovT* 29 (1987), pp. 254-64.
2. P. Minear (*I Saw a New Earth: An Introduction to the Visions of the
Apocalypse* [Washington, DC: Corpus Books, 1968], pp. 276-78) articulates this
notion of transcendence but does not make the qualitative distinction with regard to
spatial reference that I think is necessary after Rev. 21.1.
3. Gundry, 'New Jerusalem', p. 262.

specific Italian city which symbolizes the present world order which denotes doomed humanity. This interplay of spatial and non-spatial is replaced by what Gundry calls 'reciprocal indwelling', significantly, only at the New Creation. There, even imagery finds unity.

The qualitative shift signaled at Rev. 21.1 should not diminish the antithetic parallelism between New Jerusalem and Babylon at numerous points. The most obviously self-conscious of these is the visionary introduction to each city:

Rev. 17.3-5	Rev. 21.10-14
So he carried me away in the spirit	And in the spirit he carried me away
into a wilderness	to a great, high mountain
and I saw a woman sitting on a	and showed me the holy city Jerusalem
scarlet beast that was full of	coming down out of heaven from God.
blasphemous names,	
and it had seven heads and ten horns.	
The woman was clothed in purple	It has the glory of God
and scarlet,	and a radiance
and adorned with gold and jewels	like a very rare jewel, like jasper,
and pearls,	
holding in her hand a golden cup full	
of abominations and the impurities	clear as crystal.
of her fornication;	
	It has a great, high wall with
	twelve gates…
and on her forehead was written a name,	…and on the gates are inscribed
a mystery:	the names of the twelve tribes…and…
'Babylon the great, mother of whores	the twelve names of the twelve
and of earth's abominations'.	apostles.[4]

A few of the more subtle antitheses here merit special note. The first vision is set in the wilderness, a place of chaos and danger (12.6, 14; cf. Mk 1.12-13 etc.); the setting of the second vision probably connotes the Mount of Olives (Zech. 14.4) or another mountain ostensibly close to God (Ps. 48.2; Isa. 2.2; Ezek. 28.14; *1 En.* 24–25). The beast upon which the woman sits is presumably the same that rose up from the sea (13.1), the place of primordial chaos; the holy city descends from heaven in angular order (21.10-21). The woman is clothed in the accouterments of worldly wealth; the city is adorned by 'the glory of God'. The whore sports multiple adornments; the city possesses the singular radiance of 'a very rare jewel'. The cup of impurities held by the whore (full of

---

4.   All biblical quotations are from the NRSV.

martyrs' blood, v. 6) contrasts to the purity of the city, which is 'clear as crystal'.

While 17.3-5 and 21.10-14 are the most explicit parallel passages, there are numerous additional antithetic connections between Babylon and New Jerusalem. The place names themselves are obvious choices for the depiction of a mythic struggle between the wealthy and powerful enemies of God and the people he will ultimately save. John incorporates material from prophetic denunciations of Egypt (Ezek. 29–30) and especially of Tyre (Isa. 23; Ezek. 26–28), but the imagery of Isaiah 47 and especially Jeremiah 51, where Babylon is personified as a lascivious female pleasure-seeker, provides the framework for Revelation 18.[5] The historical reason for this is confirmed by contemporary Jewish usage: it was Babylon, not Egypt or Tyre, that destroyed Jerusalem in 70 CE.[6]

Another obvious contrast is that between whore and bride. Babylon, like the beast upon which she rides (cf. the red dragon, 12.3), is arrayed in sinful scarlet, displaying her cup full of 'the impurities of her fornication' (17.4); the bride wears 'fine linen, bright and pure—for the fine linen is the righteous deeds of the saints' (19.8; cf. 15.6).[7]

The contrast between the dragon or beast(s) and the Lamb provides additional parallels which, while not as clearly identified with the two cities, certainly contribute to antithetically parallel realities that *involve* the cities. There is a clear movement from 'I saw a beast rising out of the sea' (13.1) and 'I saw another beast that rose out of the earth' (13.11) to 'Then I looked, and there was the lamb, standing on Mount Zion!' (14.1). The beast requires a mark to be worn on the hand or forehead (13.16-18); the Lamb writes his name on the forehead of the saints (14.1; cf. 3.12; 7.3; 22.4). A destructive flood gushes from the mouth of the dragon (12.15); a life-giving fountain springs from the throne of the lamb (22.1-2).

There are numerous other antithetic parallels more directly related to the two cities. The New Jerusalem is characterized by a glory which obviates 'light of lamp or sun' (22.5; 21.23-24); the present world is

---

5. A thorough list of the correspondences is contained in C.H. Dyer, 'The Identity of Babylon in Rev. 17–18', *BSac* 144 (1987), pp. 433-49; see also C. Deutsch, 'Transformation of Symbols: The New Jerusalem in Revelation 21.1–22.5', *ZNW* 78.1-2 (1987), pp. 106-26.

6. L.L. Thompson, *The Book of Revelation: Apocalypse and Empire* (Oxford: Oxford University Press, 1990), p. 14. See *Sib. Or.* 5.143, 158-60; *2 Bar.* 67.7.

7. R.W. Wall, *Revelation* (Peabody, MA: Hendrickson, 1991), p. 206.

progressively plunged into darkness (8.12; 16.10) until Babylon hears the lament, 'the light of a lamp will shine in you no more' (18.23). The New Jerusalem is accompanied by songs of praise which, among other things, declare that 'mourning and crying and pain will be no more' (21.4); Babylon's demise is accompanied by dirges expressing 'torment and grief' (18.6). Rev. 18.11-17 enumerates the lost wealth of the merchants, including 'gold, silver, jewels and pearls' (18.12); Rev. 21.18-21 employs the same terms to depict what is found in the New Jerusalem. In Babylon's destruction the kings, merchants and mariners lament the commercial losses that supported their lives of luxury and impurity; in the New Jerusalem there is no depiction of individuals luxuriating, and the community grandeur is described repeatedly as 'pure' (21.11, 18, 21).[8]

To the extent that Gundry's thesis concerning the New Jerusalem 'as people' is correct, these parallels suggest that Babylon also denotes primarily people; that is, humanity in chaos and in rebellion against God. This is not to set aside social and political criticism of Rome as the immediate setting of Revelation, but it is to suggest that John has in view a broad conflict of which Rome is central or typical but not all-inclusive.[9]

From the beginning of Revelation, it is apparent that John's vision is broader in scope than even the wide borders of the empire could encompass. Granted, Babylon receives the cooperation and submission of 'the kings of the earth',[10] but John envisions this as a future development (17.12) in which the kings of the earth ally themselves with and subsequently devastate Babylon (17.16-17) before joining with one another and the beast to war against God (16.12, 14; 19.19; 20.8-9). After 19.3 Babylon is out of the picture, but John's purpose is wider,

---

8.   For this reason I am not fully persuaded by Gundry's argument that the wealth of the New Jerusalem is material ('The New Jerusalem', p. 261). The notion that the saints *are* the wealth is more consistent with co-inherence at other levels (temple, Lamb, people, etc.).

9.   See the discussion of the relation of myth and rhetorical strategy to the socio-historical situation in E. Schüssler Fiorenza, *The Book of Revelation: Justice and Judgment* (Philadelphia: Fortress Press, 1985), pp. 181-99. On the portrayal of Rome itself in ch. 18, see A.Y. Collins, *Crisis and Catharsis: The Power of the Apocalypse* (Philadelphia: Westminster Press, 1984), pp. 121-24. On the portrayal of the general social situation as reflected in Revelation see Thompson, *Revelation*, pp. 95-132, 186-97.

10.   Rev. 16.14; 17.2; 17–18; 18.3, 9; 19.19.

encompassing 'many peoples and nations and languages and kings' (10.11); that is, all humanity, which Babylon merely rules for a time (17.15). The kings of the earth and their people are apparently drawn into alliance by the desire for luxury (17.2; 18.3) and by guile (13.3-4, 13-15), and even after they knock off the beast's rider they continue to follow the beast itself (13.7-8; 19.20).

The generalization of humanity's rebellion beyond John's immediate situation is a recurrent theme in Revelation. Long before any mention of Babylon or other imagery construable as pertaining to Rome, Jesus is proclaimed as ruler of the *kings* (pl.) of the earth (1.6), and judgment falls generally on the earth[11] and on all humankind, which is universally unrepentant.[12] This generalization should not undercut the immediacy and poignancy of John's thinly-veiled attack of Rome in chs. 13 and 17–18, but it does underscore the point that Rome's evil is *constituent* or *symptomatic*. Thus to 'come out of her so that you do not take part in her sins' (18.4) is not to change geographic locations—where would one go in an entire world under judgment?—but to 'conquer' spiritually; that is, to obey the directives issued in Revelation 2–3. Thus if the New Jerusalem is people, a perfectly ordered community, then so is Babylon people, a rebellious chaos. Rome is the transient historical vehicle and Babylon the type for the ongoing and ultimate danger of allegiance to the beast and enmity toward God.

The Sea in Jewish Cosmology

The cosmic struggle between the beast and God for human allegiance is the context for the sea imagery in Revelation, imagery which will contribute further to the notion of people as place. The complexity of the imagery demands some background in the Jewish cosmology upon which John draws.

Most commentators acknowledge John's general dependence on a Jewish cosmology in which the sea is a symbol of chaos. Originally the imagery emanates from Mesopotamian stories of the earth (god) being established over the sea and river (gods) or even a sea dragon.[13] In

---

11. Rev. 3.10; 6.1-10; 7.1; 8.5, 7, 13; 9.3; 12.12; 14.16; 18.10; 19.2; cf. 11.6.

12. Rev. 9.20-21; 11.10; 13.8, 16; 16.9, 11.

13. See L.I.J. Stadelmann, *The Hebrew Conception of the World* (Rome: Pontifical Biblical Institute, 1970), pp. 1-24; B.W. Anderson, *Creation versus Chaos: The Reinterpretation of Mythical Symbolism in the Bible* (New York: Association Press, 1967), pp. 15-26, 78-79.

Genesis, God overcomes the formless waste by 'gathering' (v. 9) the waters and establishing the earth and sky above them. The common elements of the ancient mythologies produce a picture of a three-tiered universe with the heaven and earth perched atop a seething, unstable chaos. A survey of Jewish literature confirms that this basic cosmology remains and that sea imagery acquires a corollary function as metaphorical representation for the *human* enemies of God.

That the sea is contained but not transformed by God's command is confirmed by numerous texts, of which the following are representative:

> [He] has enclosed the sea in the midst of the waters,
> and by his word has suspended the earth over the waters (*4 Ezra* 16.58).

> He binds up the waters in his thick clouds,
> and the cloud is not torn open by them.
> He covers the face of the full moon,
> and spreads over it his cloud.
> He has described a circle on the face of the waters,
> at the boundary between light and darkness.
> The pillars of heaven tremble,
> and are astounded at his rebuke.
> By his power he stilled the Sea;
> by his understanding he struck down Rahab.[14]
> By his wind the heavens were made fair;
> his hand pierced the fleeing serpent (Job 26.8-13).

> When he established the heavens, I was there,
> when he drew a circle on the face of the deep,
> when he made firm the skies above,
> when he established the fountains of the deep,
> when he assigned to the sea its limit,
> so that the waters might not transgress his command (Prov. 8.27-29).

> I placed the sand as a perpetual boundary for the sea,
> a perpetual barrier that it cannot pass;
> though the waves toss, they cannot prevail,
> though they roar, they cannot pass over it (Jer. 5.22).[15]

---

14. On Rahab and Leviathan as monsters symbolizing the sea, see E. Dhorme, *A Commentary on the Book of Job* (Nashville: Thomas Nelson, 1967), pp. 29-31; D.J.A. Clines, *Job 1–20* (WBC; Dallas: Word Books, 1989), pp. 86-87; cf. Ps. 74.13-14; 89.9-10; Isa. 51.9-10; *4 Ezra* 6.49-52.

15. See also Job 7.12; 9.8; 28.25; 38.8-11; Ps. 24.2; 74.12-17; 77.16; *4 Ezra* 4.19; 6.41-42; Sir. 43.23; Pr. Man. 3. We might add passages that affirm generally God's power over the sea (Job 12.15; 26.5 Pss. 65.7; 77.16; 89.9; 93.3-4; 147.18; Isa. 50.2; 51.15; Jer. 31.35; Hab. 3.8, 15; Hag. 2.6; *4 Ezra* 16.12; Wis. 5.22; 14.3)

God's sovereignty over the sea is often focused on its essential demonstration in the Exodus sea-passage of Israel.[16] 'He divided the sea and let them pass through it, and made the waters stand like a heap' (Ps. 78.13); 'He rebuked the Red Sea, and it became dry; he led them through the deep as through a desert' (Ps. 106.9). Isa. 51.10 promises that just as God 'made the depths of the sea a way for the redeemed to cross over, so the ransomed of the Lord shall return'. Wis. 19.6 asserts that in this event, the whole creation was re-made by God (ὅλη γὰρ ἡ κτίσις... πάλιν ἄνωθεν διετυποῦτο).

The hymn of thanksgiving in Exodus 15 contains the interesting image that God's enemies 'became as still as a stone until your people, O Lord, passed by' (Exod. 15.16). This, following the description of Exod. 14.22 of 'the waters forming a wall for them on their right and on their left', suggests an identification between the waters of chaos and the enemies of God. This identification becomes common in the Old Testament:

> You silence the roaring of the seas,
> the roaring of their waves,
> the tumult of the peoples (Ps. 65.7).

> He reached from on high, he took me,
> he drew me out of mighty waters.
> He delivered me from my strong enemy,
> from those who hated me;
> for they were too mighty for me (2 Sam. 22.17-18).

> I called to the Lord out of my distress,
> and he answered me;
> out of the belly of Sheol I cried,
> and you heard my voice.
> You cast me into the deep,
> into the heart of the seas,
> and the flood surrounded me;
> all your waves and your billows passed over me.
> Then I said, 'I am driven away from your sight;
> how shall I look again upon your holy temple?'
> The waters closed in over me (Jon. 2.2-5a).[17]

and his creation of it (Pss. 95.5; 104.3, 24-25; 135.6; 136.6; 146.6; Amos 5.8; 9.6; Jdt 9.12).

16. See also Pss. 77.19-20; 114.3-5; Isa. 43.16-17; 63.12-13; Zech. 10.10-11; *4 Ezra* 1.13; Wis. 10.18; Sir. 39.17.

17. See also 2 Sam. 22.5-6; Pss. 18.16-17; 32.6; 42.7; 46.1-3; 69.1-2, 14-15;

The last passage quoted points to another recurrent Old Testament theme which may serve as a backdrop for imagery in Revelation. That is, the apposition of Sheol or the Pit (the place of the dead) and the sea: 'The shades below tremble, the waters and their inhabitants. Sheol is naked before God, and Abaddon has no covering.'[18] In two passages the interchangeability becomes even more complex, as the human enemies of God's servants are added to the equation between sea and death:

> I call upon the Lord, who is worthy to be praised,
> and I am saved from my enemies.
> For the waves of death encompassed me,
> the torrents of perdition assailed me;
> the cords of Sheol entangled me,
> the snares of death confronted me (2 Sam. 22.4-6).

> Rescue me from sinking in the mire;
> let me be delivered from my enemies and from the deep waters.
> Do not let the flood sweep over me,
> or the deep swallow me up,
> or the Pit close its mouth over me (Ps. 69.14-15).[19]

Thus the sea, primordial chaos, the abode of the dead, sea monsters, and human enemies of God, are realities so closely linked in the minds of Jewish writers as to be interchangeable in some instances. As we will observe below, this interchangeable terminology provides a rich source of imagery for the major prophets and later apocalyptic visionaries.

The Sea in Apocalyptic

Pronouncements of judgment against Israel's enemies may involve either sea associations or sea metaphors, both of which contribute to the

---

88.7; 107.23-32; 124.4-5; Isa. 17.12-13; 43.2; Jer. 7.2; 51.55; Lam. 3.54; Hab. 3.8, 12-15; *Sib. Or.* 3.678-79; cf. 1QH 2.12-13a: 'The assembly of the wicked raged against me and roared like storms upon the seas when their billows rage throwing up slime and mud'.

18. Anderson, *Creation*, p. 94; Stadelmann, *Conception*, p. 170. See Job 26.5-6; 38.16-17; Ps. 88.3-7; Ezek. 26.19-20; 28.8; 31.14-15; 1QH 3.12-18.

19. Cf. 1QH 2.16, '[And all] the men of deceit roared against me like the clamour of the roaring of great waters, and the ruses of Belial were [all] their [thou]ghts; and they cast down towards the Pit the life of the man by whose mouth Thou hast established the teaching'.

notion of place as people. In these contexts we also begin to see direct links to Revelation.

The judgments against sea power Tyre (Isa. 23; Ezek. 26–28), which are integral to the construction of Revelation 18, involve both association and metaphor. The city, which is given female personification *as the sea* in Isa. 23.4, laments with words similar to Rev. 18.7, 'I have neither labored nor given birth, I have neither reared young men nor brought up young women'.[20] In Isa. 23.11, sea and political enemy are superimposed: 'He has stretched out his hand over the sea, he has shaken the kingdoms; the Lord has given command concerning Canaan to destroy its fortresses'. Later in the same series of prophecies concerning Tyre, a general promise that the Lord will 'punish the inhabitants of the earth for their iniquity' (26.21) is followed by the metaphorical representation of Tyre as a sea monster:

> On that day the Lord with his cruel and great strong sword
> will punish Leviathan the fleeing serpent,
> Leviathan the twisting serpent,
> and he will kill the dragon that is in the sea (Isa. 27.1).[21]

Judgment texts incorporating sea imagery can take a reciprocal form; that is, those who live by the sea die by the sea. In Ezekiel's prophecy against Tyre, the sea as a double metaphor for political enemies and death becomes the means of destruction for the maritime power:

> See, I am against you, O Tyre!
> I will hurl many nations against you,
> as the sea hurls its waves (Ezek. 26.3).

> When I make you a city laid waste, like cities that are not inhabited,
> when I bring the deep over you, and the great waters cover you,
> then I will thrust you down with those who descend into the Pit
> (Ezek. 26.19b-20).

Similar imagery is employed by Jeremiah in the diatribe against Babylon in texts upon which Revelation is directly dependent:

---

20. Cf. Isa. 23.15-17, where Tyre is described as a prostitute.

21. J.W. Watts, *Isaiah 1–33* (WBC; Waco, TX: Word Books, 1985), p. 349, cf. pp. 298-99. Leviathan may represent not Tyre here but God's enemies more generally: O. Kaiser, *Isaiah 13–39* (Philadelphia: Westminster Press, 1974), pp. 221-23. The political significance of the sea monster pertains in either case. Dragon imagery is similarly employed in Ps. 74.13-14 and *T. Ash.* 7.3.

You who live by many waters, rich in treasures
your end has come, the thread of your life is cut (Jer. 51.13; cf.
Rev. 17.15; 18.19).

The sea has risen over Babylon;
she has been covered by its tumultuous waves (Jer. 51.42).

Their waves roar like mighty waters,
the sound of their clamor resounds;
for a destroyer has come against her, against Babylon (Jer. 51.55b-56a).

When you finish reading this scroll, tie a stone to it, and throw it into the middle of the Euphrates, and say, 'Thus shall Babylon sink, to rise no more' (Jer. 51.63-64a).	Then a mighty angel took up a stone like a great millstone and threw it into the sea, saying, 'With such violence the great city will be thrown down and will be found no more (Rev. 18.21).

It is significant that there is no perceived contradiction in the fact that
the city is both drowned and dried in the same passage. In Jer. 51.36,
God says of Babylon, 'I will dry up her sea and make her fountains
dry'. This pronouncement represents another strand of apocalyptic that
is dependent on the same background. That is, the sea can represent
metaphorically not only the means of judgment (other nations) and the
destination of judgment (realm of the dead) but also the *object* of
judgment—the wicked generally or a particular nation, especially when
the nation is a maritime power. Thus God's general ability to control the
sea is specified in the form of drying the sea which is identified with a
given city—Babylon here and in Isa. 44.27; 50.2; Nineveh in Nah. 1.4.
Several post-biblical apocalyptic works continue this sea-drying theme:

And the sea all the way to the abyss will retire,
to the sources of waters which fail.
Yea, the rivers will vanish away.
For God Most High will surge forth, the Eternal One alone.
In full view will he come to work vengeance on the nations.
Yea, all their idols will he destroy (*Ass. Mos.* 10.6-7).

A great star will come forth from heaven to the wondrous sea
and will burn the deep sea and Babylon itself
and the land of Italy, because of which many
holy faithful Hebrews and a true people perished (*Sib. Or.* 5.158-61).

In the last time, one day the sea will be dry,
and ships will then no longer sail to Italy (*Sib. Or.* 5.447-48).

It is not quite accurate to cite these passages as parallels to Rev. 21.1.[22] In the *Sibylline Oracles* the drying is, as in Jer. 51.36, local rather than global in scope; the last citation continues, 'Great Asia then will be water, bearing all cargo' (*Sib. Or.* 5.449). In the *Assumption of Moses*, the judgment appears to be global, but it denotes the infliction visited on the wicked, not the renewed creation given to the elect. *T. Levi*, similarly, shows that drying signifies pain rather than pleasure: 'For even when stones are split, when the sun is extinguished, the waters dried up, fire is cowed down, all creation is distraught...men will persist in their wrongdoing'. It is noteworthy that, as common as the 'new heaven and earth' and 'New Jerusalem' themes are in writings contemporary with or earlier than Revelation,[23] none of these writings contains parallels to 'the sea was no more'.

Before moving to the text of Revelation itself, we should note two more pertinent aspects of the sea imagery in apocalyptic literature. The first of these is the association of the sea with Satan and demonic forces:

> And she who is big with the Asp is prey to terrible anguish
> and the billows of the Pit (are unleashed) unto all the works of terror.
> And they shake the foundations of the rampart
> like a ship on the face of the waters,
> and the clouds roar in a noise of roaring.
> And they that live in the dust are, like them that sail the seas,
> terrified because of the roaring of the waters.
> And their wise men are for them like sailors in the deeps,
> for all their wisdom is destroyed because of the roaring of the waters,
> because of the boiling of the deeps upon the fountains of the waters.
> [And] the waves [are turb]ulent (rearing) into the air
> and the billows resound with the roaring of their voice.
> And Sh[eo]l [and Abaddon] open in the midst of their turbulence
> [and al]l the arrows of the Pit (fly out) in their pursuit;
> they let their voice be heard in the Abyss.
> And the gates [of Sheol] open [to all] the works of the Asp,

---

22. As, e.g., R.H. Charles, *The Revelation of St John* (2 vols.; Edinburgh: T. & T. Clark, 1920), II, pp. 204-205; G.E. Ladd, *A Commentary on the Revelation of John* (Grand Rapids: Eerdmans, 1972), p. 276; J.M. Ford, *Revelation* (AB, 38; New York: Doubleday, 1975), p. 361.

23. Isa. 65.17; 65.22; Ps. 102.25-26; *1 En.* 45.4-5; 72.1; 91.6; *4 Ezra* 7.75; 13.36; Wis. 19.6; *Jub.* 1.29; *2 Bar.* 4.2-7; 32.6; 44.12; 57.2; Heb. 13.14, 2 Pet. 3.7, 13.

and the doors of the Pit close upon her who is big with Perversity,
and the everlasting bars upon all the spirits of the Asp (1QH 3.12-18;
cf. 3.26-36).

A final pertinent aspect of apocalyptic sea imagery is the notion of evil
figures rising up out of the sea. The following texts do not explain the
meaning of the sea image, which presumably represents in a very
general sense the source of evil. In Daniel 7 the sea produces political
entities opposed to God: 'I, Daniel, saw in my vision by night the four
winds of heaven stirring up the great sea, and four great beasts [four
kings, v. 17] came up out of the sea' (Dan. 7.2-3). The fourth beast has
ten horns (7.24; cf. Rev. 13.1; 17.7) and speaks against the Most High
(7.25; cf. Rev. 13.5-6; 17.2) prior to its destruction. The literary context
of Daniel makes for an easy transition to association by John with
Babylon/Rome. *The Apocalypse of Baruch*, describing portents of the
beginning of the revelation of the Anointed One, predicts that
'Behemoth will reveal itself for its place, and Leviathan will come from
the sea, the two great monsters which I created on the fifth day of
creation' (*2 Apoc. Bar.* 29.4; cf. Rev. 13.1, 11). While no interpretation
is offered in the text, the monsters are presumably political powers,
symbols of irresistible dominance: Leviathan from the sea, Behemoth
from the land (cf. Rev. 13.1, 11).[24] The fifth vision of *4 Ezra* has an
eagle arise from the sea (11.1), an eagle that is identified later as the
fourth kingdom of Daniel 7 (12.10-12). It is overcome by a lion aroused
out of the forest (11.36) which is identified as the messiah (12.31-32).[25]

The developing complexity of imagery requires a brief review
before moving into the text of Revelation. We have observed interchangeable terminology for the sea, primordial chaos, the abode of the
dead, sea monsters, the demonic realm, and—most importantly for our
purposes—human enemies of God and his people. These terms may be

24. The two beasts (elephant and crocodile) appear together in such character in
Job 40.15–41.34 and *4 Ezra* 6.49-52; cf. *1 En.* 60.8, 24. Only Leviathan is mentioned
elsewhere in the Old Testament: Job 3.8; Ps. 74.14; 104.26; Isa. 27.1.

25. The second beast represents a shift, of course, in that the land beast is good
(cf. *2 Bar.* 29.4; Rev. 11.1). A more radical shift occurs in the sixth vision, when the
human figure who comes out of the sea (13.3) is the Messiah (13.25-26), and he
fights against a multitude 'gathered together from the four winds of heaven' (13.5; cf.
Rev. 7.1). The sea in this case cannot be evil; rather, it represents mystery: 'He said to
me, "Just as no one can explore or know what is in the depth of the sea, so no one on
earth can see my Son or those who are with him, except in the time of his day"'.

metaphorical (and at more than one level), apposite or proximal without regard to logical inconsistencies. As we will observe below, Revelation both represents and advances this complexity.

Sea Imagery in Revelation

Revelation fairly drips with water imagery. The fifty-plus references comprise by far the greatest concentration of such imagery in the Bible or in contemporary apocalyptic literature.[26] A catalogue of the most important references reveals a concentration of metaphorical imagery in the later chapters of Revelation:

> the sea by which dragon stands, from which beast emerges (12.18–13.11)
> 'many waters' upon which the whore/Babylon sits (17.1, 15)
> the sea as commercial empire (18.11-20; cf. blood judgment, 8.8-11; 11.6; 16.3-4)
> the sea as symbol for Babylon's *Untergang* (destruction) (18.21)
> the sea as abode of the dead (20.13)
> the lake of fire (19.20; 20.10, 14-15; 21.8; cf. the bottomless pit, 9.1-2, 11; 11.7; 20.1-3)
> 'the sea was no more' (21.1)

The organization of the catalogue and the obvious background of most references in literature cited above[27] pose the question of relationships between the references. The view through John's multi-faceted apocalyptic lens may initially seem kaleidoscopic, but closer inspection reveals a fundamental unity which confirms the original thesis that sea imagery denotes primarily people and not place.

The sources upon which John draws provide warrant to meld rather than separate the complex series of images for hostile powers in the

26. The Psalms, by comparison, contain about one-third the frequency of water references; *The Apocalypse of Baruch*, the next 'wettest' apocalyptic text, about half. By classification, the references in Revelation involve *simile* (1.15; 14.2; 19.6; 20.8), *metaphor for evil* (12.15, 16, 18; 13.1; 17.1, 15; 20.13; 21.1; 22.1, 2), *metaphor for good* (4.16; 7.17; 15.2 [2×]; 16.5; 21.6; 22.1; 22.17), and *literal reference* (5.13; 7.1, 2, 3; 8.8, 9 [2×]; 9.14; 10.2, 5, 6, 8; 11.6; 12.12; 14.7; 16.3 [2×], 4, 12; 18.17, 21).

27. Even those water references in Revelation not directly relevant to the argument here evince the Jewish cosmology described above; see, e.g., the three-tiered view of creation in 10.6 and 14.7; and the sovereignty displayed in 5.13, 7.1-3, 10.2 and 14.7. The sea of glass that stands before God's throne (4.6; 15.2) may be an antithetic parallel to the lake of fire, but it may also derive from the older cosmology in the sense of a tamed chaos.

latter chapters of Revelation. Linkages between images abound. The dragon takes his place by the sea (12.18), from which he calls up the beast (13.1). The dragon is Leviathan (Isa. 27.1), who after judgment is reduced to carrion (Ps. 74.13-14; *4 Ezra* 6.49-52). In Revelation it is technically rebellious humanity who become carrion (19.17-21), while the dragon is temporarily bound (20.2) prior to his ultimate demise in the lake of fire (20.10), where he is joined by rebellious humanity, dredged up from Hades *and the sea* (20.13). Babylon sits on the beast (17.2) but also sits on 'seven mountains' (17.9)[28] and on 'many waters' (17.1). The beast ascends from the sea (13.1) but also from the bottomless pit (11.7; 17.8); and while he sits on a throne which is actually the dragon's throne (13.2), he himself *is* the throne—that is, the mount—of the whore (17.3). The beasts's seven heads and ten horns are interpreted as specific kings (17.9-13), but later these kings are distinguished from the beast (17.16) and are still later generalized as all humanity deceived by the beast (19.18)—or the dragon (20.3, 10). This deception is perpetrated by frog-like[29] demons emanating from the dragon, the beast, and the beast's prophet (15.13-14). In 12.15, it is the dragon who vomits a river of persecution, but in 11.7 and 13.7 it is the beast who makes war on the saints. If these overlapping images are not themselves sufficient to muddy the waters (sic), it might also be asked in nearly every case if the referents are individual, corporate, political, ecclesiastical or demonic. Can such a confusing array be unified?

Attempts to harmonize these images consider Revelation in terms of contemporary historical referents: the city of Rome rides on a beast (the emperor) and is sustained by its dominance of the 'many waters' of the empire (maritime commerce) until other equally anti-Christian nations overwhelm the empire just prior to their own destruction. But this scheme raises serious questions. Is the distinction between city, emperor, and empire plausible? How is it that the city rides the emperor rather

28. Code for Rome, according to virtually every commentator, and supported by Horace, *Carm. Sec.* 7; Virgil *Aen.* 6.782; *Georg.* 2.534; Martial 4.64; Cicero *Ad Att.* 6.5; Propertius 3.10 (see Charles, *Revelation*, II, p. 69). *1 En.* 24–25, however, describes seven mountains made of jewels which constitute God's throne and upon which God will sit when he descends. Given John's penchant for allusion to apocalyptic imagery, might this passage rather than Rome lie behind 17.9?

29. Note the similarity here to the judgment against Egypt, in which frogs came up out of the waters (Exod. 8.6), and compare the summary of Exodus plagues in Ps. 105.28-35 to the judgments in Revelation.

than vice versa? Why is the emperor described in 13.2 as Daniel describes a kingdom? How can the emperor arise from the sea if the sea represents commerce? How can the emperor hate the city (17.16) and survive to lead humanity after the city is overthrown (19.19)?

The historical approach suffers not only from intrinsic implausibility but from inattention to clues of John's broader vision in Revelation. We have observed the generalization of judgment to include not only Babylon but all of humanity in rebellion against God. Attention to the interconnectedness of sea imagery in Revelation confirms this generalization and places the judgment scenes in their proper focus as antonymous, and prerequisite, to the New Jerusalem.

For example, the incongruity between the (smoking, 9.2-3) bottomless pit and the (presumably wet) sea, both of which spawn the beast, is resolved by noting the connection between Sheol, Gehenna, and the abyss as overlapping images of the place of the dead and the abode of demons. The sea (along with Hades) is also the place of the dead in 20.13. The lake of fire is the destination of the dead.[30]

The association of the sea and its denizens with the human enemies of God constitutes another composite image. The dragon and the beast and the maritime commercial enterprise of Babylon all contribute to a historical focus on Rome, but the imagery is generalized throughout Revelation to include 'peoples and multitudes and nations and languages' as the ultimate sea of God's enemies. Babylon is symptomatic. Desire for the pleasures of this world and susceptibility to deception do not end with the fall of Rome. Finally it is *all* flesh that rises like a tide against the King of Kings and then falls back sizzling into the lake of fire.

Somewhat more problematic is the overlapping imagery involving the demonic and human elements in the forces aligned against God, but this is a problem throughout the New Testament. Who is to discern when 'the devil made me do it'—or are demonic and human evil mutually defining? At the very least it can be said that Revelation and other New Testament writings describe the sea of politics, like the physical sea, as a place inhabited and provisionally controlled by unseen forces of evil.

The three associations just outlined, linking the sea with death, sin and demonic forces, are of course themselves interrelated. While specific scenes are at times incongruous, the connections are—there is no better word for it—*fluid*. They flow together and back to the original simple

---

30. M. Rissi, *The Future of the World: An Exegetical Study of Revelation 19.11–22.15* (London: SCM Press, 1972), p. 68.

notion of the sea as chaos. By definition, therefore, it cannot be changed—it must be eliminated. And so by definition people who are aligned with chaos cannot be changed but must be eliminated. Because John sees this as no seer before him saw it, his statement 'the sea was no more' looms in importance as a simple one-line summary of the final judgment described in ch. 20. Human chaos must go in order to make possible a perfect community into which nothing unclean can ever enter (21.26).

Summary

The theme demands the most *structured* summary possible. Greimas's semiotic square is in fact very helpful. It consists of three sets of axes: the vertical denoting implication, the horizontal denoting contrariety, and the diagonal denoting contradiction. While in a given text the presence of any *seme* (S) assumes the other three, the text of Revelation conveniently includes all four sequentially (moving clockwise from upper left): S = community (chs. 1–3), S' = this world (chs. 4–18) S = eschatological chaos (chs. 19–20), and S' = new community (chs. 21–22).

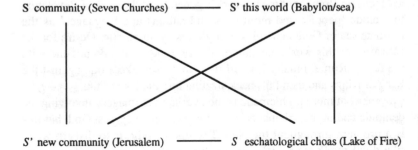

S community (Seven Churches) ———— S' this world (Babylon/sea)

S' new community (Jerusalem) ———— S eschatological choas (Lake of Fire)

The diagrammatic summary highlights the parallelism which transcends the complex chronological scheme of Revelation. On the vertical axes of implication, the New Jerusalem is essentially an extension of the obedient church; eternal punishment is essentially an extension of the world order at enmity with God. On the horizontal axes of contrariety, the churches at enmity with this world and the eschatological realities are mutually exclusive. On one diagonal axis of contradiction, the temporal Church must endure in the face of unjust suffering, while the eternally damned must face eternal just punishment. On the other diagonal axis of contradiction—that which has occupied the bulk of this article—the present world order inexorably collapses on itself, while the new community descends gracefully in perfect order. At all of these levels, the diagram points to the fundamental antonymy in Revelation between chaos and community.

Postscript: Chaos and Salvation in the New Testament

The notion of heaven as antonymous to the present world order which dominates Revelation is in fact contiguous with eschatological depiction in New Testament epistolary literature. That is, salvation is not deliverance from its opposite, a future hell; rather, salvation is from that which is 'earthly', from the chaotic way of life characteristic of this world:

> You were dead through the trespasses and sins in which you once lived, following the course of this world, following the ruler of the power of the air, the spirit that is now at work among those who are disobedient. All of us once lived among them in the passions of our flesh, following the desires of flesh and senses, and we were by nature children of wrath, like everyone else. But God, who is rich in mercy, out of the great love with which he loved us even when we were dead through our trespasses, made us alive together with Christ—by grace you have been saved—and raised us up with him and seated us with him in the heavenly places in Christ Jesus, so that in the ages to come he might show the immeasurable riches of his grace in kindness toward us in Christ Jesus (Eph. 2.2-6).[31]

Heb. 13.14 puts it succinctly: 'For here we have no lasting city, but we are looking for the city that is to come'. This is not to deny cognizance of eschatological punishment on the part of New Testament writers (*S'* requires *S* by contrariety), but such a negative reality is of minimal importance in their conveyance of beliefs. The stress is on deliverance *now* followed by a life of hope in a glorious promise. The future that reaches back into the present, motivating believers to conquer, is not the penultimate depiction of judgment. Rather, it is the ultimate vision of a perfected community, where the chaotic sea of sin, sorrow and death *is no more*.

---

31. Cf. Eph. 6.12; Col. 1.21-22; 2.20; 3.2, 5-6; 2 Tim. 4.10; Tit. 2.12. Heb. 13.14; Jas 1.27; 3.5, 15; 2 Pet. 1.4; 2.4-17, 20; 3.5-7, 10-13; 1 Jn 2.15-17; 3.13; 4.4-5; 5.4-5.

INDEXES

INDEX OF REFERENCES

OLD TESTAMENT

NEW TESTAMENT

PSEUDEPIGRAPHA

INDEX OF AUTHORS

JOURNAL FOR THE STUDY OF THE NEW TESTAMENT

Supplement Series